RELIGION AND POLITICS
IN LATIN AMERICA

RELIGION AND POLITICS IN LATIN AMERICA

Liberation Theology and Christian Democracy

Edward A. Lynch

New York
Westport, Connecticut
London

Library of Congress Cataloging-in-Publication Data

Lynch, Edward A.
    Religion and politics in Latin America : liberation theology and
Christian democracy / Edward A. Lynch.
        p.   cm.
    Includes bibliographical references and index.
    ISBN 0–275–93774–7 (alk. paper)
    1. Liberation theology.   2. Christian democracy—Latin America.
3. Christianity and politics.   4. Communism and Christianity.
I. Title.
BT83.57.L95   1991
261.7′098—dc20   90–48694

British Library Cataloguing in Publication Data is available.

Library of Congress Catalog Card Number: 90–48694
ISBN: 0–275–93774–7

First published in 1991

Praeger Publishers, One Madison Avenue, New York, NY 10010
An imprint of Greenwood Publishing Group, Inc.

Printed in the United States of America

The paper used in this book complies with the
Permanent Paper Standard issued by the National
Information Standards Organization (Z39.48–1984).

10 9 8 7 6 5 4 3 2 1

Contents

Acknowledgments

To list everyone who deserves acknowledgment for this work is a daunting task. My study of religion and politics goes back to my earliest days as an undergraduate student, and few are the professors and courses that have not contributed to my thinking on this important issue in some way.

In the interests of brevity, however, I will highlight the contributions of those most directly involved in this book. David Jordan of the University of Virginia sparked my interest in Liberation Theology years ago. He helped me to develop the specific topic and was of indispensable assistance in maintaining a scholarly balance between the world-sized issues that I treat and the need for digestible chapters. His colleagues Michael Brint and John Norton Moore read early versions of this book and provided helpful insights and corrections. I am particularly indebted to Michael, since he provided the perspective most different from my own.

John J. Schrems and Lowell Gustafson here at Villanova University did me the favor of listening to me talk about this project and providing intellectual guidance and friendly encouragement in the right proportion. Villanova's Department of Political Science also aided the process significantly by providing access to word processing and copying facilities. I am, of course, solely responsible for what appears here.

Finally, for bearing with all the sacrifices and hardships that come with a spouse who is writing a book, for reading each edited copy, and for just being there, I thank you, Jacquie.

Introduction

The relationship between religion and politics has recently become a pressing question for political scientists. Events in the Middle East are unintelligible without an understanding of the religious conflicts that motivate political actors in that part of the world. Perhaps because of the violence connected with sectarian strife, the importance of religion is most obvious in the Middle East.

In Latin America, although the stakes are less dramatic, they are no less important. Religious belief is the primary motivating factor for many of Latin America's politically active citizens. Nevertheless, North American scholarship on religion and politics in Latin America has tended to fall into one of two less-than-useful categories.

On the one hand, many scholars treat religious belief as though it is necessarily merely a veil for some other sort of interest. No one can actually believe in religion, we are told; people only use religion to hide their real motivations. On the other hand, many scholars treat religious politics as thought this were the purview just of ecclesiastics. To know what relationship exists between religion and politics in Venezuela, for example, a scholar need simply interview the bishops and clergy. This ignores the substantial hold that religious belief has over laypeople, including many well-educated and sophisticated citizens.

This book treats the two most important lay religious movements in the Latin American Catholic Church: Liberation Theology and Christian Democracy. There is a great need for original scholarly treatment of these movements. Existing literature on Liberation Theology is written either by unabashed proponents or by its most bitter enemies. Literature on Christian Democracy, while much better, is becoming dated. Edward Williams's book, for example, is now 23 years old.

I offer, then, a necessary and timely contribution to the understanding of what drives religious people to act in politics. I seek to start many more discussions than I will resolve. Some of my conclusions will be controversial; this is the essence of genuinely original scholarship.

Over 100 years ago, Friedrich Engels discovered the potential usefulness of revolutionary religion. He found that, particularly at the start of the Protestant Reformation, social revolutionaries clothed their beliefs in the garb of religious faith. The theorists of Liberation Theology refined his discovery and brought it up to date. Today, Latin America is alive with theorists who insist that the love of God requires political revolution of a Marxist economic and social stripe.

Although its proponents lost a good deal of Marxist orthodoxy in the transition, Liberation Theology retains just enough Christianity to pose a significant threat to orthodox Catholicism. Believers who are disgusted with the enormous disparities of wealth in Latin America, and impatient with gradual solutions, can see in Liberation Theology the justification to do what they want to do anyway: lead a Christian revolt against injustice. Liberation Theology requires the rejection of orthodox Catholicism as a necessary first step.

The Catholic Church, for its part, seeking to counter the claims and promises of Marxism, and perhaps anticipating the Liberationist challenge, developed a concise, coherent, and principled social doctrine at the beginning of the twentieth century. Catholic social thought rejects Marxist emphasis on mass man by celebrating the individuality of the human person. It rejects Marxist totalitarianism by promoting independent social groupings to protect individuals from state power. It rejects collaboration with Marxism in any form, recognizing its own philosophy's fundamental incompatibility with Marxism.

The political movement that sought to bring Catholic social thought to the political realm was Christian Democracy. At first, Christian Democrats in Europe, and later in Latin America, adhered closely to Catholic social thought. But in the period just after World War II, when European Christian Democrats were thrust into positions of power, they made debilitating compromises in the social doctrine of the Church.

The Catholic emphasis on individuals was lost as the Christian Democrats sought greater societal "organization" to achieve quicker and more complete electoral success. The mistrust of the state was lost in a doomed attempt to use the state to achieve social goals. On the question of Marxist collaboration, most Christian Democrats followed the example of Christian Democratic theorist Jacques Maritain, who dithered endlessly over the question before concluding that collaboration was acceptable. In making these compromises, the Christian Democrats jettisoned the clear philosophical bases for opposing radical movements, including Marxism.

In Latin America, Christian Democracy failed to present a clear alternative to the centralizing and statist trends of twentieth-century Latin American politics. Like their European counterparts, Latin American Christian Democrats abandoned the defense of individual persons and autonomous society in the quest for electoral success and the redirection, rather than the limiting, of state power. Offering no discernible alternative, Latin American Christian Democracy has withered as a political movement.

In Venezuela, although Christian Democrats were instrumental in bringing democracy to that country, they sacrificed much of their intellectual clarity in the process. They came to be perceived merely as less courageous and less committed shadows of the more radically statist Social Democrats.

Meanwhile, Liberation Theologians took advantage of the dearth of imaginative and orthodox Catholic political champions to gain strength and influence among politically active Latin Americans. Nowhere was their political strength more evident than in the struggle against Nicaraguan dictator Anastasio Somoza. Liberation Theology radicalized anti-Somoza feeling in Nicaragua, allowing the most radical Marxist opposition party, the Frente Sandinista de Liberacion Nacional (FSLN), to lead the post-Somoza government. In one of the few direct juxtapositions of Liberation Theology and Christian Democracy, the Nicaraguan Christian Democratic party went from willing collaboration to impotence and near extinction.

Liberation Theology is now influential in almost every Latin American country. Venezuela is a significant exception because the failure of Liberation Theology to take hold there is not due to its strong Christian Democratic party, but rather because of the steadfastness of the Venezuelan hierarchy in upholding the principles of Catholic social thought. Venezuela's bishops did not forsake the intellectual and philosophical bases for opposition to massification, statism, and collaboration with Marxism.

By contrast, the Nicaraguan hierarchy did collaborate with a radical Marxist movement, only to see their independence, and later their very existence, threatened after the Sandinista Triumph. As they began to undo the damage from their earlier enthusiasm for the Sandinistas, the Nicaraguan bishops moved closer to traditional Catholic social thought. They rejected both Liberation Theology and Christian Democracy, seeking to motivate their faithful with a new Catholic movement, based on ancient principles. The future of Liberation Theology and Christian Democracy will be profoundly influenced by the fall of Sandinismo.

I

The Ideologies in Theory

1

Marx, Engels, and Religion

Most proponents of Liberation Theology claim that they are mixing Marxism and Christianity. They overcome the apparent differences between Marxism and Christianity by ignoring certain aspects of Marxism. Marxism, they say, is for them merely a tool of social analysis. They can use this tool without accepting Karl Marx's attitude toward religion.

I will show that Marx himself was consistently hostile toward religion. Moreover, his attitude toward religion was evident in so many different aspects of his thought that any attempt to separate these ingredients from his social analysis is, necessarily, a misinterpretation of Marx. Of the collaborators on *Capital* and *The Communist Manifesto*, it was Friedrich Engels who understood the revolutionary potential of religious belief and sought to make use of it. Liberation Theology draws its inspiration from Engels, not from Marx, and it is Engels's writings on religion that provide the most important clues to understanding Liberation Theology.

THE HOSTILITY OF MARX TOWARD RELIGION

To the extent that Marx considered religion at all, he was frequently disgusted with it, sometimes dismissing religion in general, and Christianity in particular, as not only irrelevant but also hypocritical. In "The Communism of the Paper *Rheinischer Beobachter*," Marx disdainfully quoted a conservative Prussian newspaper, which editorialized: "If only those whose calling it is to develop the social principles of Christianity would do so, the Communists would soon be put to silence."[1] He goes on to respond that the "social principles" of Christianity justified slavery, serfdom, and the oppression of the proletariat. Such a cruel religion, it seems, was beneath his criticism.

Christianity was cruel, according to Marx, because it was so easily turned into a tool of the ruling classes. Writing in "The Leading Article of No. 179 of Kolnische Zeitung," Marx said: "Christianity teaches, as a religion must, submit to the authority, because all authority is ordained by God."[2] Marx states baldly that religion is *necessarily* a prop of the ruling classes.[3] In this sense Christianity cannot be blamed for fulfilling this role. But in a more important sense, this one statement seems to preclude the possibility of revolutionary religion.

Yet the dependence of some European governments on religious belief prevented Marx from ignoring religion altogether. Criticism of religion was, for Marx, the beginning of all criticism. Even here, though, the criticism was merely tactical. Attacks on religion were, in the 1840s, the only effective means of attacking existing social relationships, since their justification was religion. In addition, Marx believed that stripping the rising working class of its religious beliefs was essential to winning them over to revolution.[4] Again, Marx assumes that religious belief and liberation are incompatible.

Surprisingly, Marx was a passionate Christian believer as a teenager,[5] in spite of the fact that he was raised in a liberal, nonreligious household. After this brief flirtation with orthodoxy, however, Marx reacted to its perceived irrelevance and hypocrisy as one taken in and determined to show beyond a doubt that he has overcome his childish fancy.

Marx's Empiricism

Marx found religious belief incompatible with many of the major strands of his thought. The first of these major strands that I will examine is his empiricism. Religion for Marx was a symptom of a badly formed self-consciousness. Marx desired contact with "reality," with which he thought religion interfered. Reality was for him sensuous and empirical, while religion was neither.

Marx's respect for the writings of John Duns Scotus and Francis Bacon, which contrast so strikingly with his sneering rejection of most premodern philosophies, is a sign of the empiricist path his thought would follow. Both Duns Scotus and Bacon were nominalists; that is, they rejected the existence of the spiritual world and concentrated their analytic efforts at understanding the world that their senses presented to them. Nominalism, Marx thought, was the first form of empiricism and empiricism was a vital element in the metaphysical position of materialism.[6]

Christianity is unavoidably hostile to nominalism. Marx attributed what he perceived to be Christianity's eternal hostility to free scientific research to this incompatibility.[7] The Christian Church, Marx seemed to believe, recognized that its tenets could not stand scientific scrutiny. Religion's, and in particular Christianity's, claim to absolute and eternal truth was fraudulent and intellectually stifling.

Marx identified himself as a philosopher, and philosophy, he thought, asked only what is true. He was not concerned with what is merely acknowledged as true, and certainly not with which truths serve the ruling class. Philosophy must be unfettered inquiry, which Marx thought was incompatible with any theology that claimed a monopoly on truth.[8] As a dedicated empiricist, Marx saw himself as religion's executioner.

Marx's Materialism

Francis Bacon, as we have seen, was one of only two premodern philosophers whom Marx respected. In his *Critique of Critical Criticism*, Marx praised Bacon's courageous belief that the senses were infallible.[9] John Locke continued in Bacon's nominalist tradition by declaring that no philosopher can be at variance with healthy human senses and reasonable deductions drawn from the evidence that the senses provide.[10]

In contrast with the favorable remarks Marx made about Bacon and Locke, he had nothing but scorn for the idealism of Georg Friedrich Hegel. Although he adopted the Hegelian dialectical system, Marx quarrelled with Hegel over the primacy of material. Marx believed that analysts could not acquire knowledge of the ideal through speculation or imagination, which Marx saw as Hegel's route.

Still less can any genuine knowledge of material things be gained through contemplation of the ideal. Rather, to understand the ideal, the analyst must first know the real. This is the basis of Marx's materialism.

This is not to say that Marx had no use for Hegel at all. On the contrary, Marx thought that Hegel's view of the existing political order, especially as described in the *Philosophy of Right*, was essentially accurate when stripped of its speculative trappings.[11] Where the *Philosophy of Right* is contradictory merely points up contradictions in the society that Hegel described. But Marx followed Ludwig Feuerbach in positing that Hegel projected the real in forming his vision of the ideal, in the same way that religious believers project their own idealized characteristics to develop an image of God.

Hegel, then, described existing society accurately, but erred in thinking that reality was a shadow of some preexisting ideal form. For Feuerbach and Marx, immediate experience is primary and any ideal world is a reflection of reality.[12] In "The German Ideology," Marx wrote that men's notions, ideas, and consciousness are, from the beginning, directly interwoven with material activity. Moreover, the same applies to men's spiritual production. "Here," Marx concluded, "there is ascension from earth to heaven."[13] Thus not only did Marx see his materialism as incompatible with genuine religious belief, but he also believed that the pseudobeliefs that pass themselves off as religion are mere derivatives of material reality.

Marx's Humanism

Marx believed that, although the defenders of religion constantly claimed that their beliefs raised man above his baser appetites and made him better, religion actually had the opposite effect.[14] Christianity in particular taught cowardice, self-contempt, abasement, submission, and dejection.[15]

Christianity demanded these subhuman emotions because it saw man as essentially sinful and depraved, according to Marx. He believed in and affirmed the essential innocence of man, following in the tradition of Jean Jacques Rousseau. Going even further, Marx would contend that man was perfectible, and that this perfection could be achieved through science. Most important, religion was an obstacle to man's eventual fulfillment.[16]

In Marx's introduction to his graduate thesis, in which he compared Epicurus and Democritus, he wrote that philosophy must reject other gods who do not acknowledge the consciousness of man as the supreme divinity. "There must be," according to Marx the humanist, "no other god on a level with [human consciousness]." In the same work he praised Prometheus as "the noblest of saints and martyrs in the calendar of philosophy."[17]

Thus Marx did not believe that one could be either a philosopher or a humanist and hold religious beliefs at the same time. Christianity was a particularly hostile belief because of its lack of absolute confidence in man. Here again, Marx rejects the possibility of synthesizing his beliefs with Christianity.

Marx's Economic Determinism

Marx the economic determinist rejected the independent existence of religion in the first place. Religion for him was epiphenomenal; that is, caused by material reality and derived from it. We saw earlier the tension between Marx's materialism and religion; the tension between his economic determinism and religion exists for the same reasons.

Marx's analysis of the relationship between ideas and social conditions first became visible in his "Theses on Feuerbach," written in 1845. Among his scorching criticisms of Feuerbach is one concerning the latter's failure to see that "religious sentiment is itself a social product."[18]

Thus the "eternal truths" that the ruling classes use to perpetuate themselves, including the principles of religion, seem eternal only because the economic condition of exploitation of one class by another is eternal, at least in "all hitherto existing society."[19]

This is not to suggest that religion alone is derived from material conditions. In "The German Ideology," Marx would add that the mass of production forces, capital, and circumstances prescribe to every generation its own "conditions of life."[20] This comprehensive term shows that for Marx, everything was derived from economics. Besides dictating these conditions of life, economic reality also dictates man's response to them. Since morals and religion have "no history, no development, but men developing their material production," consciousness itself is a product of economics.[21]

Christianity is, according to this analysis, the result of changing economic conditions in the ancient world. In his *Review of the Religion of the New Age*, Marx writes that the rise of Christianity was preceded by the complete collapse of the ancient world. This collapse created new economic and social conditions of which Christianity was the "mere expression."

Similarly, the bourgeois revolution at the end of the Middle Ages spelled the end of the Catholic Church's dominance over civil society. As economic conditions changed, the mediating institutions that stood between man and the state, such as estates, corporations, and guilds, disappeared. Significantly, these were tied in some way to religious belief. Marx believed that their religious bases were artificial, and tied them directly to prevailing economic conditions.[22]

Marx could therefore predict with confidence that religion would disappear after continued contact with science, both because of the knowledge science would bring and because of the hoped-for dedication of science to bring about the economic conditions that would make religion irrelevant. Primitive religion was particularly vulnerable and died when increased knowledge reduced the uncertainty of daily life and scientific technology allowed man to coerce nature without the use of magic.[23]

Christianity also feeds on uncertainty. In the modern world, religion exists to provide solace for economically exploited man. As science lays bare the true roots of that exploitation and directs its energies at creating new economic conditions, the priests will lose their function. As one commentator puts it, religion is a "pain killer" that will eventually have to give way to a "genuine, therapeutic remedy."[24]

The Atomization of Religion

His economic determinism led Marx to link post-Reformation Christianity with bourgeois society through his concept of alienation. In *Cap-*

ital he wrote that Protestantism is the most fitting form of religion for bourgeois society because it is based on the cult of abstract man. In other words, a society whose economic conditions have already reduced man to the status of a commodity will naturally produce a religion in which man's best qualities are abstracted and put out of his reach.[25] Like Max Weber, Marx linked Protestantism with capitalism, basing the link on their common belief in radical individualism and "abstract man."

In his earlier writings, Marx uses this linkage to belittle the efforts of Jews to emancipate themselves from a Christian society that was hostile to them. Because religion is only the reflection of civil society, itself the reflection of economic relationships, it is these that must be attacked, and not religion per se.[26] This led Marx to a discussion of the rise of the state, a condition that meant greater hardship for man but which, through the dialectical process, hastened the advent of the hoped-for revolution.

The end of feudalism and the rise of capitalism, according to Marx, resulted in the alienation of *individual* man, first from his fellow men and ultimately from himself. Society based on the principles of economic capitalism became atomized, responding to each man's determination to advance his own economic interests without regard to his fellows.[27] An interesting admission in this analysis is that individual man was better protected from state power under feudalism than under capitalism.

Thus the rise of capitalism is coincident with the rise of egoism and the atomization of society. Under such conditions, capitalism and the cult of private gain enabled the economic sector to escape the informal and nonstate communal control that had marked feudal society.[28] Once communal controls are abolished through alienation and atomization, the consolidation of state power is inevitable.

Capitalism thus went on to create a state that was unfettered by communal control. Since the state must consolidate its power to promote the conditions conducive to revolution, Marx's writings will support its growth, even though the capitalist state is the real source of man's oppression.[29] In the "Jewish Question," Marx backs the dominance of state power over religion, calling it an inevitable step in the battle against civil society.

This "perfection" of the state required the perfection of materialism in society. Thus any existing religion must not threaten materialism, for in so doing it would retard the necessary growth in state power. It was in this regard that Marx would come to accept Protestantism as the most appropriate religion for the capitalist age.

Most Protestant sects demand the separation of church and state, thus freeing the state from religious control. Since the process of atomization thus begun feeds on itself, religion tends to separate itself from any proceedings that involve the state. As an example of this separation, Marx says that modern Christians are much more likely to institute assault charges in a civil court than they are to "turn the other cheek."[30]

Religion, reduced to private piety, no longer serves man's civil needs. This in turn builds state power. Marx himself wrote: "Under Protestantism, there is no supreme head of the Church, so the rule of religion is the religion of rule; the cult of the government's will."[31] Thus the atomization of religion does not threaten the fundamental materialism of society, nor does it impede the consolidation of state power.

Marx often refrained from value judgments about social change because he thought such developments were inevitable. Yet it is clear from his writings that he favored the consolidation of state power, since it would bring on the revolution, and thus favored the atomization of religious belief that prevented the Church from standing up to the state as an independent entity. Once this occurred, religion became a strictly private matter and irrelevant to politics.

In spite of his hostility to religion, therefore, Marx never advocated destroying it forcibly. Capitalism, he thought, would do that for him by privatizing religion. Thus Marx looked favorably on the extreme atomization of organized religion that he saw in the United States.[32] He believed this to be an inevitable result of religion's privatization and a valuable aid to the dialectical process.[33]

State Power

But the process does not end here. Even in private life, religion still makes man forget his "species nature," which is absolutely necessary for a truly revolutionary understanding to develop.[34] Once state power has been consolidated, it must then be attacked for the dialectic to continue moving forward. In this regard, the attack on private property and the attack on private religious belief are related.

Both private property and private religious experiences reflect the egoism of civil society, and communism will negate both forms of egoism. By affirming man's essential nature as a member of a species, communism will make men aware of their solidarity, and such true consciousness will mean the end of alienation and the rise of "practical humanism."[35] Thus at one stage private religious belief is useful, and any religion that promotes such emphasis on the private aspects of salvation is a progressive step. Later, however, these beliefs will have to give way to the revolutionary synthesis, in common with all other sources of human alienation.

MARX AS THE CREATOR OF A NEW RELIGION

What is striking about this summary of Marx's attitude toward religion is his unshakable confidence in man and in state power. Also striking about Marx is his conspicuous failure to provide a rational source for this confidence. Where explanation is necessary, Marx often provides only dogmatic pronouncement. He left the world with a salvific vision of man's eventual redemption that is nonrational and requires faith at key points.

For example, Marx's metaphysics provided no solution to the problem of movement or the problem of original knowledge. By skipping the necessary explanations for these phenomena, Marx left behind not so much a philosophy (to say nothing of a science) but rather a religio-political dogma.[36] Marxism's status as a religion becomes even clearer when one considers the normative aspects of his thought. Certain economic conditions, he thought, were conducive to "true humanity." This is going beyond simple empiricism, which Marx shared with other philosophers, to apocalyptic dogmatism, which marks him as the creator of a new religion.[37] This status as creator, in addition to what we have already seen, makes Marx inescapably hostile to a rival religion such as Christianity.

One of the major elements of this new religion is its commitment to humanism, and the cult of human perfectibility. Christianity, which along with capitalism sees human nature as something received, rather than something man himself creates, detracts from the independent power with which Marx wishes to endow the human race.[38] By using materialism to explain man's nature, Marx can posit that this condition is the result of malleable material forces. He can then attribute what he does not like about man to these material forces and conclude that man is not a fallen creature, but merely misguided.

In fact, material man ceases to be a "creature" at all. Marx's particular contribution to political philosophy was ridding mankind of the concept of creaturehood, which of necessity calls out for a creator. By removing God from the place of creator, and failing to show that no creator was necessary (this is the unsolved problem of movement), Marx puts man in God's place. The creature becomes creator.[39] This, I suggest, is the basis of a religious belief.

Besides a creation myth, Marx also offers salvation. The rivalry with Christianity again becomes clear in the source of this salvation. Since the curse of modern man is alienation, the cure is not a god, but labor and the realization that men are members of a class. This realization comes through the actions of men who follow the dictates of Marxism. The more strict their adherence to Marx, the better.

THE CALL TO ACTION

Marxist dogma is not a matter for armchair philosophers. Inherent in Marx's analysis of the world is a normative element and a call to action. In this way Marx will distinguish his philosophy from all previous philosophy, and all theology, which, he said, could not change the real world of politics and economics. Such unsophisticated and unprogressive beliefs could only seek to change man's perception of his economic reality. Since perceptions grow out of reality, even this was a waste of time.

Whereas other philosophers perceived the purpose of philosophy as searching for truth, Marx says in "The Leading Article" that the purpose of philosophy is publicity.[40] Even allowing that this is an extreme statement made to drive home a point, it is evident that the emphasis is on philosophy as an agent of change, and not an intellectual pursuit.

It is even more evident in the "Theses on Feuerbach." As helpfully radical as his philosophy was, Feuerbach was still only trying to understand the world, when he should have been trying to change it. Even the materialists, according to Marx, err in conceiving reality as an object of contemplation, not as an arena for action.[41] To stop with a good interpretation of the world is to only go part way. The point of philosophy is to change the world.[42]

For some analysts, Marx's creation of a new religion means that Marxism can blend with other religions. As one sympathetic commentator wrote: "Marxism is a religion in itself. So it doesn't do away with religion, it merely begins a new chapter."[43]

As I have shown, however, the social analysis of Marx and the praxis of Marx are intimately and inextricably related, and both are fundamentally opposed to Christianity. Marx was sufficiently hostile toward religious belief to allow us to conclude that he did not develop a religion consciously. Moreover, to interpret Marxism as a form of religious belief, which I do, is not to suggest that it can therefore coexist with Christianity. Quite the opposite is true. The religion of Marxism rejects the most basic tenets of Christianity and, in fact, sees them as diametrically opposed to its own tenets.

ENGELS AND RELIGION

Engels's Apparent Hostility to Religion

It would be left to Engels, and not Marx, to find the path through which religion and Marxism could seemingly be made compatible. Yet

at first glance, Engels seems a particularly poor source for such a reconciliation, since he appeared to be as hostile to religion as Marx himself.

In their joint writings, Engels joined Marx in regarding the Catholic
Church as a remnant of the feudal world that was, in modern times,
outmoded and beneath criticism. For Engels, Catholicism ceased to be
important sometime in the fourth century when it became an established
religion. The only religion worthy of analysis in the eighteenth century
was German Protestantism.[44]

Like Marx, Engels devoted relatively little of his writing to religion as
such. The only book of the Bible he accepted as "authentic Christianity"
was Revelation, and even this, he believed, was an outgrowth of vulgar
religion, based on warmed-over Stoic philosophy. He claims that the
Epistles that are usually attributed to Saint Paul are really word for word
copies of the Stoic Seneca's writings.[45]

Even if Christianity could claim an existence apart from its alleged
plagiarism of Seneca, Engels would still be hostile to it. He saw religion
in general, and Christianity in particular, as fundamentally conservative
and useful as a tool to prevent the lower classes from claiming their
economic rights.

As a materialist, Engels agreed that religion grew out of material conditions and was a response to them. On the more primitive level, religion
consoled those bothered by the uncertainty of nature and their inability
to control natural forces. Later, it served the same function for those
buffeted by nonresponsive social forces.[46]

Engels also shared Marx's absolute confidence in human reason. In
"The Peasant War in Germany," Engels praised a Reformation scholar
who equated the Holy Spirit, the traditional source for inspired revelation, with human reason. This is nothing short of the deification of
man and Engels speaks favorably of it.[47] By making men into God, Engels
released them from human categories of good and evil. Such things
were meaningful only in context of place and time. Once man
superseded these, he became eternal. While other humanists turned
away from this extreme implication, Engels did not. Rather, he willingly
placed man on the altar that God had formerly inhabited.

Finally, Engels rejected religious belief because of his economic determinism. Economic and social conditions begot religious belief. Thus,
when the Roman legions disrupted traditional social and economic patterns in the Mediterranean, a new religion appeared. Later, the fall of
Rome changed the face of Christianity. Still later, the capitalist revolution
changed it again.[48]

Pantheism

But to all of these elements of opposition to religion that Engels shared
with Marx, he added something equally important: pantheism. In the

"Jewish Question," Marx quoted the German theologian Thomas Munzer, who said that it was intolerable that God's creation should be made into property. Creation too, Munzer said, must be liberated.[49]

While it is apparent that Munzer was not talking about inanimate objects, but rather animals, Engels would eventually come to believe that matter itself was not only living, but eternal. The clue to this belief, according to one author, is Engels's rejection of entropy and the consequent belief that matter must be able to create itself.[50] Thus Engels's materialism was far more radical than Marx's. For Engels, matter is alive, on the move. It is unnatural, he believed, not to perceive this reality and live with it.

In this regard, Engels came to view religions that increased the number of gods as progressive steps toward pantheism. Thus his preference for German Protestantism. In the exponential growth of Protestant sects, there are a variety of gods being worshipped. The resulting diversity gives Engels room for philosophical maneuver necessary to reconcile Marxism with revolutionary religion.

Religion as Revolution

Thus Engels goes further than Marx in distinguishing religions. More important, he adds a meaningful criterion for distinction: a religion's revolutionary potential. Engels, unlike Marx, came to see that some brands of Christianity had revolutionary potential, and could in fact be used as weapons of the oppressed rather than of the oppressor.[51] Coming to this conclusion in 1882, he could now examine the features of Christianity that made it so useful.

The first of these was the tendency of Christianity to seek its disciples among the poor and downtrodden, offering little solace to the rich.[52] At the same time, Christianity made the poor indifferent to wealth, thus precluding the possibility of the poor being dissuaded from revolution by incremental material amelioration. Rather, the poor are taught to despise material goods and own them in common, an essential feature of theoretical Marxism.[53]

Early Christianity's second important feature was the way in which it survived through active propaganda, unrelenting struggle, through the proud profession of its revolutionary standpoint, and, finally, through martyrdom.[54]

Third, the early Christian movement bore, in Engels's mind, a striking resemblance to the Working Men's Associations of his time. Both were movements of the oppressed, both promised forthcoming salvation, both were made illegal movements and persecuted, and both "forged irresistibly ahead" in spite of all these obstacles.[55] Early Christianity had an eagerness for struggle and a certainty of victory that modern Christianity completely lacks, but which modern socialism has in abundance, according to Engels.[56]

Fourth, both socialism and Christianity seemed to Engels to justify the use of violence. Engels used quotations from both the Old and New Testaments to justify regicide and other forms of revolutionary violence.[57] Later, he would find that Revelation, the only reliable expression of "pure Christianity" to him, preached revenge through the voices of martyrs at the throne of God. This book, he added, made no mention of baptism in water. Rather, the gathered saints were washed in the *blood* of the Lamb.[58]

The fifth similarity was the tendency of both movements to be diffuse, attracting a broad range of "malcontents and nonconformists." The many ways in which the Romans could oppress the lower classes required a broad-based, diverse revolutionary movement.[59] This is vitally important because it is here that Engels found another useful Christian attribute: its universality.

Engels was struck early on by Christianity's lack of distinctive and exclusive rituals. "By addressing itself to all peoples," Engels wrote, "it becomes the first possible world religion."[60] Christianity has only one firm dogmatic point: its faithful have already been saved by the sacrifice of Christ. This notion negated the need for further sacrifices, and thus for exclusive rituals, making Christianity at least potentially a world religion.[61]

This involved making another major shift from the philosophy of Marx. Since Christianity also attracted people across class lines, and not just national boundaries, Engels had to give up the Marxist notion that religion, like all other psychic phenomena, was economically determined. The fact that he abandoned this central tenet indicates that Engels thought he found something more valuable: a religion both potentially revolutionary and potentially global. Engels concluded that a less strict adherence to Marxism was a small price to pay for such a prize.

Engels attempted to recover the class nature of his religious revolution by interpreting the religious wars of the sixteenth century as class struggles in disguise. He went on to praise Catholic heretics who accepted the notion that Christianity was reserved for the lower classes. More important, he wrote approvingly of heretics who stayed in the Catholic Church rather than forming a schism.

The Example of Thomas Munzer

Engels concluded that Martin Luther, the most famous schismatic of the Reformation, was tactically unimaginative and hopelessly bourgeois.[62] His efforts brought nothing more than a reformed "burgher Church." Like any bourgeois reformer (the phrase is used with contempt) Luther had to navigate between the Scylla of true revolution and the Charybdis of reaction, in the form of Catholic restoration. The result for Luther was paralysis and missed opportunities to take over the Church from within. Engels found his hope in the more radical movement of Jan Hus and his followers, specifically Thomas Munzer.[63]

The first true and useful expression of communist strains in the Reformation, according to Engels, came from Munzer.[64] A Catholic theologian, Munzer began his career as a parish priest in Allstet, Switzerland, an almost lawless border town. There, while still in the Church, Munzer married a former nun and began adding personal changes to the liturgy, such as having the congregation recite the words of consecration with him.[65]

Unlike Luther, Munzer did not leave the Catholic Church, but continued to claim true Catholicism.[66] Munzer constantly fought with orthodox authorities while at the same time using his political connections to secure the post of chaplain to a nunnery in Halle, a German state where he could be assured of protection. While there he organized his passionately devoted followers into armed bands. One of these bands destroyed a miraculous shrine to Mary, devotion to whom was a sign of loyalty to orthodox Catholicism.[67]

Although he was a student of Luther, Munzer broke with him on the supposed distinction between the earthly and heavenly realm. Social justice, Munzer thought, was for the here and now, not for the heavenly future.[68] The Utopia of God's empire on earth was Munzer's goal. Engels also pointed out that Munzer broke with Luther on the need for human action to bring about desired social and political changes. For Munzer, people had an obligation to combat social injustice, a form of good works that Luther rejected.[69] Related to this was his rejection of the notion that Christians did not have to suffer because Christ had already done all the suffering necessary. Action and sacrifices on behalf of the cause were integral parts of Munzer's theology.

Munzer developed a theory of the legitimate right of revolution on the basis of Holy Scripture. When he spoke of God, it was the vengeful God of the Book of Daniel and the Book of Revelation. Salvation for Munzer was reserved for the poor. The "rich and fat" were excluded from heaven on the basis of their wealth, and not on the basis of their neglect of the poor or other sins. Wealth itself was the sin.[70]

Engels completed his treatment of Munzer's career by saying that after the Peasant War, revolutionary Christianity was nursed back to health by the secular hands of the socialists. The appeal of Christianity and its usefulness to revolution were too valuable for Engels to dismiss.[71]

Yet Engels also saw that this adherence to Christianity need not be genuine in order to be useful. One of the characteristics of Munzer that Engels praises is the "dual effect" of his activity. Munzer, Engels noted approvingly, spoke the language of religion to the people, since it was the only language they could understand. But he used a different sort of language to the "initiated" who were close to him. Only to this elite group did he reveal his ultimate plans. Engels acknowledges that Munzer's organized party was an elite of revolutionaries that was never more than a small minority of the German people.

Engels believed that these first uprisings of peasants and plebeians, including the various uprisings of the Middle Ages, required "religious masks" in order to have a chance at success. Implied here is the idea that first attempts at revolution in other backward areas, such as Catholic Latin America, may also require the same masks to cover the same sort of deception regarding ultimate ends. I shall show in Chapter 2 that Liberation Theology is well suited to perform this task.

NOTES

1. Karl Marx, "The Communism of the Paper *Rheinischer Beobachter*," in Reinhold Niebuhr, ed., *Karl Marx and Friedrich Engels on Religion* (New York: Schocken Books, 1964), 83.

2. Karl Marx, "The Leading Article of No. 179 of Kolnische Zeitung," in Niebuhr, *Marx and Engels on Religion*, 37

3. See E. P. Thompson, *The Making of the English Working Class* (New York: Random House, 1966).

4. Trevor Ling, *Karl Marx and Religion in Europe and India* (London: Macmillan 1980), 16-17.

5. Delos B. McKown, *The Classical Marxist Critique of Religion: Marx, Engels, Lenin, Kautsky* (The Hague: Martinus Nijhoff, 1975), 15.

6. Niebuhr, *Marx and Engels on Religion*, ix.

7. Marx, "Leading Article," 24.

8. Ibid., 26.

9. Karl Marx and Friedrich Engels, "The Holy Family, or the Critique of Critical Criticism," in Niebuhr, *Marx and Engels on Religion*, 65

10. Ibid.

11. See Joseph O'Malley, "Editor's Introduction," in Karl Marx, *Critique of Hegel's "Philosophy of Right"* (Cambridge: Cambridge University Press, 1970), xxii.

12. Ibid., xxvii-xxx.

13. Karl Marx, "The German Ideology," in Niebuhr, *Marx and Engels on Religion*, 73-74.

14. Marx, "Leading Article," 22.

15. Marx, "Communism of the Paper," 84.

16. William Lloyd Newell, *The Secular Magi: Marx, Freud and Nietzsche on Religion* (New York:, Pilgrim Press, 1986), 4.

17. Karl Marx, "The Difference Between the Natural Philosophy of Democritus and the Natural Philosophy of Epicurus," in Niebuhr, *Marx and Engels on Religion*, 13-15.

18. Karl Marx, "Theses on Feuerbach," in Niebuhr, *Marx and Engels on Religion*, 71.

19. Karl Marx and Friedrich Engels, *The Communist Manifesto*, Penguin Classics (New York: Penguin, 1967), 79.

20. Marx, "German Ideology," 78.

21. Ibid., 74-75.

22. Geoffrey Hunt, "The Development of the Concept of Civil Society in Marx," *History of Political Thought*, 8,2 (Summer 1987): 266.

23. McKown, *The Classical Marxist Critique*, 27.

24. Rubem Alves, *What is Religion?* (Maryknoll, NY: Orbis Books, 1981), 56.

25. Karl Marx, *Capital: A Critical Analysis of Capitalist Production* (London: William Clashier, 1920), 135.

26. Karl Marx, "On the Jewish Question," in David McLellan, ed., *Karl Marx: Selected Writings* (Oxford: Oxford University Press, 1977), 50.

27. Ibid., 55.

28. McKown, *The Classical Marxist Critique*, 38.

29. Marx, "Jewish Question," 39.

30. Marx, "Leading Article," 35.

31. Quoted in Ling, *Marx and Religion*, 10.

32. Marx, "Jewish Question," 43.

33. Ibid., 47.

34. Newell, *Secular Magi*, 42.

35. Ibid., 28.

36. Niebuhr, *Marx and Engels on Religion*, ix.

37. Marx and Engels, "Holy Family," 67.

38. Newell, *Secular Magi*, 29.

39. Ibid., 16.

40. Marx, "Leading Article," 31.

41. Marx, "Theses on Feuerbach," 69.

42. Ibid., 72.

43. Alves, *What is Religion?* 58.

44. McKown, *The Classical Marxist Critique*, 81-82.

45. Friedrich Engels, "Bruno Bauer and Early Christianity," in Niebuhr, *Marx and Engels on Religion*, 195-98.

46. Ibid., 202.

47. Friedrich Engels, "The Peasant War in Germany," in Niebuhr, *Marx and Engels on Religion*, 111.

48. Engels, "Bruno Bauer," 201. See also Friedrich Engels, "On the History of Early Christianity," in Niebuhr, *Marx and Engels on Religion*, 334-35.

49. Marx, "Jewish Question," 60.

50. Newell, *Secular Magi*, 67.

51. McKown, *The Classical Marxist Critique*, 89.

52. Engels, "Bruno Bauer," 196.

53. Engels, "Early Christianity," 320.

54. Ibid., 345.

55. Ibid., 316.

56. Ibid., 330.

57. Friedrich Engels, "Peasant War," in Niebuhr, *Marx and Engels on Religion*, 113-14.

58. Engels, "Early Christianity, 337-45.

59. Ibid., 335.

60. Engels, "Bruno Bauer," 203.

61. Friedrich Engels, "The Book of Revelation," in Niebuhr, *Marx and Engels on Religion*, 206.

62. Engels, "Peasant War," 104.

63. Ibid., 101.

64. Ibid., 103.

65. C. Gordon Rupp, "Thomas Munzer: Prophet of Radical Christianity," *Bulletin of the John Rylands Library*, 48, 2 (Spring 1966): 468-70.

66. Engels, "Peasant War," 109.

67. Rupp, "Thomas Munzer," 470.

68. Steven D. Martinson, *Between Luther and Munzer: The Peasant Revolt in German Drama and Thought* (Heidelberg: Carl Winder, 1988), 28-29 fn.

69. Ibid., 25.

70. Ibid., 27-33.

71. McKown, *The Classical Marxist Critique*, 85.

2

Liberation Theology and Marxism: The Limits of Comparison

As we saw in Chapter 1, Karl Marx failed to see the revolutionary potential of religion. In fact, his attitude toward religion was consistently hostile throughout his life. Insofar as there was any "development" in Marx's thought about religion at all, it was movement from outright enmity to silent disdain. Thus Marx would be among the first to deny the possibility of collaboration between his philosophy and Christianity.

One friendly commentator defends the use of Marxism by Christians by pointing out that one does not have to be a Marxist to recognize class differences in Latin America.[1] He goes on to point out that Liberationists like Miguel Bonino accept the Marxist notion of class struggle without accepting the rest of Marxism.

The Liberationist group Christians for Socialism made one of the clearest statements in this regard in 1971: "As Christians, we do not see any incompatibility between Christianity and Socialism. Quite the contrary is true. . . . [I]t is necessary to destroy the prejudice and mistrust that exist between Christians and Marxists."[2]

Moreover, we also saw in Chapter 1 that Marx considered his philosophy a seamless whole. Marx rejected the idea of taking only part of it, such as his analysis of the great disparities of wealth in nineteenth-century Europe, and ignoring the rest, such as his materialism, humanism, or economic determinism. For this reason as well he would be likely to oppose the attempt by some Christians to apply his social analysis, apart from the rest of Marxism, to investigate the current situation in Latin America.

Thus, Liberation Theology is not Marxist.[3] Instead, the thought of most Liberation Theologians has more in common with Friedrich Engels than Marx, although even here there are important differences. At the same time, I will also show that Liberation Theology accepts enough of the Marxist philosophic worldview to separate itself irrevocably from Christianity.

REASONS FOR A CHRISTIAN-MARXIST DIALOGUE

New Competitors for Souls

Many Catholics in Latin America perceive the need for the Church to compete with Marxists for the hearts and minds of their people. The conferees gathered at Puebla, Mexico, in 1979 for the Third Conference of the Bishops of Latin America (CELAM III) deplored the Church's loss of its position as social critic and blamed its preoccupation with the next life as the reason the Church was losing ground to Marxism and "other atheistic solutions."[4]

According to one commentator, the demographic and socioeconomic changes of the twentieth century have made it necessary for the Church to provide a "new reward system" to compete with both Marxists and Protestant Evangelicals. This new system must provide the same rewards in the areas of economic and personal salvation as these competitors.[5]

Imitation as an approach to competing philosophies is nothing new to the Catholic Church. At the start of the Protestant Reformation and the beginnings of modern capitalism, many Catholics made the same arguments for "updating" the Catholic faith to make it more "responsive" to perceived current needs. More traditional Catholics wondered how far the Church could go in accommodating itself before compromising its essential beliefs.

An important part of the attempt to win back those segments of the population that have been lost to Marxism is the Church's "preferential option for the poor." The Catholic Church adopted this option long before the appearance of Liberation Theology and based its theology on the Bible instead of on Marx or Engels. Liberationists, for their part, both ignore the original doctrine and claim that it does not go far enough. Based on nothing more than the superficial coincidence that both Christianity and Marxism address the fact of poverty, some Latin Americans assert that they must therefore work together.

The Traditional Church

A second tactical reason for linking with Marxism is the Liberationist criticism of the traditional Church. The Catholic Church began to go wrong in colonial times, according to some Liberationists. Penny Lernoux, a North American sympathizer with the new theology, is typical in her portrayal of the colonial Church when she says: "From the very beginning, the region's Church was a dependent partner of the state, a condition which has survived to the present day."[6]

This criticism and disdain for the perceived role of the Church takes several forms. The first accusation levelled at the traditional Church is that it is nontransformative. That is, the Church makes no effort to effect fundamental changes in man or earthly society.

A natural outgrowth of this, according to one observer, is what he calls popular providentialism. This fills the believer with naive expectations about what God can do for him and promotes petitionary prayers to bring about divine intervention. The task of changing things for the better is left to the Almighty, and until He takes action, there is nothing to do but suffer patiently.[7]

A Partner in Exploitation?

A second, and more serious, accusation made about the traditional Church is its alleged linkage to the existing power structure. Gustavo Gutierrez, a Peruvian who was among the earliest theorists of Liberation Theology, exhorts the Church to stop identifying itself with the rich and powerful, whom he calls the agents of dependence.[8] What Gutierrez does not say is that this identification was wrested from the Church in the form of the colonial and postcolonial *patronato*, which the official Church in Rome fought throughout the centuries.

Nevertheless, Liberationists paint the non-Liberation Church as a "kept" Church, forced to play politics and thus become part of, rather than aloof from, the political process.[9] The advent of anticlerical regimes in parts of Latin America has forced the Church to fight political battles just to survive, which has also reduced its independence.

For some Liberationists, the fact that the Church raises funds makes it a part of the oppression of the masses. Juan Luis Segundo, an Argentine Jesuit, argues that since the Church gets its money from the bourgeoisie, and this class gets its charitable surplus, directly or indirectly, from the exploitation of the poor, the Church is thus a partner in this exploitation.[10]

For Liberation Theologians, therefore, the path of traditional Catholicism is unacceptable, because of the "kept" nature of the traditional Church. Committed Christians, they believe, must actively strive to create a new order for society. It is in their diagnosis of existing society, and in their prescription for curing society's ills, that Liberationists and their critics find so many areas of agreement with Marxism.

LIBERATION THEOLOGY AND MARXISM: POINTS OF CONTACT

Importance of History

An understanding of the meaning and importance of history is crucial to the Liberationists' analysis of society. How Liberation Theologians interpret history, however, is only superficially congruent with Marxist historical analysis.

According to Enrique Dussel, an Argentine Liberationist known primarily as a Church "historian," God reveals himself in history. For Dussel, each divine revelation takes place within a specific historical context and can be properly understood only within that context. Reading the Gospel message is not enough. The message must be read within the tradition in which it was given.

Dussel uses the example of God speaking to Moses in the burning bush. Moses heard the voice of God not abstractly, but through his everyday shepherd's existence. The voice that he heard carried a message of enslavement. This message would have been unintelligible without the historical knowledge of the Israelites' captivity in Egypt.[11]

Dussel chooses the example of Moses because he interprets the story of the Jewish Exodus as an example of a historical liberation; that is, the fusing of the timeless and transcendent God with a specific set of historical circumstances. By extension, he makes the argument that such a liberating process may be at hand in contemporary Latin America, citing the examples of Fidel Castro's Cuba or Salvador Allende's Chile.[12]

Marx also believed in the importance of historical context in the understanding of various revolutionary processes, but the preoccupation with history is by no means unique to him. It does, however, present certain problems for the Christian theologian. If historical context is so important, does it not necessarily follow that the message of the Gospels must be relative to history? Does this not mean that the message changes from one time to another? This runs counter to the Christian belief that the Word of God, by its very nature, must be absolutely true, not just true in certain contexts.

It is not difficult to find Liberation Theologians who profess a belief in the relativity of the Bible message. Dussel makes one of the more moderate approaches when he says: "The only way to seek God's eternal truth is to reiterate it in fresh terms for every new age and generation."[13]

Gutierrez goes a step further than Dussel when he approvingly quotes Henri Bouillard: "A theology which is not up to date is a false theology."[14] Juan Luis Segundo continues in this theme by saying that Liberation Theology must be based upon "the continuing change in our interpretation of the Bible, which is dictated by the continuing change in our present-day reality."[15] Hugo Assmann, a Brazilian known for his particularly radical statements of Liberationist precepts, expresses the logical conclusion of these thoughts when he says baldly: "The Word of God is no longer a fixed Absolute"[16] and that the worst temptation for a theology is to engage in absolutes.[17]

Besides being relative to time, the Gospel message is also relative to space, according to the Liberationists. The Gospel has a different message for Latin America than for the rest of the world. Proponents of Liberation Theology frequently emphasize the need for a strictly Latin American theology, even though many critics of Liberation Theology point to its roots in German theology and even though many important Liberation Theologians were educated at the Louvain Catholic Institute in Belgium.[18]

Dussel makes the clearest call for such a particularistic theology by hailing the 1968 Medellín Conference of Latin American Bishops (CELAM II or simply Medellín) as the start of a Latin American theology, distinct from theologies in use in other parts of the world. He adds: "Other churches cannot show us the way."[19] Penny Lernoux praises the rebirth of CELAM as "the first timid step away from Rome's tutelage."[20]

The difficulty with this relativism for orthodox Christian believers is twofold. First, it challenges those who believe that the Word of God is the same for all peoples and all generations. Second, it is easier, once the need for strict orthodoxy is discarded, to make adaptations and compromises in the faith.

For example, Dussel cites the need to "reexamine" the rules of the priesthood since not as many young men want to join as previously. The restrictive rules of the past are no longer applicable and, presumably, should be relaxed.[21] The willingness to apply this same relaxation to matters of doctrine is present in the suggestion by Segundo that the doctrine "Jesus died on the Cross [and] God raised his son, Jesus Christ, from the dead," be replaced by: "No love is lost on this earth."[22] Thus, however close Liberation Theology might find itself to Marxism, a more important question is how far it has strayed from Christianity.

An Inductive Theology

Unlike traditional Catholicism, which has a God-based and deductive metaphysics, Liberation Theology is human-based and its method of analysis is inductive. Gutierrez, for example, praises the formation of local Christian communities and asserts that the actions and deliberations of these communities must form the basis of Liberation Theology. He adds later that Liberation itself, and the path to Liberation, must come from the oppressed.[23] Jon Sobrino, a Spanish Liberationist who would do most of his writing in El Salvador, writes that the proper starting point of theology should be the "underside of history," or the underclass.[24] José Miguel Bonino, an Argentine Protestant, agrees that Liberation Theology must be inductive, coming from the experience of the oppressed.[25]

This dependence on the contemporary earthly experience of poor people for the truths of a theology is directly at odds with the Christian vision. For orthodox Christians, truth is not only revealed by God himself through revelation, but is also the starting point for understanding human life. Liberationists have reversed this relationship, based on their confidence in man, and specifically poor man, to find truth on his own.

Humanism

This confidence in man pervades Liberationist thinking and provides another point of comparison to Marx. The two philosophies also have similar views of the potential of human beings. Like Marxists, Liberationists have a very optimistic view of man's capabilities.

Rather than accepting the traditional Catholic view that man is limited by his creaturehood and by original sin, the Liberationists see man as the master and transformer of his own fate. Paulo Freire, a Brazilian who is not, strictly speaking, a Liberation Theologian but whose writings are quoted approvingly by most adherents to the new theology, describes man as a subject who acts upon and transforms his world.[26]

Man has the ability to create and control his future, and must learn to overcome his perception that he is the creation of a more powerful Being. This Liberationist belief underscores the importance of the human agent in the Exodus. According to Gutierrez, Moses liberated the Israelites by calling upon them to transform their world and in so doing, to become truly human.[27] The conscious acceptance by men of this responsibility for their own destiny is the essence of Liberation.

None of this would be contrary to traditional Catholic thought if it were not for the extreme view of man's capabilities that the Liberationists take. This is most concisely demonstrated by looking at the goal of Liberation, which is nothing short of the creation of a "New Man." This New Man will be the "artisan of his own destiny,"[28] unshackled by anything that previously bound him, including original sin. Liberation Theology accepts the Marxist notion of earthly paradise for man and earthly perfection.

Perfectibility of This World

The Liberationist view of the world is driven by their view of man. If man can be made perfect, then he must also be able to create the perfect society. This recalls the religion of Thomas Munzer, which Engels found so exemplary. Leonardo Boff describes the Kingdom of God as the "realization of a fundamental Utopia of the human heart, the total transformation of this world."[29] This was the promise of Christ, and, according to Boff, He showed that it was achievable in this world. Dussel also anticipates the temporal reign of God when he says: "Jesus is of the future." It is clear that he is talking about an earthly future.[30]

The most ardent prophet of this earthly paradise is Jose Porfirio Miranda, a Mexican Liberationist who is, incidentally, the theorist who draws the closest connection between Jesus and Marx. Miranda writes that Marx follows in the footsteps of Saint Paul, who, he says, believed that injustice and sin could be eliminated. Like Marx, Paul found imperfection embedded in "earthly principalities and powers."[31] For Miranda, faith in Christ necessarily entails the belief that the Kingdom of God can be achieved here on Earth.

Class Struggle

The methods for achieving this earthly perfection also provide points of comparison to Marxism. Liberation Theologians routinely begin their analysis of Latin America with lengthy descriptions of the poverty of the continent, contrasting this with its abundant natural resources. Most analyses also point up the enormous disparities of wealth, and argue that these disparities are growing.

More important, Liberationists link poverty to the wealth of some members of society and their determination to oppress the poor. Liberationists apply a strictly earthly standard to poverty and reject it utterly, in contrast to the traditional Catholic notion that true piety and devotion to God sometimes require a poor existence. Oppression is broadly defined as any hindrance to the pursuit of self-affirmation, but, interestingly, the discussion is normally limited to the economic sphere. Human beings are reified by oppression, becoming economic tools for the use of another.[32]

To correct this situation, the Liberationists suggest class struggle. For this reason, their theology is directed toward the lower classes exclusively. Most Liberationists make it clear that the rich are beyond salvation. Gutierrez, for example, writes that "Liberation expresses the aspirations of oppressed classes and peoples," underlining "the conflictual aspect of the social, economic and political process."[33] Class struggle for Gutierrez is inevitable, because those in power consciously keep the lower classes in submission. Segundo continues the theme, defining conscientization as "any form of social mobilization that seeks to inculcate an . . . awareness of the real interests, especially class interests, at work in society."[34]

Miranda uses two Gospel quotations to justify directing his evangelization efforts exclusively at the poor, recalling that Christ directed the rich young man to renounce all his property as a condition of salvation (Mark 10:21) and elsewhere reminded his listeners that only the poor can enter the Kingdom of God (Luke 6:20). Assmann agrees that the poor are more open to Liberation and that both class struggle and revolution are necessary to bring about that liberation.[35] Dussel goes even further, saying that this preference for the poor is the only way out of idolatry.

The difficulty, once again, is not the compatibility of Liberation Theology with Marxism, but its compatibility with the fundamental beliefs of Christianity. Liberationists accept almost without question the peculiarly twentieth-century view of collective enterprise and collective responsibility. For Christians, a man is guilty not because he is rich, but because he, personally, lied, cheated, or stole to acquire his wealth. Similarly, a rich person who forsakes the things of God because of his wealth is a sinner. But his neighbor, equally wealthy, might be innocent of any wrongdoing.

In any case, it is a person's soul, and not his bank account, that determines guilt or innocence. What is particularly troubling about the Liberationist acceptance of class struggle is not its superficial similarity to Marxism, but its fundamental incompatibility with Christianity.

Revolutionary Praxis

If a widening and dehumanizing separation of classes is Liberation Theology's diagnosis of society's ills, revolution is its prescription. Segundo, for example, writes that neutrality in the cause of liberation is immoral. Moreover, the theology designed to bring about that liberation must serve the needs of revolution.[36] Sobrino consciously follows Marx in rejecting a "philosophy of knowing" for a "philosophy of action."[37]

Gutierrez agrees that theology must strive to change the world, not just to understand it.[38] Boff adds that a "critical" Christology must be needs-directed and future-oriented. It must also be open to dialogue and committed to change in the status quo. Most important, the critical Christologist must remember that correct action is more important than correct beliefs.[39]

The imitation of Marx and his revolutionary praxis is notable, but not as important to a proper understanding of Liberation Theology as the divergence from traditional Catholicism.

Marx himself believed that religion, per se, was unable to perform the action-directed role he envisioned because religion is committed to the truth. Such a commitment greatly reduces the amount of maneuvering room available to a philosophy which is also committed to a predetermined course of action.

What the Liberationists are doing with their emphasis on praxis is denying the need not only for strict orthodoxy, but also for truth itself. Truth, for the Liberation Theologians, is that which serves the revolution. Truth, in other words, is put to the service of a desired social end. Traditional Christianity holds that the Truth must be discovered first and that this Truth must be applied to existing social conditions second. A course of action must then be determined, based on discovered Truth, and not deleterious to it. Liberation Theology reverses the order of priorities, and whatever similarity with Marxism this entails, its underlying dissimilarity with Christianity is more striking.

More revealing is the rejection of gradual or incremental reform. This will, according to Freire, only lead to a perpetuation of the oppression and domination that must be eliminated. "Generosity" by the wealthy, in the form of higher wages or social legislation, is merely a method of maintaining control, preferable to outright conquest, but having the same end.[40]

A more insidious method of self-perpetuation, however, is what Freire calls manipulation. This involves pacifying the dominated masses with the myth that they might rise out of their poverty and enter the bourgeois system themselves.[41] By rejecting such a possibility out of hand, the Liberationists rule out the hope for a better life within the existing social framework.

This domination is structural and inseparable from the most basic assumptions of capitalistic society. Liberation Theologians attack the legitimacy of private property. Dussel calls the right to private property a mere positive (man-made) right, and not a natural (God-given) right.[42] He adds in a later work that when God gave man possession and dominion over all the earth (Genesis 1:28–29) He was giving everything to everybody. Exclusive ownership is the result of original sin and not part of God's plan.[43]

What is important about this belief is not its closeness to the Marxist attitude toward private property, nor the identification of private property with original sin. Neither of these attitudes is unique to Marxism or marks their holders as Marxist. What distinguishes the Liberationists from orthodox Christian believers, and in particular orthodox Catholics, is their determination to undo the effects of original sin here on Earth. Where the Christian believer accepts an imperfect world and seeks only to soften its rough edges, the Liberationists declare the world perfectible and rely on radical solutions to achieve this perfection.

Reforms are thus not helpful and could be harmful insofar as they delay the advent of the revolution. Gutierrez writes: "Only a radical break from the status quo, that is, a profound transformation of the private property system . . . would allow for the change to a new society."[44]

Violence and Its Justification

Liberation Theology's revolutionary praxis generates strident opposition. The opposition certainly comes from members of the former dominating classes and may even come from the masses themselves. Having "internalized the oppressor," perhaps the result of paternalism, "generosity," or manipulation, the masses may fear freedom.[45] To deal with opponents above or below, Liberation Theologians unabashedly justify and even advocate the inclusion of violence in their revolutionary praxis.

The most restrained advocacy of violence comes from the Belgian Liberationist Jean Comblin, who wrote that violence is justified only if the alternative is no action. Even then, the failure to act must, in itself, condone or acquiesce in the continuation of oppression.[46] Violence, in other words, must meet the stringent conditions laid down by the Catholic just war doctrine. Comblin's attitude is condemned by many of his fellow Liberationists as hopelessly conservative.

Liberationists draw upon a statement from Pope Paul VI, writing in *Populorum Progressio*, to defend their embrace of violence, even though Pope Paul VI was probably condemning violence in the statement. Noting the grievous reality of poverty in much of the Third World, the Holy Father warned that the situation was so bad that "the recourse to violence, as a means to right these wrongs to human dignity, is a grave temptation."[47]

This is a condemnation of violence, along with a condemnation of the situation that makes violence so tempting. If recourse to violence were morally justifiable, the pope would not have referred to it as a "grave temptation." The word "grave," in papal parlance, is an indication of seriousness and disapproval. To use it to sanction violence is arguing to a conclusion.

Pope Paul VI also provided another opening for Liberationists to justify their acceptance of violence. By pointing up the injustice of existing economic relationships, Paul VI accused the rich and powerful of violence. For Liberation Theologians, then, what they advocate is not ordinary violence. It is closer to self-defense; a response to aggression.

Dussel compares Liberationist violence to that which a parent might use to defend a child, or that which the Jesuits in colonial Paraguay used to defend the Indians under their charge from Brazilian slave-hunters.[48] This "second violence" is not sinful and is distinguished from the "first violence" of the attackers, which is sinful.

Rubem Alves, a Brazilian theologian, defines violence as "anything that keeps humans from realizing a better future."[49] This definition puts the onus completely upon the ruling classes. According to Freire, oppression is a form of violence which can only be initiated by the oppressors. The oppressed, by definition, cannot initiate violence.[50]

The violence of oppression is inherent in the existing economic structure and any violence used against this structure is, again by definition, defensive. One European commentator on the notion of structural violence says that violent revolution will divide people into two camps: those who see the revolution as a crisis and those who feel that the old order was already a permanent crisis.[51]

The Liberationists are hardly alone in their condemnation of existing political, economic, and social relationships. As early as 1967 the assembled bishops of Latin America, Africa, and Asia maintained that revolution might be an appropriate means to overcome injustice, and went on to denounce the rich nations of the world as "inciters to violence."[52] The Latin American Bishops' Conference has condemned existing economic relationships as "institutionalized violence."[53] The Paraguayan delegation drew a distinction between force, which is used in the service of justice and is sometimes necessary, and violence, which is structural and never necessary.[54]

The episcopal conferences and the more radical Liberation Theologians had different attitudes towards violence. For the bishops and for Pope Paul VI, violence was a last resort, to be taken when all other means to improve the temporal situation had failed. This is consistent with the Christian notion of an imperfect world and the necessity for reasoned improvement that does not bring about greater suffering.

For the Liberationists, however, the world is perfectible and any means are acceptable to achieve this perfection. Violence against the structural violence of economic disparity is not the last resort but the first resort. Indeed, it seems to be the only choice. The revolution and subsequent establishment of the Kingdom of God on Earth are not only desirable and worth whatever sacrifices are necessary, they are also inevitable.

By asserting that revolution is the only way to the ideal society, Liberation Theology implies that it is the just way.

Socialism

The Liberationist vision of the achievable perfect society also links its believers with Marx and separates them from Christianity. Liberation Theologians are united in their call for socialism to replace the current political, economic, and social system. Not surprisingly, adherents to the new theology describe socialism optimistically.

José Miranda, for example, equates socialism with the more equitable handling of financial resources and contrasts this ideal with the terrible reality of capitalist economic disparity. Gutierrez goes further, suggesting that socialism is the only fruitful way to achieve an ideal society. Socialism for Gutierrez will necessarily lead to man's control over nature, the socialized acquisition of wealth, and the abolition of the private acquisition of excessive wealth.[55]

To a certain extent, the Liberationists' rosy view of socialism's possibilities is understandable. At the time that they were writing, socialism enjoyed a more generally favorable reputation among social scientists. In the last decade, however, the colossal failures of socialism around the world, combined with the revival of private enterprise, make their boundless enthusiasm for socialism seem almost quaint. Nevertheless, there is a serious breach from Christianity involved here.

This advocacy of socialism could involve more than just the surrender of excessive wealth by the rich. Segundo calls for certain concessions by the Church as well. He suggests that all Church institutions, including schools, universities, and any Church-operated media outlets be turned over to the new socialist state.[56] Such a suggestion could only come from someone with an extraordinary confidence in properly directed state power. Such confidence marks the proponents of Liberation Theology.

Herein lies the difference with Christianity. For traditional Christians, the state is something to be distrusted. As an agent of secular power, the state required guidance from the Church. Such oversight power could only be exercised by an independent Church. What the Liberationists suggest is that the Church and state combine. Any fear about what such a combination might do to the traditional role of the Church is left out of Liberationist writings. Equally absent is any admission of the possibility that the Church could become tied to another political order after Liberation occurs.

Even within the secular realm, the Liberationist confidence in state power raises concerns. To assert that the state has the ability, let alone the disposition, to correct all social evils is to take an enormous risk. For the questionable chance to eliminate poverty, the Liberationists risk losing precious freedom and autonomy. The danger that liberty might be sacrificed while economic nirvana remains as far away as ever seems not to have occurred to the adherents of Liberation. At the same time, they risk tying the Church to whatever oppressive state apparatus they do create.

CONCLUSION

Marx thought that religion and empiricism were incompatible. Religion, he thought, was committed to particular articles of faith, and therefore religion was incapable of the sort of free and unfettered "scientific" inquiry on which Marx depended. Marx also believed that because traditional religion is dependent on the next life for its source of justification and solace to the masses, that it was also antihumanistic. By positing heavenly values as the ultimate ones, religion relegated human values to no better than second place.

Furthermore, religion was primarily oriented to the search for truth, either by understanding "revelation" or commenting upon revelation myths. Such a belief system necessarily assigned active praxis to a subordinate position. Marx saw his action-oriented philosophy as incompatible with anything that was willing to put action at the service of truth rather than vice versa.

What is striking about Liberation Theology is that it meets almost none of Marx's criteria for religion. Liberation Theology is no enemy of empiricism, for example. Many of its adherents insist that they approach truth inductively, based on "scientific" examination of the life of the oppressed classes. Liberation Theology emphasizes the human needs of the here and now at the expense of the divine needs of eternal salvation. Thus it is as humanistic as Marxism. Finally, it is action-oriented, with prominent Liberationists insisting upon the primacy of action over reflection, action over philosophy, and even action over absolute truth.

Moreover, Marx believed that any religion which was progressive would increase human alienation and atomization. The role of unifying mankind and giving a sense of community would be taken over by a philosophy that responded to the emotional emptiness left by a purely private religion. Yet for the Liberationists their new theology will play this unifying role, a role Marx said religion was not able to play.

As I argued above, it was Engels and not Marx who came to realize the revolutionary potential of "religion." A closer look at what Engels found to be useful in religion is revealing. Engels saw revolutionary aptitude in Christianity because it preached to the poor and downtrodden, offering them a better life. Early Christianity was eager for struggle and even martyrdom, so certain was it of final victory. It justified the use of violence, at least according to Engels's questionable interpretations of Revelation and the Epistles of Saint Paul. Finally, because it required no exclusive rituals, Christianity could become a universal religion.

I suggest that all these characteristics can be attributed to numerous political philosophies, and are not particular to religion as opposed to philosophy. In other words, many kinds of belief systems can do what Engels wanted Christianity to do and yet not have any of the more fundamental characteristics of religion. These include devotion to a revealed set of truths, an immutable set of moral laws, and a metaphysics that goes beyond the material to the spiritual.

Whatever compatibility Liberation Theology has with Marx, it has more compatibility with Engels. Even here, however, Engels asks Christianity to give up what is most fundamental to emphasize what is more superficial. The result is a convincing copy of surface Christianity, which can serve to hide the more basic differences.

In effect, Marx created a new religion, complete with creation myths and promises of salvation. This new religion of Marx is incompatible with Christianity. Liberation Theology, because it also presents itself as a new religion, and because it accepts all of the elements of Marxism that make that philosophy opposed to Christianity, will be as hostile as Marxism to traditional Christian belief. Insofar as Liberationists seek to downplay their differences with the core values of Christianity, it can be more deceptive and therefore even more difficult to counter than Marxism.

NOTES

1. Deane William Ferm, *Third World Liberation Theologies: An Introductory Survey* (Maryknoll, NY: Orbis Books, 1976), 33.

2. John Eagleston, ed., *Christians and Socialism: Documentation of the Christians for Socialism Movement in Latin America* (Maryknoll, NY: Orbis Books, 1975), 4.

3. Some authors have remarked that a concept that finds no support in the writings of Karl Marx may still be Marxist. See especially Steven Lukes, *Marxism and Morality* (Oxford: Clarendon Press, 1984). I agree with Cardinal John Ratzinger, who wrote in the 1984 *Instruction on Certain Aspects of the "Theology of Liberation"* (Sacred Congregation for the Doctrine of the Faith. Official Vatican translation. Boston: Daughters of St. Paul):

It is true that marxist thought ever since its origins, and even more so lately, has become divided and has given birth to various currents which diverge significantly from one another. To the extent that they remain fully marxist, these currents continue to be based on certain fundamental tenets.

The implications of philosophies calling themselves Marxist but diverging from Marx in the fundamentals is beyond the scope of this chapter.

4. Conference of Latin American Bishops, "La Iglesia Nace del Pueblo Latinoamericano," in *Los Obispos Latinoamericanos Entre Medellin y Puebla: Documentos Episcopales* (San Salvador: UCA Editores, 1978), 18–19.

5. Ivan Vallier, *Catholicism, Social Control and Modernization in Latin America,* (Englewood Cliffs, NJ: Prentice-Hall, 1970), 58.

6. Penny Lernoux, "The Long Path to Puebla," in John Eagleston and Philip Schrarper, eds., *Puebla and Beyond: Documentation and Commentary* (Maryknoll, NY: Orbis Books, 1979), 3.

7. Vallier, *Catholicism,* 28

8. Gustavo Gutierrez, *A Theology of Liberation* (Maryknoll, NY: Orbis Books, 1973), 139.

9. Vallier, *Catholicism,* 7.

10. Juan Luis Segundo, *The Hidden Motives of Pastoral Action* (Maryknoll, NY: Orbis Books, 1978).

11. Enrique Dussel, *History and the Theology of Liberation: A Latin American Perspective* (Maryknoll, NY: Orbis Books, 1976), 2-3, 18.

12. Ibid., 121.

13. Ibid., 150.

14. Gutierrez, *Theology*, 13.

15. Juan Luis Segundo, *The Liberation of Theology* (Maryknoll, NY: Orbis Books, 1976), 8.

16. Quoted in W. Dayton Roberts, "Where Has Liberation Theology Gone Wrong?" *Christianity Today*, XXIII, 24 (1979): 28.

17. Hugo Assmann, *Theology for a Nomad Church* (Maryknoll, NY: Orbis Books, 1976), 104.

18. See James V. Schall, *Liberation Theology in Latin America* (San Francisco: Ignatius Press, 1982), and Ferm, *Third World Liberation Theologies*.

19. Enrique Dussel, *Caminos de Liberación Latinoamericanos* (Buenos Aires: Latinoamericanos Libros, 1972), 147.

20. Lernoux, "The Long Path to Puebla," 11.

21. Dussel, *History*, 82.

22. Segundo, *Hidden Motives*, 115.

23. Gustavo Gutierrez, *The Power of the Poor in History* (Maryknoll, NY: Orbis Books, 1983), especially Chap. 7.

24. Jon Sobrino, *Christology at the Crossroads* (Maryknoll, NY: Orbis Books, 1978), 353.

25. José Miguez Bonino, *Doing Theology in a Revolutionary Situation* (Philadelphia: Fortress Books, 1975).

26. Paulo Freire, *Pedagogy of the Oppressed* (New York: Seabury Press, 1970), 12.

27. Gutierrez, *Theology*, 159.

28. Ibid., 91.

29. Leonardo Boff, *Jesus Christ Liberator: A Critical Christology for Our Time* (Maryknoll, NY: Orbis Books, 1972), 49.

30. Dussel, *Caminos*, 112.

31. José Porfirio Miranda, *Marx and the Bible: A Critique of the Philosophy of Oppression* (Maryknoll, NY: Orbis Books, 1974), 277.

32. Dussel, *History*, 145.

33. Quoted in Fernando Moreno Valencia, *Christianismo y Marxismo en la Teologia de la liberación* (Santiago de Chile: Editorial Salesiana, 1976), 18-19.

34. Segundo, *Hidden Motives*, 21.

35. Hugo Assmann, "The Faith of the Poor in their Struggle with Idols," in Paulo Richard et al., *The Idols of Death and the God of Life* (Maryknoll, NY: Orbis Books, 1983), 228.

36. Segundo, *The Liberation of Theology*, 27.

37. Jon Sobrino, "Theological Understanding in the Theology of Europe and Latin America," in *Liberación y cautiverio* (Mexico City, DF: 1976), 207.

38. See Gutierrez, *Theology*.

39. Boff, *Jesus Christ Liberator*, 63.

40. Freire, *Pedagogy*, 29.

41. Ibid., 132.

42. Dussel, *History*, 136.

43. Dussel, *Caminos*, 132.

44. Gutierrez, *Theology*, 26-27.

45. Freire, *Pedagogy*, 75-76.

46. Ferm, *Third World Liberation Theologies*, 45.

47. Paul VI, *Populorum Progressio* (On the Development of Peoples), official Vatican translation (Boston: Daughters of St. Paul, 1967), para. 30.

48. Dussel, *History*, 126.

49. Rubem Alves, *A Theology of Human Hope* (St. Meinard, IN: Abbey Press, 1969), 163.

50. Freire, *Pedagogy*, 40-41.

51. Johan Galtung, *A Structural Theory of Revolutions* (Rotterdam: Rotterdam University Press, 1974) 10.

52. Bishops of Latin America, Africa and Asia, "Letter to the Peoples of the Third World," quoted in Ferm, *Third World Liberation Theologies*, 10.

53. Quoted in Segundo, *Hidden Motives*, 57.

54. Conference of Latin American Bishops, "Entre las persecuciones del mundo y los consuelos de Dios," in *Los Obispos*, 95.

55. Gutierrez, *Theology*, 30.

56. Segundo, *Hidden Motives*, 79.

3

The Roots of Christian Democracy

In the analysis of a political philosophy, one crucial area of judgement is how that political philosophy reacts to the strain of actual political power. Does it abandon its principles in the quest for short-term political success? Christian Democracy's record in this regard is, at best, mixed.

In this chapter I will examine the philosophical roots of Christian Democracy, which lie in Catholic social thought and in the thought of Jacques Maritain. I will argue that there are important differences between Christian Democracy and these antecedents. These differences exist on a philosophical level and are even more visible in the practice of Christian Democracy. As Christian Democracy has moved away from Catholic social thought, it has, perhaps unwittingly, moved closer to Liberation Theology.

TRADITIONAL CATHOLIC SOCIAL THOUGHT

Proponents of Liberation Theology contend that theirs is the only version of Christianity that demonstrates any real concern for the poor. In fact, some adherents to Liberation Theology have accused the official Catholic Church of allying itself with the rich and powerful. At best, they contend, the Church preaches a sullen forbearance of earthly suffering, holding out the hope of eternal happiness as an alternative to constructive action. This characterization of Catholicism ignores a century of Catholic response to changing social conditions.

Catholic social thought is contained in what are usually referred to as the "Social Encyclicals" of several popes. Encyclicals are official papal letters to the Catholic faithful, usually dealing with the application of Catholic faith to a particular situation. They do not have the force of a pronouncement on faith or morals and their conclusions are not binding on the faithful. They contain no claim of infallibility. They do, however, represent the last word on the position of the Catholic Church. No opinion at variance with an encyclical can claim to be "Catholic" opinion.

The Social Encyclicals are: *Rerum Novarum* (1891), *Quadragessimo Anno* (1931), *Divini Redemptoris* (1937), *Mater et Magistra* (1961), *Populorum Progressio* (1967), and *Pacem in Terris* (1968). Later papal documents written after the development of Christian Democratic theory include two by Pope John Paul II: *Laborem Exercens* (1981) and *Sollicitudo Rei Socialis* (1987). Most observers expect a further effort from John Paul II in 1991 to mark the 100th anniversary of *Rerum Novarum*.

The traditional Catholic view of man is that he is, because of original sin, imperfectible. This attitude toward man, however, does not detract from man's responsibility to make changes for the better. Pope John XXIII devotes several paragraphs of *Mater et Magistra* to the theme of how man can and must improve himself.[1]

He emphasizes, as did many of his predecessors, that such improvement must be achieved by individuals, as individuals. Liberation Theology, for its part, defines both earthly and other-worldly salvation in collective terms. This obscures, and even excludes, the importance of individual salvation.[2]

Pope John Paul II began his pontificate by calling for the Church to give priority to the liberation of man from sin. For John Paul II, a better society is one in which the spiritual needs of man are met. This does not mean that his economic and physical needs are neglected. On the contrary, John Paul II argues that unjust economic and social structures are the result of spiritual lapses.[3]

Thus, for traditional Catholic social thinkers, giving priority to economic, political, or social problems is putting the cart before the horse. A society faithful to orthodox Catholicism would seek the development of man's spiritual nature, and through this development also seek the improvement of economic and social conditions. The biblical basis for this ordering of priorities consists of two statements from the Gospels. Jesus's disdain for material wealth is visible in many places in the Gospels, but rarely is it clearer than when he asks: "What does it profit a man to gain the whole world, yet lose his immortal soul?" (Matthew 16:26) Elsewhere Christ exhorts his followers to "Seek first the Kingdom of God . . . and all of these things will be yours as well" (Matthew 6:33).

Knowing that an improved society is, in fact, possible, what types of means may man employ to achieve this progress? The popes emphasize first that any amelioration of the human condition will be gradual. Pope

John XXIII stated: "It is the nature of things for growth to be gradual and that therefore in human institutions no improvement can be looked for which does not proceed step by step, from within."[4] This statement reveals none of the impatience with incremental solutions that mark the writings of Liberation Theologians.

Second, those who seek to reform society must never lose sight of the common good. For most spokesmen for traditional Catholic thought, and specifically for Pope Pius XI in *Quadragessimo Anno*, this good must be the effective directing principle of reform efforts.[5] The popes emphasize the unity of the social body, as well as the strong bonds of service for the good of all mankind.[6] This organic theory of society, however, does not detract from the primacy of individuals.

The priority given to the pursuit of the common good becomes especially important in the discussion of the nature of private property, one of the main areas of disagreement between traditional Catholic social thought and Liberation Theology. The Catholic Church has always defended the right of man to own property. Pope Leo XIII, who inaugurated modern Catholic social thought with his watershed encyclical *Rerum Novarum*, argued that land, as the product of capital earned through labor, should be inviolate as the remuneration itself.[7]

Pius XI marked the fortieth anniversary of this sentiment by adding that God gave man the right to private ownership so that he could provide for himself. Also part of God's plan, according to Pius XI, is providing sufficient incentive to man, in the form of private gain, to insure that he actually produces those goods destined for all mankind.[8]

In defending the right to private property, the popes also lay upon the owners certain duties, which, they say, are inherent in that ownership. These duties relate to how the land is to be used. To quote *Rerum Novarum* again: "Whoever has received from the Divine bounty a large share of temporal blessings, . . . has received them for the benefit of others."[9] Later popes have reiterated this idea that wealth carries a "social mortgage." John Paul II repeated this statement at Puebla as a pointed rebuke to those present who reject all forms of private property.[10]

The papal encyclicals use very harsh language to condemn both pure capitalism and pure socialism. Pius XI wrote in *Divini Redemptoris*: "There would be today neither socialism nor communism if the rulers of the nations had not scorned the teachings of the Church. . . . Socialism and communism come out of the failures of lay Liberalism."[11]

Pius XI restated an earlier sentiment, having written in *Quadragessimo Anno*: "Just as the unity of human society cannot be founded on the opposition of classes, so also the right ordering of economic life cannot be left to a free competition of forces."[12] Pius XI refers to individualism and collectivism as "twin rocks of shipwreck, the former denying the social and public character of man, and the latter denying the private and individual character of man."[13]

The popes blame capitalism in its unbridled form for an excessive concentration of wealth in few hands. This in turn has led to a despotic "economic dictatorship in the hands of a few."[14] Thus the Roman Catholic Church acknowledges the need for social justice and its absence in existing society. It also acknowledges the appeal of Marxism, which seemingly provides a plan for attaining social justice.

Nevertheless, before World War II the official Church also explicitly rejected any collaboration with Marxism to bring about a better society. Pius XI rejected communism because of both its naturalistic metaphysics and its intent to sharpen class antagonisms in order to achieve the synthesis of Marxist Utopia.[15] He added the very strong statement that communism is intrinsically wrong and that no one who would save Christian civilization may collaborate with it in any undertaking.[16]

The harshness of the traditional Catholic condemnation of capitalism and communism is matched by skepticism about the efficacy of balancing the power of capitalists by extending and consolidating state power. The popes condemn socialism because it proposes a remedy far worse than the evil it tries to eliminate. Statist philosophies in general are suspect because they give greater importance to society as a whole than to the individuals who comprise it.

Although individuals have certain duties vis-à-vis the societies in which they live, popes in the era before World War II were very skeptical about increasing the power of the state to enforce these obligations. To depend upon the state to solve societal problems was to take an enormous risk, according to Leo XIII and Pius XI.

Early social encyclicals emphasized the need for individuals to protect themselves from encroaching state power by entering into a series of professional and interprofessional organizations. Such mediating structures must adhere to Catholic principles to fulfill the role the popes assign to them. First, they must be based on mutual cooperation and freedom of association. No one should be compelled to join.[17]

Second, the supremacy of God and the dignity of individuals must be foremost. "Society," wrote Pius XI, "is for man . . . in the sense that only man is endowed with reason and a morally free will."[18] Individuals may seek to increase their strength relative to state structures, and the popes place no limits on this process save to remind the associations that disobedience to civil law must be based on a genuine conflict with conscience.[19]

JACQUES MARITAIN

Christian Democracy began as an intellectual movement before it became a political movement. At this formative stage, the basic elements of Catholic social thought animated the writings of Christian Democracy's European theorists. The men behind these movements were determined to express their Catholicism in a political manner, keeping in mind what the popes wrote about the nature of man, his place in society, the insufficiency of capitalism, and the anxiety about increasing the power of the state.

Jacques Maritain, while not primarily a political philosopher, had a profound effect on the course of Christian Democratic thought. As we shall see in Chapter 5, his thought was also the conduit for Christian Democratic thought to Latin America. A brief sketch of his life and a detailed treatment of his philosophy is therefore in order.

Jacques Maritain was born on 18 November 1882 in Paris, France. His religious upbringing was Huguenot and he was initially attracted to the study of science. It was during this early period of his life that he briefly flirted with Marxism. The arrogance of "scientism" that he found at the Sorbonne repelled the intellectually developing young man and he turned to the study of philosophy.

In 1904 he married Raisa Oumansoff, a Russian-Jewish student. Two years later, both Jacques and Raisa converted to Catholicism. Both pursued intellectual careers, with Jacques turning to philosophy and his wife becoming a well-regarded poet and social scientist in her own right.

The Nazi occupation of France in 1940 drove Maritain from his homeland and he arrived in the United States for what proved to be a long stay. During the war years he served as visiting professor at Princeton and Columbia, while travelling to other universities in the East.

After the war, he served as French Ambassador to the Holy See, resigning that position in 1948. Returning to the United States, he taught at Princeton from 1948 until his retirement in 1960. Prior to his retirement from teaching he established the Jacques Maritain Center at Notre Dame University. Continuing to write and lecture even after leaving Princeton, he lived to age 90, passing away on 28 April 1973.

Maritain comes from the tradition of the medieval scholastics, and especially Saint Thomas Aquinas. These philosophers were known for their self-confidence in man and their belief in the inherent goodness he acquired through redemption. This gratuitous gift from God, while leaving man still incapable of perfection, nevertheless tempered the effects of original sin.[20] Maritain is critical of Niccolò Machiavelli, for example, because of the latter's failure to realize that "human badness is not radical." To assume this, Maritain says, is to cancel the image of God in man and make man purely animal.[21]

Maritain thus differed with other Christian thinkers, such as Reinhold Niebuhr, who had a more pessimistic view of man and of the change in man's nature that resulted from the Fall. He also differed from the "scientific" analysis of man held by the rationalists like Jean Jacques Rousseau. "Naturalistic" humanism, based on the celebration of man as the measure of all things, Maritain said, ignored the spiritual side of man.[22]

True humanism, or integral humanism, on the other hand, recognized not only that man had both a physical and a spiritual nature, but also that his spiritual nature was superior. Only by recognizing this could a philosophy claiming to be humanistic tend toward the greater *human* fulfillment of man.[23] Thus Maritain followed the popes in believing that addressing man's spiritual shortcomings would lead to social improvements as well.

The "naturalization" of the Natural Law that came with the nineteenth-century philosophes, therefore, was a terrible disaster, which led to what Maritain calls man's ultimate error: believing that he is saved by his strength alone.[24] Karl Marx accepted all of the worst aspects of this rationalism, which Maritain deplored. Marx's deification of man, and particularly of the working class, would compound the "ultimate error" by moving man's salvation from heaven to earth, and redefining it in economic terms. Even before the evils of Stalinism were generally known, Maritain warned that "the Communist path" would lead to the abuse of individual persons.[25]

Maritain's philosophical position between the pessimism of the Calvinists and the unbridled optimism of the philosophes led him to emphasize the subordination of the state to man's needs and to embrace gradual change for the better over radical revolution. He disapproved of the messianic solutions of Marxism because of their preoccupation with the perfectibility of man, which led them to accept any means to achieve this goal.

Writing in *Integral Humanism*, Maritain maintained that political and economic change must develop on the individual level. His social solutions revolved around organic, ongoing improvement, which, he emphasized, will not lead to earthly perfection. "The Christian," he concluded, "must work for a proportionate realization . . . of the Gospel exigencies and of Christian practical wisdom in the sociotemporal order."[26] Maritain repeated this injunction in *Christianity and Democracy*, advising his readers to "aim for the better, not for the perfect."[27]

This "better" for which persons must aim is the fuller realization of man's earthly and spiritual destiny. With this emphasis, Maritain explicitly rejects the Marxist subordination of human needs and desires to those of the state or the party. For him, the desires of the state are subordinate to the genuine needs of the people who live under that state.

At the same time, Maritain does not aim for the elimination of the state. He believes, with Aristotle and Aquinas, that political society is required by the nature of man. The human person is incomplete, unable to survive on his own, and thus required to become a part of society.

This, according to Maritain, is the insuperable cause of tension between man and the state.[28]

Again following Aristotle and Aquinas, Maritain believes that the state must be directed toward the common good and that the state has a duty to respect the needs and desires of the body politic.[29] This entity, made up of families as basic units, is endowed with essential rights and freedoms beyond the reach even of a thoroughly just state. The state is "a work of art created by man. An agent of man."[30]

Maritain followed Catholic social thought closely on most issues. Like the popes, he emphasized that the good of society must be based upon a recognition of the primacy of the spiritual, the importance of individuals, the necessity of incrementalism, and distrust of the state. One area in which Maritain broke from the Church is the question of collaboration with communists. I shall examine his attitude toward this question in Chapter 4.

THE EUROPEAN MODEL

Of course, Jacques Maritain did not spring from a vacuum. Other French philosophers wrote along the same lines. Jean Baptiste Henri Lacordaire, for example, thought as early as the 1850s that the kind of social reform on which Catholics should insist could only be achieved through political action. Similarly, Felicité Robert de Lamennais desired to see Catholics get involved in politics, at the same time that he wanted the official Church out of politics.

Under the traditional *modus vivendi* of the Catholic Church and France's Bourbon monarchy, the Roman Catholic Church ceded the right to name bishops to the Bourbon kings. In return, the Church expected these monarchs to provide official protection. Under a series of treaties, called concordats, the Church made similar arrangements with other Catholic monarchies. Both the Hapsburgs and the Spanish branch of the Bourbons brought the Church to Latin America under such an agreement.

For Lamennais, these concordats were a terrible mistake. Commenting specifically on the French example, he said that the Concordat tied the Catholic Church to all of the excesses and political reaction of that monarchy without softening its Bourbon repression and heavy-handedness in any significant manner. The only dividend for the papacy, official protection, was too dearly bought in the coin of disillusioned Catholic believers. Lamennais suggested a new ally for the pope: the lay Catholic believers, acting on their own.[31] Yet in spite of his apparent concern for the Church's future, neither Lamennais nor Lacordaire received a sympathetic hearing from the popes. Evidently, the time was not yet ripe.

After World War II, Christian Democratic parties established themselves in many parts of Western Europe. For the purposes of this discussion, the examples of Italy and France are the most applicable. Not only did these parties appear in countries dominated by the Catholic Church, the same Church that dominated politics in Latin America, but the Latin American Christian Democratic leaders also deliberately followed their example.

Early Successes in Europe

Within five years of World War II, two-fifths of the lower houses in the parliaments of the first six members of the European Community were Christian Democratic.[32] In Italy, the Christian Democratic Party (DC) won the first postwar elections and has dominated Italian politics ever since. In France, the Popular Republican Movement (MRP) was part of the French Constituent Assembly and the Fourth Republic. Other Christian Democratic parties appeared in West Germany, Belgium, Austria, and Spain.

Yet as an overtly political movement, Christian Democracy had, for all intents and purposes, begun with the immediate prewar period. Thus, unlike political movements like socialism, or even liberalism, Christian Democracy became an important political force before it had matured ideologically.

As a result, the development of its ideology was inhibited by the pressures of political responsibility. The Italian Christian Democratic Party, for example, was founded in 1943 and came to power in 1948. It was never able to develop its autonomous self separately from a close and intimate relationship with the state.

THEMES OF EUROPEAN CHRISTIAN DEMOCRACY

One of the initial problems that European Christian Democratic leaders had to overcome was the traditional reluctance of many devout Catholics to get involved in politics. After the unification of Italy by a liberal, anticlerical movement in 1870, the popes exhorted their followers to stay aloof from politics. At the time of the virulently anti-Catholic phase of the French Revolution, many French Catholics adopted similar positions of separation and intransigence.

Both the French Revolution and the Italian unification were accompanied by substantial increases in state power. This meant significantly less respect for traditional ecclesiastical prerogatives. The Church and many faithful Catholics reacted to this state usurpation by attempting to withdraw from the political system and withholding their cooperation.[33] This attitude split the Catholic faithful, with some believers maintaining that they ought to participate in politics, even under a liberal, anticlerical state, to "Christianize" the political process.

By the beginning of the twentieth century, the official Church position toward the liberal state had softened somewhat. In 1891, Pope Leo XIII lifted a long-standing ban on political activity by Italians. Leo evidently came to agree with those Catholics who pressed for a Catholic presence in politics. He also concluded that, as dangerous and rapacious as the liberal state was, it was less threatening than Marxism and socialism.

The central theme of Christian Democracy is the determination to reconcile the values and traditions of premodern society with the demands of the twentieth century. Christian Democrats are particularly determined to save traditional ideas of the importance of the family, the inviolability of private property, and the value of social diversity.

A related theme is the determination to redirect the political system toward more human ends. Human beings must be primary in the state-individual relationship. The state must *respond* to man to be a just state. Making this happen in the context of the modern world is one of the challenges of Christian Democracy.

For many Christian Democrats, the persistent conflict between the Church and state, which absorbs so much energy that other concerns are never addressed, has denied to Christians their proper role in the political system. Thus a third theme of Christian Democracy is its determination to resolve this conflict and to "restore to the political sphere criteria of action and values that had been discarded because of the Church/state conflict."[34]

Thus many Christian Democratic theorists stressed their independence from the official Church and sought to "resolve" the Church/state conflict by ignoring it. The existence of a Christian Democratic party in a political system, with no official connection to the Church, would force the secular authorities to address other important Christian concerns. Friction between the Church and various Christian Democratic parties would become the norm, although with important differences of degree.

As we saw above, Leo XIII and Pius XI blamed the existence of Marxism and socialism on the failures of liberal capitalism. Yet neither the popes nor the early Christian Democrats wanted to do away with capitalism altogether. Socialism and Marxism were, after all, the real enemies. Whatever its faults, capitalism did at least limit the power of the state. By reserving the sphere of economics for individuals, capitalists restrained state power and thus were at least partially on the side of the Church, which also wanted a restrained state.[35]

Left on its own, however, the liberal state could cause many Catholics to fall into the hands of the Church's sworn enemies.[36] Given this analysis, it is logical to fight these antiethical philosophies by improving upon liberalism, thus dealing with the root causes of Marxism. The liberal state required an active and obvious Catholic presence to provide compassion and smooth off the rough edges of capitalism.

Yet this involved the same risk about which Lamennais warned the eighteenth-century Church: Catholics would legitimize the liberal state with their participation while failing to alter it significantly. To participate in politics, therefore, Catholics required a coherent philosophy, of adequate sophistication and complexity, to allow them to withstand the trials and pressures of the political world. Christian Democracy was developed to fulfill this requirement.

As the twentieth century progressed, Christian Democracy came to mean organized political action by Catholics and their allies, acting in a self-consciously Catholic manner, within a democratic political framework. Maritain gave the movement an even simpler definition when he wrote that Christian Democrats were simply Christians who were serious about their faith.[37]

Diversity

Most European Christian Democratic parties are really coalitions of a number of different political tendencies.[38] Disagreements over exactly what it meant to be a politically committed Christian led to great ideological diversity among Christian Democrats. The grave situation of postwar Europe, including as it did a strong communist electoral challenge, also encouraged diversity.

Christian Democrats realized that a wider ideological straddle yielded a broader electoral base, especially in the exhausted world of postwar Europe.[39] Imprecise ideology also allowed the Christian Democratic parties to display slightly different faces, depending on the political needs of the moment. In the words of one analyst, Christian Democrats maintain their electoral base by acting like an "ideological chameleon."[40] In the Italian party, ideological diversity became official, with different factions, known as *correnti*, acknowledged in the party bureaucracy.[41] This willingness to bend ideology to fit immediate political goals would become more pronounced.

Its early success, therefore, distorted Christian Democracy. Its entry into power, and its determination to remain in power in Italy and to remain influential in other European states, forbade the sort of incremental ideological development that leads to greater cohesion and coherence. In many cases, it seemed that Christian Democracy could be defined as that philosophy most likely to appeal to large numbers of voters.

Pluralism in Society

Perhaps because of the different factions in European Christian Democratic parties, one area in which Christian Democrats were able to agree, at least in theory, was the importance of societal diversity. By this I mean the importance of nongovernmental groups in society to act as buffers between individuals and state power. Christian Democrats believe that man should be political, and act in politics, but that he should also participate actively in what traditional Catholics call the "natural structures" of society: the family, the community, perhaps a trade union.[42]

This emphasis on pluralism avoids both of the twin rocks of shipwreck against which Pius XI warned so forcefully. On the one hand, identification with groups and the recognition of their importance prevents the sort of atomistic individualism that has stripped modern society of so many of its "human" features and rendered it vulnerable to Marxism. Marx himself, it will be remembered, believed that atomization was an inevitable result of modernization. The Christian Democrats hold that this need not be.

Stressing the importance of groups also prevents the state from exercising too much power. Realizing that it is much more difficult for the state coercive apparatus to operate against groups than against individuals, Christian Democrats sought to protect the autonomy of groups and thus protect the individual. For Christian Democrats, a vibrant human society was made up of a myriad of social groupings. Such a society also tended to be more respectful of the prerogatives of the Christian churches. Any society in which state power is limited is more congenial to an independent entity like a church.

Furthermore, the proliferation of autonomous social structures was part of Christian Democratic socioeconomic ideology as well. Starting with Leo XIII, the Catholic Church has actively tried to counteract the Marxian notion that society is inevitably and irreconcilably divided into economic classes. Leo XIII wrote of the necessity to develop intermediary bodies, such as trade unions, not only to protect workers' rights, but also to show workers that their true interests lay in cooperation.[43]

The goal of the Christian Democratic movement was to appeal across class lines, and in general to de-emphasize the importance of such lines in the first place. To do this, members of classes must identify themselves not just as bourgeois or proletarian, or even primarily in this fashion. Rather, they must think of themselves, simultaneously, as members of a class, a church, a union, a family, and several other associations as well. Only then can a member of society see what interests he has in common with his fellow citizens. To concentrate on separation is pointless and counterproductive.[44] Christian Democrats in Europe often began with working-class associations in their efforts to develop more independent social groups.

Protection of the family was also important to Christian Democratic theorists. Maritain, for example, emphasized the need for independent schools in which Catholic parents could direct the overall spiritual development of their children.[45] The demand for religious education, independent of the state, was an important part of the Christian Democratic agenda.

One observer deplores what he thinks of as the inordinate importance given to the "schools question" by Christian Democrats. Their insistence on their own schools, he says, has prevented some European Christian Democratic parties from forming coalitions with other centrist parties and thus has hampered the effectiveness of the movement.[46]

Such criticism misses the importance of the schools question. It is essential to the larger question of whether society will be protected from state power. To allow the state a monopoly on education is to sacrifice the vitals of Christian Democratic social theory. If parents cannot direct the content of what their children learn, then they are not truly independent.

Theoretical Attitudes toward State Power

It is the duty of the state to get along with the independent structures that make up society, according to Christian Democracy, and not the other way around. Otherwise, the societal diversity that is so important will soon disappear. Christian Democratic theory, before the various parties came to power, was characterized by skepticism about the role of the state in society. Early Christian Democrats wrote that social groups would provide a "guarantee against the *spontaneous* totalitarianism of the state."[47]

The family, according to Leo XIII, is older than the state and has rights and duties which are quite independent of state power. Maritain added that the state is but an agency, an instrument in the service of man. Reversing this, according to both, is a political perversion.

Etienne Gilson, a follower of Maritain and a Christian Democratic theorist, also emphasized the autonomy of groups and added that the [French] Political Revolution had produced such a perversion in the form of "centralized elitism." Such an elitism would start among the industrial giants but would soon try to gain control of the state apparatus. Safety existed only in limiting the state.[48]

Similarly in Italy, Luigi Sturzo, a Catholic priest and the founder of the Italian Popular Party, a precursor to the modern Christian Democratic Party, wrote of the need for local self-government and individual freedom, especially from the control of a pervasive central government.

Free schools and free trade unions were of particular importance to him.[49]

European Christian Democratic parties adhered to this line until they tasted state power for themselves. The Christian Democratic French Popular Republican Movement (MRP) was one of several parties competing for power in France after the Liberation. The MRP started out opposing an expanded role for the state in France's economy. Such a state role, the MRP leadership held, would create economic relationships as "between governor and governed."[50]

The MRP also advocated significant internal checks and balances, on the American model, to make governing more cumbersome and difficult. Their aim was to prevent undue increases in state power. Also part of their immediate postwar program was a demand for bicameralism in the French Parliament, with a "house of second thoughts."[51]

Changes in Attitude Once in Power

Yet in spite of these antistatist attitudes evident in Christian Democratic theory, the various parties would fail to present a clear alternative to the statist trend in European politics during the postwar period. Rather, most European Christian Democrats would offer a slower or less committed version of statism, promising to use the state to benefit certain interest groups, while somehow continuing to protect society from encroaching state power. Christian Democratic fear of capitalism, and the search for electoral success, would overwhelm the movement's antistate attitudes.

Christian Democrats started their rapprochement with the state with the discovery of what the state could do and how it could be helpful in accomplishing traditional Christian Democratic goals. Even as early as the 1896 Congress of the pre-Christian Democratic French Cercles d'Etudes, Christian Democratic theorists stated that the state should not only protect the family, but use its power to promote measures to help the family.[52] While the Congress made it clear that it did not want a greatly expanded state role, it nevertheless opened a door. After the war, Christian Democrats in France would seek to make use of the state, not to avoid it.

Also in France, Albert deMun, a Catholic social thinker and member of Parliament, favored state intervention and legislation to improve social conditions and, by the use of state power, to enforce the "social mortgage" of traditional Catholic social thought.[53]

This tentative rapprochement with the state would grow more manifest as the European Christian Democrats exercised more actual political power. Christian Democrats played a major role in the French and Italian Constituent Assemblies after World War II. Working in the lingering shadow of the Third Reich, these assemblies concentrated almost single-mindedly on protecting human rights.[54] In the process, they added economic and social rights to the political rights enumerated in the Atlantic Charter and the American Bill of Rights. These new rights require not the restraint of government power, but its judicious employment and, frequently, its expansion.[55]

Again, their demands began with state enforcement of important parts of Christian Democratic social theory. For example, traditional Catholic social thought requires that workers be paid a "family wage." This, as defined by the medieval scholastics, is a wage sufficient for a family to survive without both parents having to work outside the home. In the constituent assemblies, the Christian Democrats began to demand that government *require* that employers pay such a wage. Until they did, they desired that the taxpayers provide family allowances to make up the difference.[56]

A second example of Christian Democratic acceptance of state power is the schools question. French Christian Democratic theorists insisted on having their schools left alone, and they deplored any state involvement. The French Christian Democrat politicians wanted parallel public and private schools, both equally subsidized by the state.[57] The MRP, then, not only invited state involvement in schools, but demanded it.

European Christian Democrats would encourage an increased state role in the national economy as well. As such, the Christian Democrats were no different from any other "moderate" party in postwar Europe. They generally accepted that market forces must be limited by government action, but they also shared a consensus that the government should abstain from major redistribution policies.[58]

The Italian DC, for example, has created one of the larger and more powerful public sectors in Europe. Almost simultaneously with coming to power, the DC strengthened and extended the reach of the state into the Italian economy.[59] By 1983, Italy had 60,000 public and quasi-public corporations, starting with the one charged with southern economic development.[60] These public corporations are dominated by members of the DC and extend to all levels of Italian society.[61]

Increasing state power was the invariable Christian Democratic response to changes in Italy's political reality. As the 1976 Italian referendum on divorce painfully demonstrated, the Catholic hierarchy can no longer deliver the votes, even on important issues. At the same time, the political influence of agricultural areas has been declining. As a result, the DC has increased its "colonization" of some of those sectors of Italian society that are the most dependent on state largess.

In other words, the DC has abandoned its early reliance on ideology to sway voters. It is now dependent on clientism. This requires an expansion of state power. A clientist system requires not only government subsidies and other handouts to survive, but also increasing numbers of government positions for clients to occupy. This is a process that feeds upon itself, creating more and more government as it creates the need for more and more clients.

Christian Democrats have also moved to centralize the state bureaucracy, while extending their patronage network within that bureaucracy. They also added to their previous interference in industry a new system of "preferments" for industry through the parastatal economic corporations.[62]

The process was repeated in France. The French Bill of Rights, on which the MRP collaborated, directs the state to lend its active support and machinery to secure for each French citizen the right to work, to economic security, to welfare and to education.[63] After serving on several early Fourth Republic cabinets, the MRP insisted that the government plan the economy for growth and progress, in order to improve the chances that each French citizen could achieve true personhood.[64] Once again, the demand for state intervention was ostensibly to accomplish a long-standing Christian Democratic goal.

In general, French Christian Democrats accepted the extensive level of state ownership that they found in France in the immediate postwar period. They favored more extensive government intervention when such intervention was consistent with private initiative and did not stifle creativity. Abandoning their traditional distrust of the state, the MRP as early as 1944 called for "an economy controlled by the state."[65] As in Italy, the perceived need for immediate economic growth provided the rationalization for increased state power. The MRP declared itself in favor of a "leading role" for the state in rebuilding the shattered French economy.[66]

Both the Italian and French Christian Democrats made substantial changes in their attitudes toward state power. In part, this is due to their perception, upon tasting political power, that such power can be used for good. This represents a departure from Catholic social thought, for which state power is invariably dangerous.

Yet having lost their fear of the state, the European Christian Democrats found a new danger: private enterprise. While Catholic social thought also distrusts capitalism, it does not prescribe increased state power to counter it. On the contrary, the popes suggested increased private ownership of productive enterprises. This same fear, as we shall see, motivated the Latin American Christian Democrats.

WORKING WITH RIVAL PARTIES

During the early period of the DC's development, it rejected a coalition with the Italian Communist Party (PCI). This rejection was based not on economic questions, but on the communists' anti-Christianity. Founding DC Premier Alcide deGasperi took pains to make it clear that his party and the PCI substantially agreed on economic policy.[67]

DeGasperi was able to make this seemingly extreme statement because the Christian Democratic critique of capitalism and individualism had advanced so far that it was more suspicious of private enterprise than it was of state power. In fact, in the words of one analyst, their state had progressed so far from the liberal ideal that it resembled the Fascist state of Benito Mussolini.[68]

Even dismissing this comparison as an overstatement, deGasperi himself described the DC as a "party of the Center moving toward the left."[69] As we have seen, this began as an effort to use state power to achieve Christian Democratic goals. Even if this were the only motivation, one could reasonably question the extent to which the DC was giving up its founding principles of pluralism and limited state power.

There were other motives as well. Concurrent with the defeat on the divorce referendum, a spurt in PCI popularity in 1976 challenged the DC's electoral dominance. After decades of occasional anticommunist rhetoric, used amidst the insistence that the DC and PCI were not really very far apart, the Italian electorate shifted to the left. Italians evidently concluded that if the DC offered only watered-down Marxism, perhaps they would be better off with the real thing.[70]

The DC reacted to this electoral reverse by trying to co-opt the communists, as they had various centrist parties. Aldo Moro became the author of the "historic compromise," which promised to end three decades of bitter electoral rivalry. According to the plan, the DC and PCI would merge in a grand coalition, both motivated by the prospect of electoral success to put aside their ideological differences. In so doing, the DC leadership hoped to retain voters put off by the party's intransigence over divorce, especially young people, intellectuals, and union members.[71] Christian Democrats could consider losing their more conservative voters unlikely, since no other Italian party would accommodate them.

Thus the Christian Democrats sought to submerge their differences with the communists. This involved substantial risks for the Christian Democrats. On the one hand, if the PCI was made up of real communists, then union with the Christian Democrats would be sterile. On the other hand, if the PCI was not a danger, or if it was really made up of well-meaning social democrats, then a substantial part of the DC's *raison d'être* would be gone.[72]

The "historic compromise" proved to be less than its lofty title promised. At the time that the DC was ready to move, the PCI saw its rival's motives as defensive, and the communists hoped to have a majority themselves very soon.[73] As this possibility faded, the DC became less interested in a grand coalition. Moreover, the murder of Aldo Moro, chief architect of the attempted union, by the communist Red Brigades in 1978 put a fatal damper on public sentiment for collaboration.

The MRP could never make an historic compromise, since it never achieved the DC's level of electoral success. After the immediate postwar period, when it contributed significantly to the French Constituent Assembly, the MRP never really found a niche in postwar French politics. The thorough dominance of Charles deGaulle in postwar France and his more successful efforts to address many MRP issues were obstacles to the MRP.

The French Christian Democrats could not prevent the polarization of French politics into a Gaullist/Socialist split. Faced with such a choice, French voters rarely risked splitting the antisocialist vote between the Gaullists and the MRP.[74] Faced with the prospect of permanent irrelevance, the party officially dissolved itself in 1969.

CONCLUSION

A political analyst can hardly express shock and indignation when a political party acts like a political party. Most political parties act differently when they exercise power and seek to use their power to perpetuate themselves. Neither the French nor the Italian Christian Democratic parties do much to distinguish themselves from their more secular counterparts.

Yet this is exactly the point. The Christian Democrats, at least at the beginning, had a divine calling. They aimed at nothing less than an approximation of the Kingdom of God on Earth. To be reduced to the tawdriness of buying votes through pandering and clientism is a different matter for Christian Democrats than it is for other, less committed parties.

Only by staking out a unique area of the political spectrum can Christian Democracy hope for sustained success. The area of greatest promise, and the one most consistent with the original principles of Christian Democracy, is a position of skepticism with regard to state power. To express serious doubts about the efficacy of state interference would indeed risk alienating the minority of voters who are dependent upon the state, but it would energize and mobilize the great majority of voters who wish nothing more from the state than to be left alone. Thus, there is no tension between ideological consistency and electoral pragmatism.

Furthermore, holding a "moderate" position on extending state power, besides being logically inconsistent, is also bound to be unproductive electorally. Once a party accepts the premise that state intervention makes an economy work better than private enterprise, it inevitably gets into a bidding war with other statist parties. A "moderate" statist party cannot win such a war, since immoderate statists can always promise more state intervention than the Christian Democrats can accept.

This makes Christian Democrats particularly vulnerable in any electoral or philosophical struggle with Socialists or Communists. As we shall see in Chapter 5, Latin American Christian Democratic parties have also succumbed to the statist temptation, and have paid a price in electoral success and originality. They have also left themselves vulnerable to the challenge of more radical statist movements, including Liberation Theology, which not only seeks to outdo their statism, but also their Christianity.

NOTES

1. John XXIII, *Mater et Magistra* (Mother and Teacher), official Vatican translation (Boston: Daughters of St. Paul), para. 73-81.
2. W. Dayton Roberts, "Where has Liberation Theology Gone Wrong?" *Christianity Today*, XXIII, 24 (1979): 28.
3. John Paul II, *Laborem Exercens* (On Human Labor), official Vatican translation (Boston: Daughters of St. Paul).
4. John XXIII, *Pacem in Terris* (Peace on Earth), official Vatican translation (Boston: Daughters of St. Paul), para. 161.
5. Quoted in Anne Fremantle, *The Papal Encyclicals in Their Historical Context* (New York: Mentor Omega, 1963), 233.
6. Paul Douglas, *Six Upon the World* (Boston: Little, Brown, 1954), 277.
7. Leo XIII, *Rerum Novarum* (On the Condition of the Working Classes), offical Vatican translation (Boston: Daughters of St. Paul), para 9.
8. Fremantle, *The Papal Encyclicals*, 231.
9. Leo XIII, *Rerum Novarum*, para. 36.
10. John Paul II, "Opening Address at Puebla," in Quentin L. Quade, ed., *The Pope and Revolution: John Paul II Confronts Liberation Theology* (Washington, DC: Ethics and Public Policy Center, 1982).
11. Pius XI, *Divini Redemptoris* (On Atheistic Communism), official Vatican translation (Boston: Daughters of St. Paul, 1937), para. 38.
12. Fremantle, 233.
13. Ibid., 231.
14. Ibid., 234.
15. Pius XI, *Divini Redemptoris*, para. 9.
16. Pius XI, *Divini Redemptoris*, para. 58.
17. Fremantle, *The Papal Encyclicals*, 232.
18. Pius XI, *Divini Redemptoris*, para. 29.
19. John XXIII, *Mater et Magistra*, para. 147.
20. The best short treatment of this is the *Treatise on Law* from the *Summa Theologica* of Saint Thomas Aquinas. Aquinas bases his discussion of law on the human faculty of reason, through which man can discover just laws.
21. Jacques Maritain, "The End of Machiavellianism," from *The Range of Rea-*

son, in Joseph W. Evans and Leo R. Ward, *The Social and Political Philosophy of Jacques Maritain* (Notre Dame, IN: University of Notre Dame Press, 1976), 294.

22. This, at least, was Maritain's view of Rousseau. See also Robert Derathe, *La rationalisme de Jean Jacques Rousseau* (Paris: Presses universitaires de France, 1948).

23. Cited in John M. Dunaway, *Jacques Maritain* (Boston: Twaynes Publishers, 1978), 64-66.

24. Jacques Maritain, *Christianity and Democracy* (San Francisco: Ignatius Press, 1986), 15.

25. John W. Cooper, *A Theology of Freedom: The Legacy of Jacques Maritain and Reinhold Niebuhr* (Macon, GA: Mercer University Press, 1985), 14.

26. Quoted in Dunaway, *Jacques Maritain*, 69-70.

27. Maritain, *Christianity and Democracy*, 38.

28. Jacques Maritain,"The Person and the Common Good," quoted in Evans and Ward, *The Social and Political Philosophy*, 85-87.

29. Maritain uses this term to refer to society as a collection of individuals a "whole made up of wholes." See especially Jacques Maritain, *Man and the State* (Chicago: University of Chicago Press, 1951).

30. Maritain, "The Person and the Common Good," 75.

31. R. E. M. Irving, *Christian Democracy in France* (London: George Allen and Unwin, 1973), 27.

32. Ibid., 12.

33. Mario Einaudi and François Goguel, *Christian Democracy in Italy and France* (Notre Dame, IN: University of Notre Dame Press, 1952), 4-5.

34. Einaudi and Goguel, *Christian Democracy*, 1.

35. Emil J. Kirchner, *Liberal Parties in Western Europe* (Cambridge: Cambridge University Press, 1988), 398.

36. Mark N. Hagopian, *Ideals and Ideologies of Modern Politics* (New York: Longman Press, 1985), 158.

37. Quoted in Hagopian, *Ideals and Ideologies*, 167.

38. Geoffrey Pridham, "Christian Democracy in Italy and West Germany: A Comparative Analysis," in Martin Kolinsky and William E. Paterson, eds., *Social and Political Movements in Western Europe* (London: Croon Helm, 1976), 147.

39. Kirchner, *Liberal Parties*, 24.

40. Pridham, "Comparative Analysis," 153.

41. Geoffrey Pridham, "The Italian Christian Democrats After Moro: Crisis or Compromise?" *Western European Politics*, 2,1 (1979): 75.

42 R. E. M. Irving, "Christian Democracy in Post-War Europe: Conservatism Writ Large or Distinctive Political Phenomenon?" *Western European Politics*, 2, 1 (1979): 54.

43. Irving, *Christian Democracy in France*, 28.

44. Pridham, "Comparative Analysis," 147.

45. Hagopian, *Ideals and Ideologies*, 165.

46. Irving, *Christian Democracy in France*, 270.

47. Ibid., 61. Emphasis mine.

48. Irving, "Distinctive Political Phenomenon?" 54.

49. Alan S. Zuckerman, *The Politics of Faction: Christian Democratic Rule in Italy* (New Haven, CT: Yale University Press, 1979), 72.

50. Einaudi and Goguel, *Christian Democracy*, 129.

51. Irving, *Christian Democracy in France*, 67-69.

52. Ibid., 34.

53. Ibid., 32.

54. Irving, "Distinctive Political Phenomenon?" 57.

55. Einaudi and Goguel, *Christian Democracy*, 30-31.

56. Irving, *Christian Democracy in France*, 59.

57. Ibid., 62.

58. Wolfgang Wessels, "Economic Policies," in Roger Morgan and Stephano Silvestri, *Moderates and Conservatives in Western Europe: Political Parties, The European Community and the Atlantic Alliance* (London: Heinemann, 1982), 245-46.

59. Antonio Pilati, "The Italian Christian Democratic Party," in Morgan and Silvestri, *Moderates and Conservatives*, 27-28.

60. Zuckerman, *The Politics of Faction*, 83.

61. Ibid., 86.

62. Pridham, "After Moro," 74.

63. Einaudi and Goguel, *Christian Democracy*, 42

64. See reports submitted to the Twenty-second National Congress of the MRP (1965), excerpted in Randolph L. Braham, ed., *Documents on Major European Governments* (New York: Alfred A. Knopf, 1966), 101-3.

65. Irving, *Christian Democracy in France*, 107.

66. Einaudi and Goguel, *Christian Democracy*, 147.

67. Ibid., 52.

68. Ibid., 70.

69. Ibid., 71.

70. Pridham, "After Moro," 81.

71. Ibid., 77.

72. Irving, "Distinctive Political Phenomenon?" 63.

73. Ibid., 63.

74. Ibid., 65.

4

Jacques Maritain and the Problem of Communism

There is one issue among the many that Jacques Maritain considered during his life that merits special attention. That is his difficulty in developing a coherent philosophical and political strategy for dealing with Marxism. It is important because many of the problems that Maritain had with the idea of collaboration with Communist Party members would trouble Latin American Christian Democrats as well.

Jacques Maritain's well-publicized call for collaboration with members of European Communist parties in the construction of his postwar "New Democracy" caused many of his former supporters to react with dismay and skepticism. Much of this skepticism came from those simply opposed to collaboration. For others, however, the negative reaction was caused by what they perceived as an unwarranted change of heart by Maritain on this important issue.

In fact, Jacques Maritain seems to have undergone not one, but three conversions on the issue of collaboration with communists during his long life. As a young man, Maritain described himself as a Marxist and wrote that he would dedicate his life to the pursuit of Marxist goals. In 1936 he wrote *Integral Humanism*, one of his first books of philosophy, which included a condemnation of communism as an atheistic philosophy. Maritain also specifically rejected separating communist social solutions from this atheism, which would seem to preclude collaboration.

Seven years later, during the antifascist struggle of World War II, he wrote *Christianity and Democracy*. In this work he included an entire chapter on the necessity of including European communists in the task of postwar political reconstruction. Near the end of his life, he wrote *The Peasant of the Garonne*, a collection of musings on a wide range of topics. In this book, Maritain returns to the harsh condemnation of Soviet atheism that appeared in *Integral Humanism*.

Critics of Maritain point to these ostensible shifts in his opinion and argue that they are the sign of an inconsistent and thus inconsequential philosophy. Even worse, Maritain's switches on communism, coming most dramatically during World War II, might also be signs of expediency, brought on by the perceived needs of the war. I will examine the development of Maritain's thought on this important issue and determine why the issue was so troubling to him that he redirected his consideration of it three times.

The Political Threat of Communism

The basic philosophical tenets explored in Chapter 3 led Maritain to distrust the cult of the state, which he saw beginning with Georg Friedrich Hegel and continuing, in an even more virulent form, in the writings of Karl Marx. Maritain's early flirtation with Marxism alerted him to what he would later call its "basic errors." These were its contempt for the person and its bureaucratic despotism.[1]

Marxism implicitly accepts the French philosophe error of supposing there to be two opposite "rhythms" of existence: the religious and the natural. In attempting to make the former subordinate to the latter, Marxists posed a significant threat to the basic rights of the body politic.

Communism, since it was based on the notion that it could provide for man's *earthly* perfection, carries with it an inevitable intolerance of other political groups or political philosophies. It is therefore a threat to pluralism in society. It is here that Maritain found the gravest threat of communism. The record of Soviet communism, he wrote, proves that the demise of private voluntary associations led to pervasive and intrusive state influence over the lives of individuals.[2]

Maritain sees voluntary associations as necessary mediating institutions for the protection of the individual from state power. Maritain finds it significant that Marxists have attacked the independence of all such voluntary associations, starting with labor unions and business corporations. Both of these institutions, in very different ways, are based on the respect for property.[3] Property, and the ability it brings to earn a living independently of the state, is an essential element of man's ability to protect himself from encroaching state power, according to Maritain.

Communism as Atheistic Heresy

Marxism, Maritain believes, is unable to perform the proper function of a just state. This is due not only to its inherent rapaciousness, but also to its rejection of its duty to promote the common good and to direct man toward his spiritual fulfillment. Central to this criticism was Maritain's perception of Communist atheism.

Because God does exist and does take an interest in the affairs of men, Maritain believed that the very act of denial of God's existence is psychologically untenable. Atheism is "unlivable" and Maritain used the psychic dissolution of Friedrich Nietzsche as an example of what awaited anyone who tried to deny the reality of man's spiritual side.[4]

Any attempt to deny the existence or the importance of God and religion would lead inevitably to the replacement of one form of religion with another. Maritain discovered early in his career that communism was itself attempting to play the role of surrogate religion in a society barren of religious belief.

Maritain describes communism as a system or doctrine for living life that purports to provide ultimate meaning to man's existence. In other words, communism is a religion.[5] As a particularly austere and insecure religion, based on a metaphysical base that is untenable, communism is unable to tolerate the existence of other religions and must work to destroy them. Again, communism threatens the independence of voluntary religious associations.

But there is more to Maritain's criticism of communism than even this. Maritain describes communism not only as a mock religion, but also as "the latest Christian heresy."[6] Its heresy appears in its mimicking of Christian notions of communion, faith, and sacrifice. In addition, Marx uses an "anthropocentric, monist metaphysics to make man take on the attributes of God."[7]

Marx also preserves the Christian notion of redemption. For Marx, however, redemption comes not from God but from man. It also comes not on an individual basis but on a class basis. Thus redemption is not available to everyone. Moreover, one group of men, the vanguard, can act as the redeemer for others, the proletariat, even though Marx believed that the membership of this vanguard would come from another class.

Distinguishing Communism from Fascism

Maritain concluded during World War II that even a Christian heresy, which is what he believed Marxism to be, was preferable to the existence of an anti-Christian and thoroughly inhuman philosophy such as fascism. Maritain took great pains in all of his later writings to distinguish between the evils of communism and the evils of fascism. These comparisons provide a vital clue to the understanding of Maritain's position on collaboration with communists.

Fascism, in Maritain's opinion, was irretrievably poisoned by its racism. In an article critical of the legacy of Niccolò Machiavelli, Maritain labels fascists "contemporary Machiavellians" who are "ferocious" in their impatience for political success.[8]

The fascist criteria for such success is the immediate, the earthly, the material, and the perversely humanistic. Maritain believed that fascism was born of the transformation of humanism to an earthly, materialistic outlook that ignores the higher nature of man to which Maritain was committed.[9] Fascism is a quintessentially modern political philosophy in that the state has assumed a sovereignty separate from the will of the people. The fact that it invokes the "people's will" in its unspeakable crimes only adds to its criminality.

However, it is no worse in this regard than any other modern philosophy. As we have seen, Maritain holds that the beginning of the end for true (or integral) humanism came with Jean Jacques Rousseau and the secularization of the body politic. Maritain once wrote of the General Will that since a "figment of [Rousseau's] imagination" cannot rule, sovereignty is inevitably transferred to the state.[10]

Still, fascism does have its distinguishing characteristics. It is marked by hate, more than any other existing political philosophy, according to Maritain. Fascism was based not on a misguided democratic principle, but on the ideology of inherent superiority based on race.[11] Unlike communism, which at least purported to offer hope and salvation for all mankind, fascism explicitly denied the right to hope, salvation, or even humanity itself to large numbers of human beings.

Committed fascists, therefore, had consciously cut themselves off from the vast majority of the human race. They had, in Maritain's eyes, forsaken their humanity and in so doing, rendered themselves almost unsalvageable. Even Rousseau's General Will, the antecedent to so much mischief, was based upon the principle of love. Fascism, embracing the principle of hate, was fundamentally different from all other modern philosophical aberrations and thus demanded different treatment.

Maritain utterly rejects any common cause with fascists. This principled stand caused him to lose many friends and admirers when he applied it to the Spanish Civil War. Some traditional Catholic thinkers, especially in rightist *Acción Française*, supported Generalissimo Francisco Franco in that conflict and even praised him as the New Crusader against the communist infidel. Maritain would have none of this and insisted that the choices in Spain's tragedy were far less clear cut.[12]

Maritain was equally impatient with the "realists" of the 1930s who advocated a policy of accommodation with Adolf Hitler's Germany. In a statement clearly directed at the appeasement policy, Maritain wrote in 1952 that "justice can never be the cause of ruin or destruction. Political injustice," such as dealing with a modern Machiavelli like Hitler, "is always dearly paid for in the end."[13]

Maritain retained this distrust of the right until the end of his life. Writing in *The Peasant of the Garonne*, Maritain said that while the left despises the "real," the right despises not only disorder, but also justice and charity. He went on to describe himself as "what people call a man of the left."[14]

Reasons for Collaboration

Maritain offered three reasons why he thought an alliance with communists was legitimate. First, collaboration itself eliminated some of the political problems connected with Marxism. If the survival of independent voluntary associations was a problem in communist regimes, it need not be one under a coalition government that included communists. Indeed, the very nature of such a *coalition* government would seem to forestall that danger.

Second, Maritain draws a distinction between communism as an atheistic philosophy and individual communists as misguided but well-meaning social reformers. Even before the war and the U.S.-Soviet alliance, Maritain said in an interview: "I have no desire to turn all Communists into ashes; I should like them to become converts to God."[15] He repeats this preference in *Christianity and Democracy*.

Third, at the time that he wrote most forcefully about collaboration, Maritain largely agreed with Marxists about the fundamental causes of social ills. Marxism responds, he thought, to many of Christendom's failures. To understand Maritain's insistence that communists were on to something important, it is necessary to understand his criticisms of modern Christianity, capitalism, and democracy.

During his early period, Maritain wrote that communism was rooted in the resentment against "a Christian world failing to live up to its principles."[16] This resentment, he argued, was misguided only in that it went beyond an impatience with individual Christians, and extended to a hatred for Christianity itself.

Nevertheless, it was the half-hearted Christians who invited this resentment, according to Maritain. Shutting up their understanding of the truth and divine light within a limited part of their existence, some Christians seemed to draw a distinction between public and private morality.[17] In the business world, such people would attend church on Sunday and then cheat their business associates on Monday. In the political realm, Maritain refers to the practice of dealing with criminal regimes, advocated by men who would never deal with ordinary criminals.

The most conspicuous failure of Christianity, in Maritain's view, was its failure to adequately provide for the needs of the working class. Maritain believes that the Catholic Church in Europe was unprepared for the new demands that would be placed upon it by the Industrial Revolution. These needs were first, to see to the spiritual needs of the workers as they moved in large numbers from the countryside to the city; and second, to persuade factory owners to maintain the traditional commitment to the just wage and to family life outside of the factory.

The Church failed in both of these missions. As a result, they lost the working classes. Maritain describes what others have called Christianity's "desertion" of the workers as a process through which the workers left the Church, and not vice versa. However, he is quick to add that this exodus took place because the workers no longer felt welcome in the "crib of Christianity."[18]

Only after the materialistic philosophies began to take hold, Maritain believed, did the Church begin to reach out to its lost sheep. Maritain was supported in this criticism of the Christian world by no less an authority than Pope Pius XI, who wrote in 1937 that the greatest scandal of the modern age was that the Church had lost the working classes.[19]

Inherent in Maritain's treatment of Christianity's failures are the failures of democracy and capitalism as well. Maritain wrote in 1943 that democracy was still important, but that it had to liberate itself from materialistic capitalism. Democracy, he thought, was a living instinct that made men reach out to their fellows in a spirit of communitarianism. Capitalism, for its part, encouraged the development of radical individualism. Thus the two were not compatible and yet many in the West felt that to defend democracy they had to defend capitalism as well.[20]

The evil of capitalism, according to Maritain, is its anthropocentric spirit that praises economic gain over all other values. Capitalism ignores man's spiritual side, and thus falls into the same trap that communism does. The particular absurdity of capitalism was that it exalted individualism as a goal yet denied this very individualism to all but the privileged few.

The great tragedy of the modern age was that the communists were the ones who revealed and analyzed the brutality of unchecked capitalism. The capitalism of Marx's time cried out for a revolution, Maritain believed, but he did not think that this revolution had to take a Marxist path. A "Christian Ghandi," he thought, "might have led a Christian social revolution."[21]

Maritain's views on the evils of capitalism would undergo a drastic change during his long stay in the United States. One of Maritain's biographers wrote that early in his career, Maritain shared Reinhold

Niebuhr's dislike and distrust of private corporations. This view, according to the author, underwent a change while Maritain lived in the United States.[22] This, I suggest, is something of an understatement. What occurred during Maritain's residence in the United States was a complete reworking of his theory of economic ethics.

Ten years after Maritain's return to America, following his stint as French Minister to the Holy See, he summarized his impressions of his adopted country. Like Alexis deTocqueville, Maritain was struck by the enormous amount of economic, social, and even political activity that took place in America outside of government control. Charitable organizations, professional fraternities, service organizations, and similar private groups all existed side by side with the most productive example of capitalism the world has known.

Maritain concluded from this that Americans had overcome what Europeans, and especially European Marxists, had labeled the "bourgeois" attitude. The United States' middle class was not self-satisfied and uncaring, as European Marxists expected them to be.[23]

What America lacked, Maritain thought, was an explicit ideology that reflected its unique contribution to social and economic relations. The beginning of the development of this ideology would be the realization that European-style, liberal capitalism had ceased to exist here.[24]

Maritain cites the power of labor unions, the ease with which many laborers rose to management positions, the "cooperative tension" between labor and industry, and institutions like profit sharing as evidence of a new economic and social reality. Far from falling into the hell of dehumanization that Marx predicted, capitalism and the wealth it produced in the United States had led its citizens to create what Maritain called "economic humanism."[25]

In so doing, America became the reality of Aristotle's and Aquinas's political society: a place where the work of reason and virtue allows men to live and work together to fulfill their highest material and spiritual aims. Thus, Maritain concluded that America was the embodiment of much of what he had written about in *Integral Humanism*, and had in fact achieved what the Marxists said only they could provide: the classless society. America had differences in wealth and opportunity, but its citizens lacked the "class mentality" that poisoned so much political debate in Europe.[26]

American capitalism, then, had robbed communism of many of its pretexts and made Maritain less certain that its analysis of the causes of social ills was as valuable as he had thought. So if Maritain changed his mind on the question of collaboration with communism near the end of his life, it is possible that the reason for this apparent change of heart was his mental rehabilitation of capitalism, at least its American version.

This explanation is inadequate. Whatever repairs Americans have made in capitalism, they certainly have not addressed the metaphysical differences between communism and Christianity, or done away with the former's open disdain for the latter. Maritain seemed keenly aware of these metaphysical differences early on, seemed to paper them over during the war, and reasserted them at the end of his life.

BASIC DIFFERENCES: HOW IMPORTANT?

Those who find inconsistencies in Maritain's political philosophy tend to emphasize his early embrace of Marxism, his thundering condemnation of it in early works such as *Integral Humanism*, his insistence on working with communists during the war, and his return to condemnation in *The Peasant of the Garonne*. One work that does not receive sufficient attention is Maritain's 1947 speech to the Mexico City conference of the United Nations Educational Scientific and Cultural Organization (Unesco). This speech represents the link in Maritain's thought and points up the single principle that adds consistency to his thought on the question of communism.

Maritain began by reminding the delegates that French culture had always tended toward universality. Tolerance for foreign manners, customs, and ways of thinking had always been part of the French experience.[27] He went on to say, however, that Unesco was not created to look after the theoretical progress of education, science, and culture in the world, but to make use of these tools in concrete and positive work. In addition, it should be the mission of the organization to promote this work through individual action, a constant Maritain theme, taken on a mass scale and, most importantly, over the heads of unenlightened governments.[28]

Since the work of the organization was important, and since it would be done outside of government sanction, as Maritain had seen so much good work done in the United States, he concluded that Unesco's work would not be harmed by the presence of what he called "some irrational currents," a reference to communists.

What was more immediately important to Maritain was agreement among coalition partners on common practical ideas. Ideological differences, he noted, were still important, and he added, "There is such a thing as truth and falsehood," but people whose metaphysics are opposed may still agree on prescriptions. Such people can and should work together to perform urgently needed tasks, without letting metaphysics get in the way.[29]

In *The Peasant of the Garonne*, Maritain repeated these opinions, demonstrating that, at least in his mind, nothing important had changed on the question of communist collaboration. He combined these ideas, moreover, with another favorite theme, the redeemability of all men.

Everyone is a potential member of the Body of Christ. Thus, all men are worthy of respect and cooperation.[30] This is the same idea that Maritain expressed in his 1939 interview, in almost the same words.

Maritain compares the task of Christian political reformers to that of Christian missionaries. While they must understand the basic differences between their beliefs and those of the heathen they must convert, they must also love the people with whom they live, and not be afraid to work with them to accomplish needed tasks. Many of these tasks will not have a metaphysical element to them in the first place.[31]

What this means is that the apparent differences in Maritain's attitude toward communists are really changes in tone, not in substance. It does not matter how severely Maritain criticizes the metaphysical underpinnings of Marxism. Whether he is denouncing communism as the newest Christian heresy or temporarily choosing not to dwell upon its deficiencies, Maritain consistently believed that collaboration is necessary and proper.

Even at his most critical, when he wrote in *Integral Humanism* that it is impossible to separate communist social solutions from its atheism, Maritain still left room for collaboration. It is not necessary to separate them. Communist atheism does not affect the question of collaboration. It is unnecessary, Maritain thinks, to first reconcile metaphysical differences before working together.

Central to the Christian life, of course, is the practice of charity. Maritain believed that this charity would eventually not only rob communism of its pretexts by rehumanizing political and economic relationships, but also win over many individual communists. Such potential converts must exist, according to Maritain, because communism is based upon love, however misguided.[32] Maritain continued to draw the distinction between communists and communism, arguing in *The Peasant of the Garonne* that Vladimir Lenin was dangerous precisely because he was "a man of the right leading a revolution of the left."[33]

Maritain calls charity "the secret weapon of Christianity." This charity will enable Christians to use the contributions of non-Christians to help the world and the non-Christians in spite of themselves.[34] Thus it is not only permissible for Christians to cooperate with communists, it may even be a duty. The real wrong would be to forsake them, as many of Maritain's contemporaries suggested.

MARITAIN'S THEORY: AN ASSESSMENT

Maritain is consistent throughout his career on the question of collaboration with communists, although differences in tone and style make this consistency hard to detect. However, his arguments about communism reveal other inconsistencies that are perhaps more troubling than a contradictory position on collaboration would be.

For example, Maritain seems to think, at different times, that communism is either an atheistic religion or merely a Christian heresy. If a Christian heresy can be atheistic and still just a heresy, Maritain fails to explain how this can be. Maritain also seemingly ignores the fact that heresy has posed greater dangers to Christian unity through the centuries than outright persecution. This history should have made Maritain more wary of labeling communism a "Christian heresy."

Second, of equal concern is Maritain's breezy confidence that Christian good intentions and fine example will blunt the edge of communism's challenge to its existence. Maritain seems to believe that only communism can be corroded by close contact between it and Christianity. In so doing he ignores the threat to individual Christian believers who lack Maritain's sophisticated outlook and are liable to be misled by seeing Christian lay leaders side by side with Communist Party members. To many believers, this represents a "legitimization" of communism.

Third, Maritain certainly changes his mind about *why* it is permissible to cooperate with communists. In his middle works, most notably in *Christianity and Democracy*, Maritain says that Christians must work with communists because they agree on the causes of social ills. It was during this period that Maritain was most critical of liberal capitalism, and most sympathetic to the social diagnosis of Marx.

Yet by the time he was addressing the Unesco conference, only four years later, Maritain was arguing that the basis for Christian/Communist Party teamwork was agreement not on diagnosis, but on prescriptions. In the intervening period, Maritain spent some time in the United States and probably began his mental rehabilitation of capitalism.

Since capitalism's inadequacy was one of the reasons for collaboration in the first place, such a basic change in his opinion of capitalism *should have* caused him to change his opinion of communism, and of the possibilities for common cause. I think that a genuine change of heart on this point would be less troubling than the almost "foolish consistency" that Maritain seems to demonstrate.

Finally, I think that Maritain's facile distinction between communism as a philosophy and individual communists as misguided reformers is overdrawn. Nor is his description of Lenin as a "man of the right" terribly reassuring. Unless the Christian coalition partners are willing to dictate which communists are acceptable, presumably based on their level of misguidedness, they will have to deal with the Communist Party leaders actually in control. In the sort of coalition effort that Maritain envisions in *Christianity and Democracy*, it is much more likely that the Lenins of a Communist Party will be involved, and not the misguided reformers.

In short, while Maritain did not change his opinion on the question of collaboration between Christian reformers and communists, he should have. His reasons for suggesting such a coalition in the first place take inadequate account of the political dangers involved. Moreover, he changed his opinion about the bases for cooperation and found new bases later on. Maritain was seemingly unwilling to abandon a favorite policy prescription and this, I suggest, is a more serious philosophical shortcoming than inconsistency.

Latin Americans of all political stripes face the same questions of coalition building, pragmatism, attaining political power, and dealing with Marxist movements. If anything, they are more pressing for Latin Americans than for Maritain and his European colleagues. How Latin American Christian Democracy has fared with these challenges will be the subject of Chapter 5.

NOTES

1. John M. Dunaway, *Jacques Maritain* (Boston: Twaynes Publishers, 1978), 68.

2. John W. Cooper, *A Theology of Freedom: The Legacy of Jacques Maritain and Reinhold Niebuhr* (Macon, GA: Mercer University Press, 1985), 106.

3. Ibid., 94ff.

4. Dunaway, *Jacques Maritain*, 67.

5. Jacques Maritain, "Roots of Soviet Atheism," from *Integral Humanism*, in Joseph W. Evans and Leo R. Ward, *The Social and Political Philosophy of Jacques Maritain* (Notre Dame, IN: University of Notre Dame Press, 1976), 252.

6. Brooke Williams Smith, *Jacques Maritain: Antimodern or Ultramodern?* (New York: Elsevier, 1976), 96. Smith's quotation is from Maritain, *Integral Humanism*.

7. Maritain, "Roots of Soviet Atheism," 255-59.

8. Jacques Maritain, "The End of Machiavellianism," from *The Range of Reason*, in Evans and Ward, *The Social Political Philosophy*, 311

9. Dunaway, *Jacques Maritain*, 66.

10. Jacques Maritain, "Problems Concerning the State," from *Man and the State*, in Evans and Ward, *The Social and Political Philosophy*, 92.

11. Maritain does not distinguish between the Nazi version of fascism and other varieties. Thus he assumes that racism and fascism are inextricably mixed.

12. Smith, *Antimodern or Ultramodern?* 39.

13. Maritain, "The End of Machiavellianism," 310.

14. Jacques Maritain, *The Peasant of the Garonne*, Cuddity and Hughes, trans. (New York: Holt, Rinehart and Winston, 1968), 21-22.

15. "An Interview with Jacques Maritain," *Commonweal*, 29, 15 (1939): 398.

16. Maritain, "Roots of Soviet Atheism," 255.

17. Ibid., 257.

18. Smith, *Antimodern or Ultramodern?* 93.

19. Pius XI, *Divini Redemptoris* (On Atheistic Communism), official Vatican translation (Boston: Daughters of St. Paul, 1937), para. 50.

20. Jacques Maritain, *Christianity and Democracy* (San Francisco: Ignatius Press, 1986), 18.

21. Dunaway, *Jacques Maritain*, 97.

22. Cooper, *A Theology of Freedom*, 103.

23. Jacques Maritain, *Reflections on America* (New York: Charles Scribner's Sons, 1958), 87.

24. Ibid., 101.

25. Ibid., 109-13.

26. Ibid., 175-79.

27. This speech is reprinted in Evans and Ward, *The Social and Political Philosophy*, 123-36.

28. Ibid., 125.

29. Ibid., 133-34.

30. Maritain, *Peasant of the Garonne*, 71-72.

31. Ibid., 74-76.

32. Maritain was also aware of the many instances of actual conversions. See Dunaway, *Jacques Maritain*, 149.

33. Maritain, *The Peasant*, 22.

34. Ibid., 62.

5

Latin American Christian Democracy

The Christian Democratic movement began in Latin America at the end of World War I. By the 1950s there were Christian Democratic parties in almost every Latin American country that permitted political parties, and Christian Democratic movements in most of the others.

Nevertheless, it was not until 1964 that any Christian Democratic party actually achieved power, with the victory of Eduardo Frei Montalva in Chile. Four years later the Venezuelan party won presidential elections there. These two victories seem to presage a Christian Democratic wave across Latin America. This wave never materialized.

Observers both in Latin America and in the United States have tended to view the Christian Democrats as moderate, slightly left-of-center reformers. These observers expect them to provide a bastion against radical leftist movements, including communism.

Such faith in Christian Democracy is ill-placed. Latin American Christian Democrats, like their European counterparts, accept too many of the basic assumptions of radical leftism to be effective anticommunists. The Christian Democrats mirror their more extreme rivals in their attitude toward capitalism, toward labor, toward nationalization of basic commodities, and, most importantly, toward the usefulness of state power.

THE LEGACY OF EUROPE

Links with Catholic Social Thought

Latin American Christian Democracy drew its inspiration from the "social encyclicals," especially *Rerum Novarum, Quadragessimo Anno, Mater et Magistra*, and *Pacem in Terris*. As the Catholic Church moved leftward in the 1960s, so did the Christian Democratic movement. What some experts describe as the more progressive elements of the Catholic laity found a social policy in these encyclicals that went beyond mere charity.[1] This was a welcome change for those Latin American Catholics who were disgusted with what they perceived as the Church's traditional defense of the status quo.

In Chile, the Christian Democratic Party (PDC) grew out of a student movement that began in the 1930s. Its leaders were determined to "put Christian doctrine in the service of the present day."[2] Its programs were designed to center political and economic life around the needs of the human person, or in the words of a PDC document, "to bring the individual to some meaningful sense of himself."[3]

This method of origin and central themes was repeated elsewhere in Latin America. In Venezuela, Rafael Caldera established a student movement in the 1930s based on the papal social encyclicals and the works of Jacques Maritain. In Guatemala, José García Bauer, a labor lawyer, started a Catholic study group that became the Christian Democratic Party in 1955.[4]

Links to Jacques Maritain

European Christian Democrats were also important to the Latin American movement. One author mentions Maritain, Yves Simon, and Etienne Gilson in particular.[5] Christian Democracy also has roots in the nineteenth-century traditionalism of José de Maistre, Jaime Balmes, and Juan Donoso Cortés.[6]

The vehicle for transmitting these European intellectual currents to Latin America was a movement that began just after World War II to establish new Catholic universities, or new philosophy or theology departments in existing universities. These universities favorably received the thought of many European Christian Democrats, most notably Jacques Maritain.[7]

Maritain's ideas came to Latin America at a propitious time. For almost three quarters of a century, the anti-Christian movement of positivism was dominant among intellectual circles. There was a need for a new philosophy that intellectuals who were determined to retain their Catholicism could call their own. The thought of Maritain, with its intellectually stimulating complexity and its fidelity to the Faith, filled this need.

No other European would equal the influence of Maritain among Latin American Christian Democratic intellectuals. Eduardo Frei, for example, was most notably attracted to Maritain, saying himself that Maritain "occupied a central position in [my] thought."[8] In another work, he cited his long friendship with Maritain and the long sessions the two spent together.[9]

Maritain's neo-Thomism animated the establishment of other Latin American Christian Democratic parties. In Brazil, Jackson deFiguereido was an important Christian Democratic theorist. He drew his inspiration mainly from Maritain.

Equally important to the Brazilian movement was Alceu Amoroso Lima. This Brazilian intellectual was active in the Christian Socialist movement. He claimed that he owed a great debt to Maritain, in particular Maritain's concern with the working classes. The great task of Christian socialism, according to Lima, was educating and cathecising labor so that it might develop a social consciousness.[10] Maritain's influence also drew Lima away from an orthodox socialist position. As we have seen, Maritain placed great importance on social pluralism. This emphasis made Lima skeptical about an evergrowing role for the state.[11] Elsewhere in Latin America, Maritain clubs sprang up, although not all of these matured into political parties.

Relations with the Catholic Church

According to one expert, Christian Democracy has a great potential in Latin America because it is a philosophy that does not break with the Catholic humanistic value system of the Latin American political tradition.[12] Nevertheless, the Christian Democrats have always been at great pains to separate themselves from their national churches, and indeed from the Roman Catholic Church itself.

On one level, this is merely good politics. To be identified as a clerical or confessional party in Latin America is to enter a world of immobile political opinions. Latin Americans who are active in politics tend to have positions on the Church/state question that are set in cement. Thus, while the Christian Democrats could depend upon loyal support from many powerful and influential people by defending the Church, they also knew that such a stand would alienate many others.

Christian Democrats also had philosophical reasons for separation from the official Church. As we saw in Chapter 2, many Liberationists see the national Catholic churches as married to the status quo and nostalgic for the sixteenth century. Christian Democrats held the same uncomplimentary view.

Frei, for example, wrote that the Church of Latin America defended the political regime in power during the colonial era, "with all the abuses of the metropolitan power and the restrictions on international trade."[13] Writing in 1971, Frei said: "During the 19th century and until the 1950s, the Church was conservative and a pillar and underpinning of the established order."[14]

The split between Frei's followers and the Chilean Church got so serious at one point that there was even talk of excommunication. Cardinal Giovanni Battista Montini, then Vatican Secretary of State, and later Pope Paul VI, rescued the fledgling movement from this punishment.

Friction between the Christian Democratic parties and national churches existed elsewhere also. In Argentina, there was no hierarchical support for the Christian Democrats.[15] In Brazil, Alceu Lima, like Frei, condemned what he saw as the Brazilian Church's close identification with the state and its neglect of labor.[16]

Yet relations between the Christian Democrats and the Catholic Church in Rome have been close and cordial. In several cases, Roman clerics played a direct role in forming Christian Democratic movements, much as they did with Alcide deGasperi in 1943. Venezuela's Rafael Caldera was inspired to found a Christian Democratic movement after attending the First Congress of Catholic Youth in Rome in 1934.

With him at the Congress were Mario Polar and Venacio Flores, influential figures in Christian Democracy in Peru and Uruguay, respectively.[17] The Salvadoran party goes back to the 1954 conference of the Pax Romana, another Vatican youth organization.[18]

Even in Chile, Roman influence was evident. Most leaders of the Falange, Christian Democracy's precursor, were students under Fernando Vives de Solar and Alberto Hurtado Cruchaga, both "progressive" Jesuits. In Latin America, as throughout the world, the Jesuits are the arm of direct Vatican control, over the heads of the national episcopal conferences.

It is this progressive Roman Church with which the Christian Democrats wish to identify themselves. Today, Frei wrote, the Church supports change and inaugurates it. He is referring to the Vatican II Church of Rome, and ignoring for the moment its Chilean branch. Thus the Christian Democrats have entered the ancient conflict between Rome and the national Churches, and have done so on the side of Rome.

THE POLITICS OF CHRISTIAN DEMOCRACY IN LATIN AMERICA

The best summary of the Christian Democratic outlook on earthly politics was given by Eduardo Frei, writing about the old and new

Catholic Church. The dividing line between these two Churches was, for him, the publication of *Mater et Magistra* in 1961.

The new Church looks favorably on change, is concerned with the present and not just the heavenly future, has accepted struggle over resignation, promotes personal responsibility over Divine Providence, affirms the inadequacy of good intentions, equates charity with efficiency and productivity, and respects manual and commercial occupations.[19]

Like their European counterparts, Latin American Christian Democrats center their social concerns on the personhood of each individual. The good of the individual must overcome opposition based on classes, consistent with Catholic social thought.[20] It must also modify the strictly economic concerns of capitalism, which can deny the possibility of human fulfillment to many individuals.

Christian Democrats insist that a revolution is necessary to bring Latin America to this humanistic understanding, but they also insist that this revolution, however pivotal in its effects, must not be violent in its means.[21] Such violence is inconsistent with the primacy of the individual.

Social Pluralism and the Role of the State

Insofar as Christian Democratic theory is consistent with Catholic social thought, there is a great emphasis on the creation and maintenance of mediating social structures.[22] The Brazilian Alceu Lima was most eloquent on this issue, which highlights his rejection of the Christian Socialist tradition.

Neo-Thomists throughout Latin America emphasized an important but *limited* role for the state, and highlighted the importance of social voluntarism as a source of consistent opposition to Marxism.[23] In Peru, Christian Democratic theorist José Luis Bustamente y Rivero criticized the statism of Marx and suggested social cooperation as an alternative.[24] In El Salvador, Carlos Alberto Siri also held the classical Christian view that the state is inadequate to provide for all human needs. For Siri, the state merely coordinates the initiatives of individuals in society.[25]

The Christian Democratic view of the state is consistent with its view of the individual. Christian Democrats view the state as egotistical and prejudiced and maintain that the claims of such an imperfect state must be secondary to the claims of the individual. The primacy of the family is also important, since the activity of the state must be limited by the anterior and comprehensive authority of the family. According to the theory, the state must also give way to local communities, to regional subdivisions, to trade unions, and to the Church.

Frei reiterated much of this in his writings. He consistently condemned collectivism "that will absorb and subjugate man."[26] While attempting to warn his countrymen of the danger of Salvador Allende, he predicted that an Allende government would mean, among other things, more nationalizations, expropriation of large landholdings, and government control of the distribution of consumer goods.[27] Communism, he said some years later, is objectionable because it places no checks on government.[28]

In Ecuador, some Christian Democrats even tried to put this antistatist rhetoric into practice. The Christian Democrat–influenced regime of Jaime Roldos, for example, made a short-lived attempt to decentralize some of the authority and functions of the state Ministry of Health. The ministry was recentralized within two years.[29]

In 1984, León Febres Cordero, at least a nominal member of the Christian Democratic party, came into office as the champion of private enterprise. Calling himself "more Reagan than Mitterrand," Febres often repeated his belief in economic liberty.[30] Such liberty, he believed, involved a decline in state power, and this he seemed determined to achieve.[31] Febres's 1984 electoral program included fewer government regulations on business, lowering of import duties, and the elimination of government price and exchange controls.[32]

Despite the apparent conservatism of some of their beliefs, Liberationists can accept much of what Christian Democrats say about "new" Christianity, capitalism, and revolution. The Liberationists differ from the Christian Democrats on the issues of violence and class struggle. This disagreement reflects a more basic difference on the primacy of the individual. If the individual is primary, he cannot be sacrificed for a worthwhile social goal.

Without this commitment to individuals, Christian Democrats lose the base for their opposition to violence and class struggle. Thus whenever they waver in their support for individual well-being, Christian Democrats risk becoming mirror images of the Liberationists.

Nevertheless, Latin America's Christian Democrats have sacrificed their commitment to the individual and have sought to redirect state power, rather than to limit it. The search for short-term political gain has seduced Christian Democracy toward rejection of the one philosophical tenet that separates it from most Latin American political movements of the right and the left. A review of Christian Democratic policies shows how this took place.

Land Reform

In theory, the Christian Democratic plan for land reform is to replace the capitalist system of "few proprietors" and the socialist system of "no proprietors" with a new system of "all proprietors." The apparent bias toward private property in this plan is tempered by the demand that the use of private property be directed toward the common good. In other words, the Christian Democrats favor private property so long as owners acknowledge the "social mortgage" emphasized by Pope Paul VI.

Christian Democrats favor land reform that expropriates large land-holdings and redistributes them to tenant farmers or sharecroppers. The reform must be responsive to the needs of the new owners. They must be allowed to form communities and to be economically viable for the reform to make any sense.[33]

A critical part of the "common good" for Frei was avoiding violent revolution. Such a revolution, born of the pent-up frustrations over the unfinished nature of the independence revolutions, is almost inevitable, Frei wrote in 1971. Because of the threat of this class-based revolution, classical economic formulas, which exacerbate tensions between classes, will not work. Great changes must take place. The first of these changes, according to Frei, is widespread land reform.[34]

In practice, Chilean land reform concentrated almost completely on the supposed rights of the new owners. The 1964 Christian Democratic campaign program called first for a new tax structure, under which land would be taxed based not on what was actually produced, but on what might have been produced.

For those landholders able to bear this fiscal strain, the near certainty of expropriation remained, beginning with irrigated holdings of more than 80 hectares.[35] This was more land than most Chileans had, but hardly a legendary *hacienda* of old. Compensation was in the form of long-term, low-interest bonds. Moreover, under the land reform bill of 1967, the Chilean government was allowed to occupy land regardless of whether payment had been made or even agreed upon.[36]

Frei's land reform program involved a basic logical contradiction, based on the ambiguous attitude toward the former landowners. If these landowners were holding their lands illegally and immorally, then there was no reason to compensate them for the loss. If their influence on Chilean society was an essentially positive one, then there was no need for land reform in the first place. If landholding itself induced the dire social irresponsibility that Frei suggested, then Christian Democracy's "all proprietors" goal would only make things worse.

Thus, the theoretical Christian Democratic commitment to "all proprietors" was soon forgotten in Chile. The expropriated land was not turned over to the supposed beneficiaries, but rather turned into government cooperatives, with the provision that they remain so for three to five years. For the peasants, gaining outright ownership of the expropriated land was nearly impossible.[37]

Nationalization of Basic Resources and Industries

Christian Democratic attitudes toward the role of foreign investment and ownership are ambiguous. As we have seen, they have a suspicion of capital investment in general, going back to Maritain and the popes.[38] Mixed with this is a particularly Latin American expression of nationalism, one that requires control over natural resources. Thus suspicion of external capitalists comes from two different directions.

Frei believed that the nationalization of resources, such as mines and fisheries, was inevitable in Latin America. The continent, he wrote, entered its modernization phase without the Western luxury of accumulated capital to use for development. For development to occur without the loss of "independence," basic resources must not be alienated to outsiders.[39]

The Christian Democrats shared this outwardly nationalistic determination with the Liberationists. Their methods of achieving economic independence, however, were different. Frei invented a "moderate" method of expropriation. Over a period of some years, Chilean government ownership of basic industries replaced foreign ownership as the government bought out the foreigners. In the case of copper, Chile's largest export, Chile's government acquired 51 percent of the American firms' holdings.[40] This gradual, nonconfrontational process was called "Chileanization."

The Chilean government did not acquire this controlling interest to pass it on to Chilean entrepreneurs. Instead, Chileanization involved a permanent government presence in the copper industry. It was an attempt by government to involve itself in exploiting Chilean resources to a degree never before contemplated in Chilean history.

The Chileanization pattern became the model for subsequent Christian Democratic positions on nationalization. In Argentina, the small Christian Democratic party promised voters nationalization of the oil industry, with the Argentine government taking over production and distribution.[41]

Twenty years later the Ecuadoran Christian Democrats, supposedly more fiscally conservative than their predecessors, started out inviting foreign participation in oil exploration. While this seemed to be an expression of confidence in foreign investment, the Ecuadoran administration allowed the foreigners to do little but explore. Once they found the oil, it went to the government.[42]

Christian Democrats in Chile and Ecuador used the nationalization issue to increase their control over their respective economies. Like Christian Democratic land reform, the Chileanization pattern did nothing to economically empower new groups in the Latin American social system, the goal of Catholic social thought and, to a lesser extent, of Maritain. Thus while such programs alienated much of the property-owning class, to say nothing of those who hoped to be property owners someday, it did little to satisfy the left.

Evidence of this comes from a leftist commentator who blasted the

Frei administration for paying over 90 percent of book value for 51 percent of Anaconda's actual Chilean copper holdings. The author goes on to say that it was left to the Allende administration to demonstrate "real" nationalism by nationalizing the remaining copper mines, as well as Chile's nitrates, iron, and coal.[43] Like many compromise solutions, the Christian Democratic answer to foreign investment pleased no one.

Like land reform, Chileanization involved a basic problem of logic. Although Frei spoke stridently of the need for Chilean control of foreign investment, and often spoke harshly of foreign investment per se, he opposed the Marxist/socialist view that such investment assets should be seized outright. If foreign investment is as detrimental as Frei often suggested, there is no justification for buying the foreigners out, as opposed to simply ordering them out. On the other hand, if foreign investment is not detrimental, then there is no reason for it to leave, compensated or not. Chileanization suggests that foreign investment is good and bad at the same time.

Labor Policy

As we have seen, Christian Democratic social and economic theories were both based on the primacy of the individual. This attitude is visible in their labor policy as well. In theory, Christian Democracy seeks to replace capitalist enterprise with communitarian enterprises, in which both capital and labor will participate in ownership, direction, and distribution of profit. It is determined to integrate the worker into society.[44]

Economically, the Christian Democrats wish to overcome the traditional labor-management split and reunite the worker with his product. The method for accomplishing this is profit sharing. According to Christian Democratic theory, the worker should obtain shares of stock through a "planned and large scale access of labor to capital."[45] In this way, the Christian Democrats hope to attain peacefully and gradually what Marx said could only be achieved violently and traumatically: the classless society.

The difference, in theory, between the two is that the Christian Democrats' classless society would be made up of all bourgeois instead of all proletarians. Workers must therefore be convinced that their true interests lay in emulating the bourgeoisie, rather than opposing it. For this reason, Christian Democrats in Latin America entered labor politics early.[46]

Chilean Christian Democrats, for example, got involved in organizing labor in the 1930s. By the 1950s, they had turned their attention to rural laborers, a promising field of endeavor since the countryside had been ignored by most socialist labor organizers. When the Christian Democrats finally came into office in 1964, they immediately rewrote the labor code to provide for rural unionization by municipality, changing the old system of patron-client unions centered around plantations. One author credits the Christian Democratic electoral gains in 1967 to this effort.[47]

Yet the way in which Christian Democrats in Chile tried to put their labor theory into practice proved to be their most serious error. Frei failed to reform the labor code and break the power of the socialists and communists in the labor movement. The numerous financial constraints on unions and shop stewards, including the requirement that most union activity be done on the workers' own time, favored the well-financed socialists and communists and made entry by newcomers difficult.[48]

Most significantly, Frei failed to enact what was, according to both Catholic social thought and Maritain, the central pillar of labor policy: profit sharing. The Frei administration failed to make any real effort to establish worker control or widespread profit sharing. While one author attributes this to Frei's preoccupation with other matters,[49] it really reflects a more basic shortcoming. After rejecting capitalism in other areas, Frei could not encourage labor to act like bourgeois. Thus he lost an opportunity to realign labor's political loyalty. Christian Democrats would compete for labor votes by trying to outbid the left, a hopeless task. Christian Democracy had become a victim of its own contradictions.

CHRISTIAN DEMOCRATS AS ALTERNATIVES TO COMMUNISM

Many people in Latin America viewed Frei's victory as the start of a new era, in which the Christian Democrats would steer a course between the right-wing nationalism of Peronist-like parties and Castro-style communism. The Christian Democratic victory in Venezuela four years later raised hopes for such a pattern even further.

The Chilean 1964 campaign was, however, an anomaly in Chilean politics. The right did not run its own candidate and thus Frei was the only alternative to Allende's Marxism. Moreover, as the campaign entered its final month, anticommunist rhetoric from the Christian Democratic camp became more intense. Frei would not have been able to do this had there been a more conservative candidate staking out the anticommunist field.[50]

The thrust of most of the Christian Democratic campaign, however, was a "Revolution in Liberty." Frei accepted most of Allende's social and economic proposals, but he promised to accomplish them more effectively and with less disruption.[51] These guarantees, combined with the last-minute scare tactics, assured a Christian Democratic victory.

Frei acknowledges that the greatest appeal of Christian Democracy is providing an alternative to communism. In fact, he attributes the right's hatred for Christian Democracy to this strength, saying that the right is haunted by past Christian Democratic successes.[52] Such successes, Frei argues, prevent the right from presenting itself as communism's only roadblock. Deprived of this, the right is fated to disappear from Latin American politics.

In the United States, Frei's 1964 defeat of Allende was greeted with enthusiasm by the Johnson administration. American policymakers, still preoccupied with the possibility of "another Cuba," saw Frei as the answer to their prayers. With Frei, the United States did not have to choose between autocratic governments and radical leftist movements. So happy was the administration with Frei that Washington was embarrassing in its offers of financial aid to his presidency.[53]

Frei's first two years in office coincided with the first flush of American enthusiasm for Latin American democratic reform. Under the Alliance for Progress, Chile received the highest per capita share of resources in the hemisphere.[54]

As the Nixon administration began, it seemed that Frei's lustre to North Americans had worn off. Richard Nixon cut aid and relations became far less cordial.[55] However, the 1970 election changed everything. In Henry Kissinger's encyclopedic memoirs, Frei is one of the few Latin American leaders of whom Kissinger speaks highly.[56] He describes the elaborate schemes the U.S. devised to circumvent the Chilean constitution, all to allow Frei to run again after the 1970 election.

Frei also received covert support from Washington. The sudden change in the tone and substance of the Christian Democratic campaign in 1964 to a hard anticommunist line led many Chileans to speculate that outside influences were at work.[57] During the Church Committee hearings of the United States Senate, it was revealed that the Central Intelligence Agency (CIA) had poured millions of dollars into the Frei campaign.[58]

Frei himself denies that the Christian Democrats took part in the activities of the CIA and points out that he and his party resisted Kissinger's plan to force a new election in 1970.[59] He steadfastly denies that the Christian Democrats had anything to do with the CIA in 1964 and insists that the anticommunist posters and advertisements were the work of independent agencies not under his control.

One defender of Frei points to the Church Committee's conclusion that CIA involvement did not affect the outcome of the 1964 election. Somewhat disingenuously, he maintains that all the CIA did was give Frei a majority, rather than a mere plurality.[60] Since this outright majority allowed Frei to carry out most of his program, a reasonable person would have to conclude that CIA involvement was a crucial factor in Christian

Democratic government. The point is, the CIA got involved because of Washington's perception that the Christian Democrats' ideology would prevent radical leftist revolution.

Some of the same patterns were visible 20 years later in Ecuador and El Salvador. In Ecuador, the Febres administration, as we have seen, identified itself with the economic policies of Ronald Reagan. It was rewarded with good relations with the United States. As Chile was the showpiece for the Alliance for Progress, so Ecuador became the show-piece for the Baker Plan on Third World debt. Conservative organizations in the U.S. also praised the Febres experiment, including the normally difficult to please Heritage Foundation.[61]

In El Salvador, the Reagan administration State Department viewed José Napoléon Duarte as that country's only hope for salvation from a serious challenge from Marxist-Leninist guerrillas. Enraging Reagan's conservative allies in the Congress, the CIA once again involved itself in a Latin American election, this time to insure a Duarte victory not against a leftist opponent, but against a conservative coalition.[62] Twenty years later, in a different part of the hemisphere, against a different sort of electoral opponent, Washington's policy remained consistent: support the Christian Democrats to undercut the Communists.

Christian Democratic Attitudes toward Communism

As we saw in Chapter 4, Maritain himself had great difficulty in dealing with the challenge of communism. Plagued by the fear of enemies on the right, Maritain concluded that a working relationship with the communist left was necessary to prevent the right from rising again. In addition, the claims of the left were essentially just, he thought, and worthy of a serious hearing. Maritain's apparent shifts on the issue of communist collaboration only point up the difficulty he had with this matter.

Maritain's imprecision on this issue is repeated by his Latin American followers, making them a weak peg on which to hang the anticommunist hopes of political leaders on two continents. Some Latin American conservatives recognize this, and have accused the Christian Democrats of being communist wolves in the clothing of Christian sheep.[63] They base this opinion, in part, on the Christian Democratic view that capitalism and communism are both unacceptably materialistic and humanistic philosophies.[64]

Like Maritain, Latin American Christian Democrats view communism and other radical leftist movements as an effect of unjust economic conditions and social injustice. Communism is not caused by evil manipulators from outside the hemisphere but by evil capitalists. As such, the real enemies are capitalists and the socio-economic conditions they perpetuate.[65]

Christian Democrats consistently attempt to lure voters away from socialists and communists by promising many of the same things. However, so far the Christian Democrats have failed to deliver. By promising a "Revolution in Liberty," for example, Frei promised a revolution less ruthless than the one Allende promised. As such, he was immediately prevented from taking the same sorts of radical actions that Allende could have taken.

The result, almost inevitably, is a "Revolution in Liberty" that restricts economic liberty, thus alienating conservatives, but without providing genuine revolutionary change, thus not only alienating the left, but also leaving the right alive and well, ready to oppose the Christian Democrats in the future. Disappointed leftists may also oppose the Christian Democrats, opting instead for what one author called "the promised revolution; this time without the last name."[66]

In this way, the Christian Democrats may be not the saviors from radical solutions, but the harbingers of radical solutions. One leftist author thanks the Chilean Christian Democrats for their radical rhetoric and moderate policies. "By mobilizing and raising expectations of peasants and proletarians in 1964–65," he adds, "[the Christian Democrats] played an important contributing role in the Marxist electoral victories of the early 1970s."[67]

The Christian Democratic strategy in Chile's 1970 election is instructive. After failing to get the leftist parties to join them in a coalition, the Christian Democrats tried to outflank them from the left, thus alienating much of the conservative support on which their 1964 victory had depended.[68] At the same time, they were unable to outbid the Popular Front candidates for support from more leftist sectors. The result was a poor third place finish in 1970.

It is interesting to note that, with only one exception, Christian Democratic presidencies in Latin America have always given way to more radical leftist movements. In Chile, Allende followed Frei. In Brazil, João Goulart followed the nominally Christian Democratic Janio Quadros. In Venezuela, the Christian Democrats alternated in power for awhile, but for the moment have been eclipsed by the leftist *Acción Democratica*. In Peru, Alan García, then the most leftist democratic leader on the continent, followed the moderate, Christian Democratic-inspired presidency of Fernando Belaunde Terry. In Ecuador, after four years of Febres Cordero, the Christian Democrats finished out of the running in the 1988 elections and the run-off was between two candidates, both to the left of Febres.

Only in El Salvador did the administration of Duarte hand over power to a more conservative, and more anticommunist, political coalition.

There are good arguments for excepting this particular case. First, the left is illegal in El Salvador. Second, even if they had a viable legal wing, the extreme violence of the armed left could serve to alienate potential voters. Third, there is serious question about whether the Christian Democrats could have won the 1984 election at all without U.S. covert aid.

Some Christian Democratic movements have even spawned radical leftist movements. In Chile, a Christian Democratic split in 1969 led to the formation of the Movement for United Popular Action (MAPU), which became a part of the Allende coalition.[69] In Bolivia, the radical Leftist Revolutionary Movement (MIR) sprang from a Christian Democratic youth group.[70] In other cases, Christian Democrats who turn to more radical solutions do not leave the parties, but try to redirect them from within. Thus even a sympathetic author notes that infiltration from "displaced Marxist Socialists" has weakened the movement.[71]

Christian Democratic Pragmatism

The standard text on Latin American Christian Democracy makes the understated comment that its ideology and its actual programs have not always matched.[72] Linking its broad analyses of social problems to everyday tactical problems has always been a shortcoming. In fact, the author concludes, the brute struggle for political power has turned the Christian Democratic promise of something more than just material progress into "a mirage on arid sands."

Christian Democrats had difficulty adhering to their political philosophy once they tasted power. Like the Europeans, they soon concluded that they could use the state to achieve many of their social goals. This meant abandoning their ideological opposition to growing state power.

In Chile, land reform resulted not in all proprietors but in state proprietorship. Nationalization increased the state's economic role. The commitment to profit sharing and worker management was abandoned to achieve other goals. This cost them dearly in the 1970 elections, raising questions about just how pragmatic these decisions were.

In most cases, Christian Democratic pragmatism has meant abandoning Catholic social thought. Febres Cordero was most clear on this point when he said he was a good Catholic, but "this does not mean that I have to agree with the Social Doctrine of the Church."[73]

Febres, as we have seen, promised to reduce state power, and offered strident arguments for doing so. After failing to win an outright majority in the first round of the 1984 elections, however, he switched from a neoconservative platform to one of traditional Latin American populism. His campaign slogan for the second electoral round was "pan, techo, y empleo."

Having used this slogan to defeat his leftist opponent, Febres made no real effort to implement his conservative policies. Once coming to power he made only marginal changes, failing to seriously challenge the hold that the Ecuadoran state had on the economy and society of that country.[74] In fact, the economic measures he proposed were not only very different from his campaign promises, they were not perceived as very different from those of the previous administration. This in spite of the fact that his greatest support came from Guayaquil, the part of Ecuador most suspicious of the Quito government.[75]

Failing to Present an Alternative

The experiences of the Chilean and Ecuadoran Christian Democrats, ending as they did in failure and replacement by more leftist regimes, seems to indicate that whatever short-term gain might have been hoped for by the pursuit of pragmatism, the long-term results were disastrous. By failing to offer a genuine alternative to the traditional statism of Latin American politics, the Christian Democrats wrote their own obituaries.

The willingness of Christian Democrats to work closely with rival parties, noncommunist as well as communist, is part of this debilitating pragmatism. In Argentina, for example, the Christian Democrats under Horacio Sueldo adopted a policy of working with the Peronists and trying to form a popular front for the 1963 elections.[76] They evidently failed to realize the minor role that they would play in any coalition with Peronismo, revealing a startling yearning for co-optation. In the early 1980s, they travelled the same route again, joining the Peronists to press for elections from the military regime.[77]

In Brazil, the Christian Democrats formed a coalition to support the candidacy of Quadros, even though he had repeatedly demonstrated that he had no ideological commitment to any party or political philosophy.[78] As a new party that had never held power, the Christian Democrats had the most to gain from presenting a clear alternative to Brazilian voters, wearied by decades of insider politics. Instead, they joined a coalition in which they could not hope to become dominant.

In Peru, the pattern repeated itself. Instead of providing an alternative to the popular APRA (Alianza Popular Revolucionaria Americana) party, the Christian Democrats joined it in various coalitions, thus assuring itself political invisibility.[79] When they did not try to work with APRA, the Christian Democrats tried to outbid and steal its constituency.[80] With Victor Haya de la Torre exerting the influence he did over Peruvian politics, the path to political survival lay in presenting a clear alternative.

In Guatemala, the Christian Democrats started out as an anticommunist party dedicated to Catholic social thought. They dropped this stance to support many of the policies of the radical Jacobo Arbenz

Guzmán regime, hoping to use this support as their path to political power.[81] They remained the weakest of three major parties into the 1970s. In Guatemala's current democratic experiment, they have managed to win the presidency, but their hold on any significant portion of the Guatemalan electorate remains tenuous.

In Uruguay, the Christian Democrats examined the long tradition of dominance by the traditional Blanco and Colorado parties and decided that the way to crack their dominance was to form an alliance of leftist parties, including communists, and use that alliance to come to power.[82] This meant accepting the statism of the left and abandoning the option of presenting a hopeful alternative, based on the teachings of the Church.

Coalitions and co-optation was the way in which some Christian Democrats sought to respond to Liberationist challenges as well. What Frei never seemed to understand was the legitimizing factor of coalitions with communists. Also like the Liberationists, Frei tried to achieve an amalgam of Marxist and Catholic teachings, starting a movement which one author said ended with an attempt to reconcile Christian teachings with Leninism.[83]

Liberationists acknowledge their debt to Christian Democrats in subtle but still discernible ways. Orbis Books, the Maryknoll publishing house and the largest single source of English-language treatments of Liberation Theology in the United States, has translated and published two of Frei's books. The translator for them was Miguel D'Escoto Brockmann, then head of Orbis Books, later the Sandinista foreign minister of Nicaragua.

Working with secular Communist Parties is also a frequent Christian Democratic strategy. In Chile, young Christian Democrats broke from the Conservative Party in 1935 to support the candidacy of a socialist/communist Popular Front coalition candidate.[84]

Frei defends his attitude toward communist collaboration in much the same way that Maritain does. He says that the communists have changed over the years, citing Eurocommunism as proof, and adds that the communists' dropping their doctrine of the dictatorship of the proletariat makes them attractive partners.[85]

Bernardo Leighton, a long-time colleague of Frei, endorsed communism even more strongly in a 1976 interview. He said that Christians should treat Marxism the same way as their own doctrine. Both, he adds, "represent a world outlook that came into being in the course of history."

Frei also attempts to defend his party from the charge that they paved the way for Allende's Marxist coalition. He speaks of the various reforms the Christian Democrats made, asks sarcastically if it is communistic to teach people to read, and concludes that if what the Christian Democrats did was communist, then only the Russian tsar was anticommunist.[86]

Frei misses the point his critics make. In his spirited defense of Christian Democracy, he asserts that all of his reform measures were "embodied in a systematic government program." He then goes on to discuss their substance. By assuming that only through the use of government power can reforms take place, Frei's Christian Democrats accepted a major premise of the communists. To see this statist thrust from a supposedly centrist party not only deprives political discourse of a nonstatist alternative, but makes the more radical statists seem different only in degree, not in kind.

CONCLUSION

Christian Democratic confidence in the efficacy of state power, like its willing collaboration with communists, like its distrust of capitalism and of independent society in general, shows a disconcerting tendency to accept the ideological underpinnings of its leftist rivals. Many people criticized Allende for suggesting to Regis Debray that he would use plebiscites to thwart congressional opposition.[87] Yet the Christian Democratic platform of 1964 demanded the president be given this very power.[88] This only served to make Allende's usurpation of power seem legitimate.

On issue after issue, the Christian Democrats in Latin America have abandoned those parts of their ideology based on the social encyclicals and on the Thomist writings of Jacques Maritain. Wherever they have abandoned these roots, they have replaced them with policy prescriptions based on the premises of Marxism or some other radical leftist movement.

In so doing, they have failed themselves and Latin America. By not providing a clear alternative to the many varieties of statism in Latin America, the Christian Democrats doom themselves to a perpetual state of marginal importance. Since Latin America's economic prospects have been so ill served by this mercantilist view of the state, the continent has also suffered from this Christian Democratic failure.

Perhaps this is why Christian Democracy has failed in most Latin American countries. After a short period of growth and progress, based upon faithfulness to their true Catholic roots, Christian Democrats become part of the problem rather than part of the solution. In only one country has a Christian Democratic party won the presidency twice. This occurred in Venezuela, and I shall examine its particular brand of Christian Democracy in Chapter 7.

NOTES

1. Miguel Jorrin and John D. Martz, *Latin American Political Thought and Ideology* (Chapel Hill, NC: University of North Carolina Press, 1970), 408.
2. "We are for unity of action of all democrats" (Interview with Bernard Leighton), *World Marxist Review*, 19, 6 (1976): 55.
3. Leonard Gross, *The Last, Best Hope: Eduardo Frei and Chilean Democracy* (New York: Random House, 1967), 158-59.
4. Robert J. Alexander, *Latin American Political Parties* (New York: Praeger Publishers, 1973), 360.
5. Edward J. Williams, *Latin American Christian Democratic Parties* (Knoxville: University of Tennessee Press, 1967), 28.
6. Harold Eugene Davis, *Latin American Thought: A Historical Introduction* (Baton Rouge: Louisiana State University Press, 1972), 219.
7. Ibid., 220.
8. Jorrin and Martz, *Latin American Political Thought*, 409.
9. Eduardo Frei Montalva, *Latin America: The Hopeful Option* (Maryknoll, NY: Orbis Books, 1978), xi.
10. Jorrin and Martz, *Latin American Political Thought*, 409-10.
11. Davis, *Latin American Thought*, 223.
12. Williams, *Latin American Christian Democratic Parties*, 267.
13. Gross, *Last, Best Hope*, 91.
14. Eduardo Frei Montalva, "The Second Latin American Revolution," *Foreign Affairs*, 50, 1 (1971): 85.
15. Robert J. Alexander, ed. *Political Parties of the Americas: Canada, Latin America and the West Indies* (Westport, CT: Greenwood Press, 1982), 66.
16. Jorrin and Martz, *Latin American Political Thought*, 411.
17. Ibid., 416.
18. Alexander, *Latin American Political Parties*, 359.
19. Gross, *Last, Best Hope*, 90.
20. Frei, *Hopeful Option*, 60.
21. Williams, *Latin American Christian Democratic Parties*, 39.
22. Jorrin and Martz, *Latin American Political Thought*, 414.
23. Ibid., 409.
24. Ibid., 421.
25. Davis, *Latin American Thought*, 228.
26. Frei, "Second Latin American Revolution," 93.
27. Gross, *Last, Best Hope*, 98.
28. Eduardo Frei Montalva, *The Mandate of History and Chile's Future*, Papers in International Studies, Latin America Series, no. 1, trans. Miguel D'Escoto Brockmann (Athens, OH: Ohio University Center for International Studies, 1977), 67.
29. Karen Ruffing Mangelsdorf, "Administrative Decentralization and Development: Some Conflicting Evidence from Ecuador," *International Review of Administrative Sciences*, 54, 1 (1988): 67–88.
30. Ramiro Rivera, *El Pensamiento de Leon Febres Cordero* (Quito: Ediciones Culturales, 1986), 33.

31. Ibid., 50.

32. David W. Schodt, *Ecuador: An Andean Enigma* (Boulder, CO: Westview Press, 1987), 160.

33. Frei, *Hopeful Option*, 64.

34. Frei, "Second Latin American Revolution," 87.

35. Alexander, *Latin American Political Parties*, 329.

36. Williams, *Latin Amercian Christian Democratic Parties*, 144.

37. Alexander, *Latin American Political Parties*, 329.

38. Frei, *Hopeful Option*, 126.

39. Frei, "Second Latin American Revolution," 94.

40. Alexander, *Latin American Political Parties*, 328.

41. Alexander, *Parties of the Americas*, 66.

42. Schodt, *Ecuador*, 164.

43. [Carlos Rodriguez, pseud. for a Chilean businessman], "The Frei Alternative," *Monthly Review*, 28, 5 (1976): 54.

44. Williams, *Latin American Christian Democratic Parties*, 116-17.

45. Gross, *Last, Best Hope*, 92.

46. Frei, *Hopeful Option*, 60.

47. Alexander, *Latin American Political Parties*, 330.

48. Ibid., 331.

49. Alexander, *Parties of the Americas*, 235.

50. Gross, *Last, Best Hope*, 109.

51. Alexander, *Latin American Political Parties*, 326.

52. Frei, *Mandate of History*, 14.

53. Jorrin and Martz, *Latin American Political Thought*, 406.

54. Mark Falcoff, "Eduardo Frei Montalva, 1911–1982," *Review of Politics*, 44, 3 (1982): 324.

55. Ibid., 325.

56. Henry A. Kissinger, *The White House Years* (Boston: Little, Brown and Co., 1979), especially chap. XVII.

57. Gross, *Last, Best Hope*, 110.

58. David Gallagher, "Chile Struggles to Save its Grapes of Freedom," *Wall Street Journal*, 14 April 1989, p. A15.

59. Frei, *Mandate of History*, 27.

60. Falcoff, "Eduardo Frei Montalva," 326.

61. Timothy Ashby, "Ecuador: A Model for Latin American Development," Heritage Foundation *Backgrounder*, no. 479 (10 January 1986).

62. Senator Jesse Helms (R-NC) was particularly vocal about administration interference in the 1984 Salvadoran election.

63. Williams, *Latin American Christian Democratic Parties* 183-84.

64. Ibid., 127.

65. Ibid., 194.

66. Albert Szymanski, "The Rise and Decline of the Christian Democratic Party in Chile: An Analysis of the 1961 and 1965 Congressional Elections," *Social and Economic Studies*, 24, 4, (1975): 473.

67. Ibid.

68. Alexander, *Parties of the Americas*, 236. Outflanking Allende was easier

than it sounds, since Allende in 1970 was attempting to create a more centrist image.

69. Alexander, *Latin American Political Parties*, 335.

70. Alexander, *Parties of the Americas*, 46.

71. Williams, *Latin American Christian Democratic Parties*, 255.

72. Ibid., 238.

73. Rivera, *Pensamiento*, 120.

74. Schodt, *Ecuador*, 157.

75. John D. Martz, "Ecuador: The Right Takes Command," *Current History*, 84, 499 (1985).

76. Alexander, *Parties of the Americas*, 66.

77. Enrique A. Baloyra, ed. *Comparing New Democracies: Transition and Consolidation in Mediterranean Europe and the Southern Cone* (Boulder, CO: Westview Press, 1987), 21.

78. Alexander, *Latin American Political Parties*, 355.

79. Ibid., 357.

80. Williams, *Latin American Christian Democratic Parties*, 214.

81. Alexander, *Latin American Political Parties*, 361.

82. Ibid., 357.

83. Jorrin and Martz, *Latin American Political Thought*, 220.

84. Alexander, *Latin American Political Parties*, 319.

85. Frei, *Hopeful Option*, 61-62.

86. Frei, *Mandate of History*, 23.

87. See Regis Debray, *The Chilean Revolution: Conversations with Allende* (New York: Pantheon 1972).

88. Gross, *Last, Best Hope*, 105.

II

The Ideologies in Practice

6

Liberation Theology in Nicaragua: Radicalizing the Opposition

Liberation Theology, confined to the musings of theologians, would seem to be of little concern to the political scientist. Only when the doctrine comes off the library shelves and begins working in the minds of people in political causes does it become a fit topic for students of politics.

Such a transfer took place in the Central American nation of Nicaragua, where in July 1979, the 40-year-old Somoza "dynasty" succumbed to enormous internal and external pressure and was replaced by the provisional junta of the *Frente Sandinista de Liberacion Nacional*. The FSLN appeared in 1963, yet it operated in almost hopeless obscurity until the mid–1970s.

Liberation Theology had a profound effect on the eventual success of the FSLN. Miguel D'Escoto Brockmann, during his days as an exiled opposition figure, wrote that the Somoza dynasty rested on four "pillars" of support. These were: the local oligarchy, the Catholic Church, the armed forces, and the United States.[1] If they saw the FSLN as a radical, Marxist-led movement, these pillars would all choose Somoza as the lesser of two evils.

Liberation Theology had the effect of both radicalizing hitherto moderate opposition to Anastasio Somoza, while at the same time making this radical opposition appear moderate. In so doing, the theology undercut Somoza's support from three of these four pillars: the local oligarchy, the United States, and the Catholic Church itself.

THE EVENTS OF THE REVOLUTION

Guerrilla violence, which had been limited to certain parts of the countryside since the founding of the FSLN in 1963, took a new and dramatic turn in December 1974. FSLN guerrillas raided a Christmas party in honor of American Ambassador Turner Shelton and took 45 people hostage. They eventually released the hostages in return for one million dollars, a flight to Cuba, and the release of twenty "political prisoners," one of whom was Daniel Ortega Saavedra, who later became the president of Nicaragua.

Somoza lifted the resulting state of siege in October 1977, in response to the pleas and pressure of U.S. President Jimmy Carter. Although sporadic outbreaks of violence continued, the situation in Nicaragua remained relatively calm until 10 January 1978. On that day Pedro Joaquin Chamorro, editor of *La Prensa*, Managua's largest daily newspaper, was shot execution-style on his way to work. He was the unofficial leader of the moderate opposition to Somoza and a member of the Broad Opposition Front (FAO), which was the most potent non-Sandinista opposition group in Nicaragua. The Nicaraguan Chamber of Commerce responded to the murder by calling a general strike in Managua. Violence in the countryside also increased.

In August 1978, Somoza's opponents made another dramatic strike in Managua. Sandinista guerrillas, operating under the command of Eden Pastora, better known as Comandante Zero, seized the National Palace, the Nicaraguan equivalent of the Capitol Building, and held between 1,000 and 1,500 hostages. Negotiating through the Catholic Archbishop of Managua, Miguel Obando y Bravo, the guerrillas agreed to release the hostages in return for the release of 59 political prisoners, a flight to Cuba, and cash. Once again, Somoza was forced to give in to demands of the FSLN, which had made its presence unmistakably felt in the very seat of the Nicaraguan government.

The following month saw the beginning of a general insurrection in the departments of León, Esteli, Chinandega, and Grenada, the four most populous departments in the country. The fighting escalated quickly as Somoza called in air strikes on the major towns and cities of these areas. It was this offensive that, after months of bitter fighting, would bring the Sandinistas to victory on 19 July 1979. Monsignor (now Cardinal) Miguel Obando y Bravo performed one of the first public acts of the post-Somoza era by celebrating a victory Mass.

I believe that this revolution would not have been successful without the efforts of many Catholics who subscribe to Liberation Theology. I further contend that it was their belief in this theology that provided both the inspiration and justification for their acts.[2]

THE THEOLOGIANS—WHO WERE THEY?

In order to prove this, it is first necessary to show that the major Catholic actors in this drama were believers in Liberation Theology. A number of important contributors to the Sandinista victory are in this category. Let us begin by looking at Miguel D'Escoto Brockmann, Maryknoll priest and former Sandinista foreign minister of Nicaragua. D'Escoto deplores what he perceives to be the traditional role of the Church, that is, silent supporter of the status quo. He praises what he calls the "process of Christianization"[3] that began with Vatican II and was "filtered down" to Nicaragua at the Medellín conference. It was at this conference that many of the tenets of Liberation Theology became a part of the official doctrine of the Latin American Church.

D'Escoto's own commitment to these tenets is quite clear. He is a bitter opponent of capitalism and argues that the Church has been illicitly involved with this philosophy for centuries. He says: "It [the Church's link with capitalism] has been a very happy wedding for a long time. I think this is the greatest sin of the Church for 150 years."[4] By contrast, he refers to Marxism as "being one of the greatest blessings on the Church."[5] On the question of Church participation in revolution, he declares: "The question is not between struggle and non-struggle. Quietism is much more readily anti-Christian."

Father D'Escoto is equally open about his feelings towards the use of violence and the blessings of socialism, two important tenets of Liberation Theology. On the former, he wrote in 1977 that violence is the only way for courageous Nicaraguans to obtain justice. In the same essay he called for the establishment of a "just, non-capitalist system."[6] That this system will be a socialist one is made clear in his support for a pastoral letter issued by the bishops of Nicaragua which calls for a socialistic type of economic plan.[7]

The same influence is visible in the words of Ernesto Cardenal, reputedly a Trappist monk, a former student of Thomas Merton,[8] and former Sandinista cultural affairs minister. Father Cardenal happily describes war and violent destruction as "more than justified if their aim is the creation of a society where men live in peace." Cardenal also has adopted the Liberationists' practice of giving words new meanings. His definition of "peace" is an example. For him, peace implies justice and can exist in the midst of war. He praises the Sandinista fighters who were the personifications of peace, especially in the act of violent revolution. Cardenal called revolution a beautiful word, a synonym for love, in another example of Liberationist use of language.

Cardenal also shares the aim of the Liberation Theologians to create a "New Man" through the advent of a truly progressive government.

He advocates a postrevolutionary Nicaraguan educational system that will "create solidarity among Nicaraguans [and create] a 'new race' of people." He adds later that not only does he believe that the creation of this "new race" is possible but that "all the programmes of our government . . . have been put into effect with the intention of creating such a new being."

Like his colleague at the Ministry of Foreign Affairs, Father Cardenal rejects neutrality on the part of believers. By equating participation in the Revolution with faith in Jesus Christ, he implies that a lack of participation indicates a lack of faith. No participation, or neutrality, must therefore indicate a total lack of faith.

Cardenal also has no difficulty with a union between Catholicism and Marxism. In fact, he is quoted at a February 1977 news conference sponsored by the Washington Office on Latin America (WOLA) as saying that "there must be an integration of the Church and Marxism."[9] Finally, Cardenal is similar to other Liberationists in that he feels no particular obligation to moderate his beliefs or his activities even at the urging of the pope. Cardenal interpreted John Paul II's rejection of violent revolution, for example, as a rejection only of terrorist violence (that is, that of the National Guard) and not "legitimate violence" (that is, that of the Sandinistas).[10]

Fernando Cardenal, Ernesto's brother, was a Jesuit priest who was put in charge of the nationwide literacy campaign that took place in the first year of the Sandinista regime. Fernando holds certain beliefs in common with the Liberationists. For example, he seems to accept the "structural violence" argument when he claims that the Somoza regime "has stimulated a constant state of agitation, causing continuous armed actions."[11] Although claiming to be against violence himself, he justifies violent action against Somoza by saying that "dictators like Somoza lead many people to believe that the only way to democracy is through blood."[12]

A clearer link between Fernando Cardenal and Liberation Theology can be found in connection with the literacy campaign, which I will discuss in greater detail below. Suffice it to say now that he drew heavily on the work of Paulo Freire and the participation of Cuban instructors to make this campaign work. His work in the field of education led one Nicaraguan soldier to refer to him as a "self-acknowledged Marxist socialist, who . . . prepare[d] the school age children with a frame of mind of social revolution."[13]

All the above discussion proves, however, is that three prominent Sandinistas accepted the major tenets of Liberation Theology. As prominent as they are, they obviously did not make the Revolution all by themselves. The bishops of Nicaragua also incorporated this philosophy into their criticism of the Somoza regime. Their opposition was obviously more important than that of the Cardenal brothers and D'Escoto because their views represented the official Church position in the country.

The Church hierarchy was active during the Sandinista Revolution. They began by condemning the alleged human rights abuses of Somoza and later called for his overthrow. In doing so they "explicitly condoned the use of violence."[14] They reiterated this sentiment in the period just before the Sandinista victory when another pastoral letter "proclaimed the right of the Nicaraguan people to engage in revolutionary insurrection."[15]

As early as 1972 the hierarchy rejected an agreement between the two major parties of Nicaragua (the ruling Liberals and opposition Conservatives) to call a constituent assembly to write a new constitution. Instead of the customary blessing, the bishops of Nicaragua's two largest dioceses declared their support for "a completely new order."[16] This new order, they said, should include the Liberationist "preferential option for the poor" and a "planned economy for the benefit of humankind."[17]

Finally, the bishops adopted the Exodus imagery of Enrique Dussel to express their joy at the victory of the Revolution. In a statement by the major Catholic and Protestant clergy organizations made only a month after the Triumph, they said: "Nicaragua has passed . . . through the Red Sea, leaving slavery behind in order to walk to the Promised Land."[18] The bishops' support for Liberation Theology, however, came more from a desire to oust Somoza than from a life-long commitment to this particular brand of Christianity. Events since the Revolution indicate that perhaps Obando y Bravo went along with D'Escoto and Cardenal hoping that they could be controlled by an episcopal presence.

ROLE OF THE LIBERATIONISTS IN THE REVOLUTION

Knowing that many vocal and powerful elements of the Catholic Church used the tenets of Liberation Theology as the basis for their opposition to Somoza does not prove that these elements were decisive in the Sandinista victory. Therefore, let us now turn to an examination of the role of the many supporters of Liberation Theology in the Revolution.

It is important to remember that the Church in Nicaragua traditionally opposed the Liberal Party, even before it became associated with the Somoza family. As early as the years just after Nicaragua's independence, the Church made its opposition known by supporting the Grenada Conservatives against the Liberals of León.[19] This was the traditional position of the Catholic Church, to side with the farmers of the interior against the tradesmen of the coast, who, in the case of León, had connections with foreign masonic lodges and were admirers of the anti-Catholic ideologies that emerged from the French Revolution.

What was new about the opposition of the 1970s, then? First, as we have seen, Obando y Bravo, along with his colleagues, rejected both parties and called for a "new order." Second, they advocated extraparliamentary means to achieve this. The effect of Liberation Theology was not to place the Church in opposition to the regime, since this opposition predated Medellín by 150 years, but to place the Church in a position of radical opposition.

An important area in which Liberation Theology and its proponents played this radicalizing role was in education. The Social Catholic movements established by Fernando Cardenal, among others, whose purpose was the "conscientization" of school age children, were important in this regard. Cardenal does not deny that this was the purpose of his education efforts, and said in 1981 that the Church's leadership in the "formation of the people" was of extreme importance. He added that the education, the aim of which was to bring "a certain consciousness to our people," had been going on for 12 or 13 years.[20]

This conscientizing education did not always take place in schools, however, and was not limited to students. The most widespread method of spreading Liberation Theology was through the Comunidades Eclesiales de Base, Christian Base Communities (CEBs). Penny Lernoux describes these as small groups of neighbors in impoverished areas which take over catechism classes and get involved in other neighborhood concerns. In their classes, the Bible is taught as a story of liberation, based on the documents of Medellín.[21] Lernoux underlines the importance of the CEBs by calling them "the heart and soul of our pastoral activity—the first prong of the attack." Harvey Cox echoes this sentiment when he calls the CEBs "the reality that made Liberation Theology possible."[22]

The effect of the comunidades in Nicaragua was profound. The first such organizations were founded in poor Managua barrios by Spanish Father José de la Jara in 1965. By the time of Medellín, another Spaniard, Father Bonifacio, was also working in the capital and the number of CEBs grew steadily into the 1970s.[23] The influence of foreigners in the movement also continued to grow, making the civil authorities suspicious of the groups.

Ecclesiastical authority was also somewhat uncomfortable with the growth of the CEBs. Although they frequently were started to relieve overworked parish priests of some of their duties, and for this received the blessing of the official Church, some began without the sponsorship or even the knowledge of the Church hierarchy. Indeed there are cases in which not even the local priests were told what was happening.

Much of the work of forming the CEBs and leading them in an overtly political direction was left to laypersons called Delegates of the Word. They specialized in developing the "Christian formation of peasants, focusing on literacy, conscientization and health."[24] The opportunities for turning these communities into centers of political opposition to Somoza were myriad. As early as 1972 such a development took place in the northern department of Matagalpa, where Father Miguel Vasquez started CEBs, "which soon produced enough political organizations to lead to conflict between parishioners and the government."[25]

The CEBs soon attracted the attention of the Somoza government. Their activities were perceived as subversive and the National Guard was sometimes used against them. The Christians trained in these communities often collaborated with the FSLN, which itself had "become more open to the Christian bases for political action."[26] Followers of Liberation Theology succeeded in mobilizing Nicaraguans to radical opposition to the Somoza regime.

The instrument of Catholic/FSLN cooperation in rural areas was the Association of Rural Workers (ATC). This was founded in March 1978 and was useful in the struggle against Somoza by changing the homes of peasant members into places of refuge, storehouses for arms, and supply depots for the guerrilla army.[27]

The ATC was an outgrowth of the Committees of Agricultural Workers, which were formed in 1976 by the FSLN and Catholic activists. These committees were outgrowths of the Evangelical Committee for Agrarian Advancement (CEPA), which was created by the Jesuit Order in 1969 with the expressed purpose of training peasant leaders to politically organize their communities.[28] Among the prominent Nicaraguans active in CEPA was Fernando Cardenal.[29] In the beginning this organization encouraged collective action by the peasants and emphasized the biblical justification for the ownership of property.

After joining the Sandinistas and forming the ATC, however, the aims of the group changed and became more radical. Some CEPA members even became armed combatants with the FSLN. This type of activity led to a split between the ATC and the Church hierarchy, with the former cutting its ties and becoming an independent Christian organization. The falling out also had to do with CEPA's active promotion of a Christian-Marxist dialogue.

Illustrative of the work of both the Delegates of the Word and the CEPA members was their influence in the huge rural department of Zelaya. Most of the priests were foreigners, and in addition, the department was home to over 900 Delegates of the Word, many of whom were also foreign.[30] As early as 1976 the Capuchin Order published a letter documenting alleged human rights abuses in Zelaya and making known its opposition to Somoza. This letter is credited with increasing the international pressure on the regime.[31] The Zelayan clergy were also important as a source of information to the United States Congress about conditions in Nicaragua. I will discuss the effect of this below.

Most of the activity by radical Catholics that I have discussed so far took place on a behind-the-scenes organizational level and occurred before the start of widespread fighting. The Sandinistas' Liberationist allies, however, did not disappear once the shooting started. According to one observer, most of the clergy, especially at lower levels, opted actively to support the Revolution.[32] Whether or not the Revolution's supporters actually constituted a majority of the clergy is debatable, but certainly elements of the Church were active in providing aid and comfort to the guerrillas.

Food and medicine, for example, were available in many churches across the country.[33] In at least one case, a small rural church was used as a drop-off and pick-up point for mail to the Sandinistas. It was usually stuck to the underside of one of the pews.[34] Churches were sometimes used as places of shelter and refuge, as sources of fresh drinking water, which was put in baptismal fonts, and even as centers for the making of bombs and the storage of arms.[35] Catholic priests were also involved in the actual fighting. Two priests led troops in combat.[36] Many other priests and nuns actively took part in the fighting as well.

The effect of this extensive Catholic participation in the Sandinista Revolution, most of which was carried out by the proponents of Liberation Theology, was twofold. First, the appearance of priests and nuns at the side of, or even among the ranks of, guerrilla fighters legitimized the Sandinistas to an extent unthinkable without their participation. The FSLN actively encouraged Catholic participation in the Revolution and the increasing radicalization of the Church coincided with the growth of the Sandinista movement.

Even sympathetic authors admit that the Sandinistas did not have much popular support until quite near the end of Somoza's reign. Richard Millet wrote as late as 1977 that the guerrillas "have continuing problems in gaining effective local support in their areas of operation."[37] Lernoux added in Congressional testimony that the guerrillas "have never enjoyed widespread peasant support."[38] Given these observations and the coincidence mentioned above, it is reasonable to conclude that Catholic collaboration was pivotal in broadening support for the FSLN.

The second effect of Catholic participation was to create enormous difficulties for Somoza. To the extent that members of the clergy were connected to the revolutionaries, to try to forcibly counter them was to appear to persecute the Church itself. Miguel D'Escoto told a Congressional panel in early 1977 that vicious National Guard reprisals had taken place against the Churches of Zelaya. Twenty-six churches in this department were allegedly used as barracks and torture chambers by the guard. In addition, the words "Christian community," used to describe the CEBs, were banned as Communist propaganda.[39] D'Escoto was careful to portray these activities as persecution. Obando y Bravo also complained of heavy-handedness in a May 1976 letter to Somoza outlining incidents of censorship of Church publications.[40]

Such difficulties were exacerbated by the use of churches as places of refuge and supply during the civil war. Large red crosses were frequently painted on the sides of the churches, forcing the National Guard to choose between disregarding the internationally recognized symbol or allowing fleeing guerrillas to escape. Restraint on the part of the Guard was not always forthcoming.

Even in the larger cities, churches were not always safe havens. Guardsmen used machine-gun fire against protesters in a León church in February 1979.[41] On the deeply religious people of Nicaragua, such a thing could not help but have the effect of disenchanting people with the government. The dilemma for Somoza and his commanders was an uninviting one and it would not have existed if not for the active support of many priests and other religious.

An insurrection with the approval of lower level clergy, as serious as this was, might have been manageable if ecclesiastic support had been limited to the lower levels. As it was, however, Somoza also had to deal with the opposition of the Catholic hierarchy. The connection between the bishops and the government was always uneasy, but it took a decidedly unfriendly turn in 1968 with the arrival of Obando y Bravo.

The split widened with the earthquake in 1972. Somoza related that Obando y Bravo was invited to join an emergency committee to oversee relief operations but refused to attend the organizational meeting.[42] The hierarchy also complained that relief supplies were to be distributed through voting precincts rather than through parish churches. Somoza replied that the latter was impossible because so many churches had been destroyed. At one point the bishop of León went so far as to hijack a supply train and claim the contents for himself, illustrating the poor relations between the Church and state.

It is clear, therefore, that the bishops had long-standing grievances against Somoza before the Sandinistas became important. As Pedro Joaquin Chamorro said in his last interview: "Somoza lost the Church a long time ago." The effect of Liberation Theology, once again, was to make this opposition progress from moderate to radical. The complaints about the earthquake relief could have been made by any Catholic bishop. Only bishops who subscribed to Liberation Theology, however, could justify revolutionary violence, as they did in a later pastoral letter.

The effect of this and similar hierarchical pronouncements was to legitimize even further the radical opposition to Somoza. When the bishops called for Somoza's resignation and "a completely new socioeconomic order" in August 1978, their letter, according to the Sandinistas themselves, got the support of Nicaragua's major banking firms. These would usually not be considered very revolutionary bodies and yet they were willing to join the Church in revolution.

It is impossible to underestimate the importance of the Church to the Somoza regime. In fact, one of the few areas in which Somoza and the Sandinistas were in total agreement was the importance of radical priests to the success of the Revolution. Daniel Ortega has said that "the best arguments the Sandinistas had urging people to take up revolutionary struggle were Christian arguments."[43] Miguel D'Escoto described the Catholic Church as one of four pillars of support on which Somoza rested. When the Church ceased to act as a pillar, it also removed some of the support of the local oligarchy, as we saw illustrated in the statement of the bankers. The Church, then, had an importance beyond its position as one of four pillars.

Somoza concludes his memoirs with this comment: "These political priests seem to be omnipresent. They were effective in Nicaragua and now they are being effective in Guatemala."[44] This is a toned-down version of a sentiment expressed earlier when Somoza wrote: "I can't stress strongly enough the role that the Communist (Somoza's term for believers in Liberation Theology) priests played in the Sandinista movement."[45]

THE EFFECT IN WASHINGTON

The effect of the Liberationists was not limited to Nicaragua, however. The battle for control of that country was not fought only in the streets of Managua or in the hills of Zelaya. It made its way into the halls of Congress as well. The Somoza family was installed by the United States at the end of the U.S. Marine Corps occupation of Nicaragua in the 1930s. To the end, the family was a loyal ally of the United States and depended heavily on U.S. support to survive. As the Sandinista Revolution grew in intensity, the need for economic and military aid grew proportionately.

Beginning with the Carter administration, however, the United States cut such aid severely, and when it gave it at all, it placed stringent limitations on it. President Carter cut off all funds in the first month after taking office. What is relevant to the present discussion is the question of whether the Church, through Liberation Theology, was pivotal in Somoza's loss of support in the U.S. This support was described by D'Escoto as the most important of his four pillars.

It is possible that the decision to cut off aid in February 1977 came in response to a pastoral letter of January 1977, which condemned alleged human rights abuses. At the same time, the decision allowed President Carter to demonstrate his new emphasis on human rights as the basis for U.S. foreign policy. The administration considered Nicaragua an ideal country for such an experiment because Somoza seemed invulnerable. This was before the Chamorro assassination and at a time when the FSLN was not a significant threat.

After the suspension of aid, the U.S. Congress soon began to hold more extensive hearings into the state of affairs in Nicaragua. With the administration's actions putting Nicaragua under the spotlight, some congressmen proposed to cut the country off completely from both military and economic aid. It was here, at the Congressional hearings, that Liberation Theology and its followers became important.

The situation in Nicaragua came under close scrutiny as a result of a series of atrocities perpetrated by the National Guard. Many of these atrocities took place in areas where Catholic missionaries happened to be stationed. These priests were able to tell the world about what had taken place in their neighborhoods.

Other Catholic witnesses, especially D'Escoto and Fernando Cardenal, made frequent appearances on Capitol Hill arguing for an end to American support for Somoza. Cardenal appeared before a subcommittee of the House International Relations (Foreign Affairs) Committee in June 1976 and presented a list of "disappeared persons" that he said he had obtained from an anonymous Catholic priest in Zelaya province. This rural part of Nicaragua was well known for its foreign Liberationist clergy.[46]

Cardenal described the Somoza regime in very harsh terms, and included the claim that Somoza's men deliberately starved prisoners to death. The importance of Cardenal's testimony is underlined by the fact that he was the only Nicaraguan witness to appear before the panel. So one-sided was his testimony that the Ford State Department submitted a document citing twelve specific errors in his prepared statement.[47] Nevertheless, the subcommittee thought highly enough of his testimony to invite him back.

In April 1977 hearings were held before the Foreign Operations Subcommittee of the House Appropriations Committee. The first witness was Charles Bray from the Carter State Department. In his five-minute opening statement, Bray made three references to Church-related sources of information about human rights abuses in Nicaragua.[48] The subcommittee members made no effort to challenge these sources. D'Escoto spoke at the same hearing and roundly criticized Somoza. Again, the subcommittee did not challenge his veracity. His clerical collar was the only credential he needed.

There are a number of such occurrences on record. In October 1978 another Congressional committee heard the statements of a number of refugees to dramatize the poor conditions in Nicaragua. The first refugee statement was that of a Spanish priest.[49] What becomes evident in reading these documents is that the statements of Catholic priests carried great weight with the congressmen. Such witnesses convinced the representatives not only that the Somoza regime was undeserving of American support, but also that opposition to Somoza was broad based, Church sanctioned, and for these reasons, trustworthy.

Much of the preliminary work of finding suitable witnesses and seeing to it that they got before Congress was done through the Washington Office on Latin America (WOLA). It was through this private organization that D'Escoto and Cardenal did most of their work in the Congress. WOLA, by its own admission, relied primarily on "Church sources" for information to present to Congress.[50] Other critics of the regime, such as Richard Fagen, drew heavily on WOLA for their information.[51]

WOLA was not, however, a disinterested and neutral observer of the Latin American scene. A memo sent from WOLA on 11 May 1976 to witnesses planning to testify the following month stated baldly: "It is imperative that [Congressional] testimony be sharp, penetrating, and critical of U.S. policy wherever *necessary*."[52]

As the hearings progressed, even more interesting facts about WOLA surfaced. Their director revealed in 1978 that the Maryknoll Order was a "faithful financial supporter of WOLA."[53] At the time that he made this statement, the head of the Maryknoll Order's Social Communications Department, which presumably had some input into where communications money was spent, was Miguel D'Escoto.[54]

D'Escoto was also the head of Orbis Books, the Maryknoll publishing house. One publication of Orbis Books was Richard Millet's *Guardians of the Dynasty*, an attack on the National Guard. D'Escoto wrote the introduction for this book. It also served as the basis for a 1978 WOLA document on land tenure under Somoza.[55]

This is a complicated web of relationships but it leaves little doubt that the Nicaraguan Liberationists were influential with the body that arranged for Nicaraguan witnesses to appear before the U.S. Congress. WOLA provided a steady stream of radical opponents to Somoza, and presented information designed to discredit the regime based on Church-related sources. It was an avenue for Liberation Theology to reach the representatives.

To see how influential these Church sources of information were in the Congress, consider their effect on just one congressman: Democrat Edward Koch of New York City. Both Somoza and D'Escoto agree that Koch was one of the most important leaders of the battle in Congress against additional U.S. aid for the Somoza regime.[56] Koch introduced an amendment to cut off aid to Nicaragua in 1977.

Koch relied heavily on both WOLA and the Nicaraguan bishops for his information about Somoza and the Sandinistas. In fact, conservative

Congressman John Murphy (R-CA) accused Koch of a "fanatical reliance" on WOLA for information. Even dismissing this phrase as purely partisan criticism, Koch's own words reveal his attitude toward clerical spokesmen.

In April 1977 hearings before the Foreign Operations Subcommittee, Koch repeatedly referred to the bishops' January pastoral letter, as though its contents were indisputable.[57] He asked one witness sarcastically: "Isn't it fair for this Committee to rely on the Archbishops [sic] of Nicaragua?" He added later: "I can't tell you how effective . . . such an encyclical or pastoral letter is because it has been my experience that the Church is reluctant to engage itself in a matter of this kind."[58]

This statement shows the danger in assuming that the Catholic Church is a monolithic organization. Koch was unaware that the bishops did not speak for their entire flock, in spite of the fact that other Catholic priests refuted the charges of WOLA at the subcommittee hearings. By failing to see the split in the Church brought by the advent of Liberation Theology, Koch was unable to distinguish between the Nicaraguan hierarchy, which was attempting to use Liberation Theology for its own ends, and "the Church" as a reliable source of unbiased information. Yet Catholic witnesses did contradict each other before Congress. Bishop Salvador Schlaeffer of Zelaya, for example, admitted that a number of atrocities attributed to the National Guard were actually perpetrated by FSLN guerrillas wearing government uniforms.[59]

The movement that opposed Somoza was, by 1979, broad and deep. Many Nicaraguans who wanted Somoza overthrown were apprehensive about a future under the FSLN. Nevertheless, the witnesses that prevailed with the congressmen were the more radical opponents of Somoza. The embrace of Liberation Theology by many Nicaraguan priests, nuns, and bishops helped to change the nature of anti-Somoza feeling and activity.

Through their appearance with the FSLN fighters, Liberationist priests and nuns legitimized radical opposition in the eyes of Nicaragua's middle class and business class, one of D'Escoto's four pillars of support. As we have seen, radical Catholic witnesses were important to the loss of support in Washington, another pillar. Counting the Church itself as a third pillar, Liberation Theology also radicalized opposition there. By the spring of 1979, Somoza was left with only the 15,000 man National Guard.

LIBERATION THEOLOGY SINCE THE REVOLUTION

The presence of representatives of the Roman Catholic Church in the Sandinista Revolution made this revolution seem more moderate and legitimate in the eyes of both Nicaraguans and North Americans. The hope among many people was that these priests, nuns, and bishops would serve to restrain the more radical tendencies of the anti-Somoza coalition.

Little moderating influence has been visible in the actions of the FSLN junta since 1979. The Church and individual Catholics have not only not exercised much moderation, but have also actively participated in one of the most immoderate of the Revolution's programs.

The Literacy Campaign

Fernando Cardenal, whose efforts to instill revolutionary conscious-ness among school children were several years old, headed the literacy effort. Fernando's brother, Ernesto, is warm in his praise for the literacy campaign. Through it, he said, Nicaragua became one large family. The effort was a "victory for Love."[60] Considering that for Ernesto, Love, Revolution, and Violence all seemed to be synonyms, this is an inter-esting comment.

There were problems with the campaign from the start. The unavail-ability of extra food for the youngsters, the need to provide many peas-ants with glasses, and the problem of getting proud Nicaraguans to admit to illiteracy all hampered the effort.[61]

An even bigger problem was the conditions under which the children had to live during the campaign. Most of them were unaccustomed to life in the country, and in spite of the forced marches that were used to prepare them, many parents felt anxious about their 13- and 14-year-old offspring. Primitive conditions and infectious diseases, including leprosy, were still prevalent in some parts of Nicaragua and this did little to reassure the participants or their parents.[62]

Cardenal and the other organizers like to call the effort voluntary and refer to the participants as volunteers. Students who did not participate, however, "were barred from matriculating the following year, and those scheduled to graduate could not receive their diplomas."[63] The need for this incentive seems to belie the "love" that Cardenal ascribes to the student teachers.

More important was the type of literacy that was taught. The model for the textbooks and methods used was the pedagogy of Paulo Freire, the Brazilian expert in "conscientizing education," which combines lit-eracy with political indoctrination.[64] One of the early phrases in the textbook, for example, is: "The FSLN led the people to their liberation." Another reads: "The Sandinista defense committees defend the revo-lution." The effect of this type of education on the people is visible when "barely literate poor people" use words like "marginalize," "sectors," and "bourgeoisie."[65] The strenuous effort to control the language, so much a part of Liberation Theology, is clearly visible here and could have an enormous long-term impact on Nicaragua.

Some 1,200 Cuban teachers were brought in to assist the Nicaraguans.[66] Defenders of the regime argue that these were to overcome a serious shortage of teachers and that Cuba was the only country to offer experts in sufficient numbers. The reason for this shortage, however, was the firing of over 5,000 trained educators by the Sandinistas for alleged pro-Somoza tendencies.[67]

In close collaboration with the Sandinistas and Cardenal on this project was the official Catholic Church. The Church and the popular organizations connected to it provided much of the logistical support needed, and endorsed the campaign in a pastoral letter five months before it began.

The immediate results of Cardenal's literacy campaign were almost universally praised. Eden Pastora, who left the ruling junta and has become a vociferous critic of his former comrades in arms, said: "If it weren't for the national literacy crusade, I would dare say to you that it is almost like the time of Somoza."[68] This is a left-handed compliment, to be sure, but clearer praise comes from a number of North American observers, including Thomas Walker and *New York Times* reporter Alan Riding.

By all accounts, the illiteracy rate fell significantly, although actual figures of conditions both before and after the campaign vary. The effort also attracted the attention of the United Nations, with Unesco awarding Nicaragua the International Nadezhda Krupskaya Prize in 1980. A sour note in this song of praise is sounded by Alfonso Robelo, another ex-Sandinista, who called using "a politicized program to overcome ignorance . . . something like a rape of the mind."[69]

THE EFFECT ON AMERICAN PERCEPTIONS

Even if only marginally successful in having an effect on the Revolution in Nicaragua, the participation of the Catholic Church had an enormous effect on the way Americans perceived the Sandinistas. This is reflected most clearly in the debates in the Congress over foreign aid to the fledgling regime. The Church created an image that did not correspond to reality. The image, in this case, is that a Catholic Church is an infallible indicator of a free and open society.

A sampling of statements by State Department officials testifying before Congressional committees shows how important the presence of the Church was to them. William G. Bowdler, assistant secretary of state for inter-American affairs in 1980, called Nicaragua a "largely open society." The first bit of evidence he gave to substantiate this claim was the fact that "Christian worship is encouraged, not repressed."[70]

Lawrence Pezullo, the ambassador to Nicaragua at that time, argued before the House Foreign Relations Committee that the Sandinista government was pluralistic. His evidence also began with a mention of the "Christian elements in the Cabinet."[71] John A. Bushnell, Bowdler's immediate predecessor, told a House Appropriations Subcommittee: "Nicaragua remains surprisingly open to moderation and pragmatic consideration. In Nicaragua, Christian worship is encouraged and not repressed."[72]

Probably the most important State Department actor at the time was William Christopher, who headed the department's committee on economic assistance. This committee has the "last word" on approving or holding up such assistance on human rights grounds.[73] In this light, the following statement by Christopher is instructive: "I am glad to say that the Catholic Church . . . [is] active in this struggle and is participating in reconstruction in a way that will strengthen their political hands."[74]

All of this testimony became important in the debate over a $75 million aid package that was passed in 1980. Senator Edward Zorinsky (D-NE), who described himself as a long-time critic of foreign aid, nevertheless supported the package because he believed that the Church leaders in government were proof that the Sandinista government had broad-based popular support.[75]

A colleague in the House, Robert J. Lagomarsino (R-CA), also supported the bill, basing his support on his belief that vigorous Church leadership would help Sandinista society evolve into a pluralistic, non-Marxist model.[76] Finally, Clarence D. Long (D-LA), chairman of the House Foreign Operations Subcommittee, gave his support to what he called "the largest foreign aid per capita that I can think of in the history of the United States" because he could not believe that a communist government would have the support of so many "Church groups."[77]

Opponents of the aid bill found it difficult to counter this perception. Although based on false assumptions that the Church was homogeneous and basically conservative, the tendency to link Catholic participation with trustworthiness was an attractive one. When the $75 million aid bill came to a vote on the House floor, every attempt by Congressman John Murphy to attach conditions to the grant was voted down. A majority of congressmen felt that refusing the appropriation, or attaching restrictive conditions to it, would be "turning [our] back on the Church."[78]

CONCLUSION

Almost no one now argues that the Sandinista Revolution turned out the way that most Nicaraguans and North Americans expected. What many hoped would be a noncommunist but genuine social revolution, one that could point the way between dependence on the superpowers, became distinctly immoderate in rhetoric and action.

There were, and are, many reasons for this, with an armed rebellion and U.S. hostility among them. This rebellion and this hostility did not appear right away, however. The Sandinista Revolution had the support of the overwhelming majority of Nicaraguans in 1979 and it had won the support of the Organization of American States. From July 1979 to January 1981, the Sandinista government received copious amounts of aid from the United States.

The basis for this honeymoon was the perception that Nicaragua would not be "another Cuba." A main pillar of this perception was the presence, and apparent influence, of "Christian elements" in the San- dinista government. In other words, the Sandinistas' victory and their initial success in winning domestic and international sympathy for their revolution were largely based on a misunderstanding of Latin American Catholicism.

The Nicaraguan Church did its share of misunderstanding too. Whether the embrace of Liberation Theology by Obando y Bravo and some of his brother bishops was based on sincere belief or mere tactical considerations is hard to tell. If it was based upon tactical considerations, perhaps in the hope that by supporting a revolution that they knew to be repugnant they could somehow make peace with it, then the bishops seriously underestimated the determination of the Sandinistas to remake Nicaragua in a Marxist-Leninist image.

On the other hand, if the bishops sincerely believed in Liberation Theology, then there would be no ideological basis for opposition to the current regime. However, the initial "era of good feelings" between the Sandinistas and the Nicaraguan official Church did not last long. While the Sandinistas often claimed Church support during and just after their victory, they also began to move to put the Catholic Church under greater control. In addition, the government began supporting a Lib- erationist "Popular Church" in opposition to the bishops. Beginning around 1982 the attitude of the Catholic hierarchy toward the Sandinistas changed. I shall examine the reasons for this change, and the results, in Chapter 10.

NOTES

1. Miguel D'Escoto Brockmann, "Nicaragua and the World," *Christianity and Crisis*, 40, 8 (May 1980): 141.

2. For concise treatments of the events of the Revolution, see Thomas W. Walker, *Nicaragua: The Land of Sandino* (Boulder, CO: Westview Press, 1981),and Henri Weber, *Nicaragua: The Sandinist Revolution* (London: Verso Editions, 1981).

3. D'Escoto, "Nicaragua," 141.

4. Ibid., 142.

5. Ibid., 144.

6. Miguel D'Escoto Brockmann, Introduction to Richard Millet, *Guardians of the Dynasty* (Maryknoll, NY: Orbis Books, 1977), 11-13.

7. U.S. Congress, House, Committee on Foreign Affairs, *Special Central American Economic Assistance*, 96th Congress, 1st session, 1979, 52.

8. Ernesto Cardenal, "Nicaragua's Revolution," *New York Times*, 30 June 1979, A19.

9. Ernesto Cardenal, "Revolution and Peace: The Nicaraguan Road," *Journal of Peace Research*, 18, 2 (1981): 201.

10. Cardenal, "Nicaragua's Revolution," 19.

11. U.S. Congress, House, Committee on International Relations, Subcommittee on International Organizations, *Human Rights in Nicaragua, Guatemala and El Salvador: Implications for U.S. Policy*, 94th Congress, 2d session, 1976, 10.

12. Ibid., 62.

13. U.S. *Congressional Record*, 26 February 1980, p. H1273.

14. Walker, *Land of Sandino*, 99.

15. House Committee on Foreign Affairs, *Special Central American Economic Assistance*, 52-58.

16. Millet, *Guardians*, 236.

17. House Committee on Foreign Affairs, *Special Central American Economic Assistance*, 57.

18. U.S. Congress, Senate, Committee on Foreign Relations, *S. 2012*, 96th Congress, 1st session, 1979, 43.

19. Walker, *Land of Sandino*, 12.

20. Quoted in James V. Schall, "Central America and Politicized Religion," *World Affairs*, 144, 2 (1981): 133.

21. Penny Lernoux, "The Long Path to Puebla," in John Eagleston and Philip Schrarper, eds., *Puebla and Beyond: Documentation and Commentary* (Maryknoll, NY: Orbis Books, 1979), 19.

22. Harvey Cox and Faith Annette Sand, "What Happened at Puebla?" *Christianity and Crisis*, 39,4 (1979): 59.

23. Michael Dodson and T. S. Montgomery, "The Churches in the Nicaraguan Revolution," in Thomas Walker, ed., *Nicaragua in Revolution* (New York: Praeger Publishers, 1982), 164.

24. Ibid., 170-1.

25. Ibid., 172.

26. Ibid., 171.

27. Luis Serra, "The Sandinist Mass Organizations," in Walker, ed., *Nicaragua in Revolution*, 107.

28. Dodson and Montgomery, "Churches," 170.

29. House Subcommittee on International Organizations, *Human Rights in Nicaragua*, 10.

30. *New York Times*, 2 March 1977, 8.

31. Dodson and Montgomery," Churches," 171.

32. Walker, *Land of Sandino*, 100.

33. Wayne H. Cowen, "Nicaragua: The Revolution Takes Hold," *Christianity and Crisis*, 40, 8 (May 1980): 140.

34. U.S. Congress, House, Committee on Appropriations, Subcommittee on Foreign Operations, *Foreign Assistance and Related Agencies Appropriations for 1978*, 95th Congress, 1st session, 1977, 518.

35. Cowen, "Nicaragua," 140, and Dodson and Montgomery, "Churches," 173.

36. Cowen, "Nicaragua," 140.

37. Millet, "Guardians," 163.

38. House Subcommittee on Foreign Operations, *Foreign Assistance Appropriations for 1978*, 551.

39. Ibid., 545-46.

40. House Subcommittee on International Organizations, *Human Rights in Nicaragua*, 163-64.

41. *New York Times*, 16 February 1979, p. 12.

42. Anastasio Somoza and Jack Cox, *Nicaragua Betrayed* (Boston: Western Islands Publishers, 1980), 11.

43. Dodson and Montgomery, "Churches," 177.

44. Somoza and Cox, *Nicaragua Betrayed*, 303.

45. Ibid., 24.

46. House Subcommittee on International Organizations, *Human Rights in Nicaragua*, 30.

47. Jeffrey St. John, "Human Rights and Revolution: A Case Study in Moral Confusion," in Belden Bell, ed., *Nicaragua: An Ally Under Siege* (Washington, DC: Council on InterAmerican Affairs, 1978), 72.

48. House Subcommittee on Foreign Operations, *Foreign Assistance Appropriations for 1978*, 1-2.

49. U.S. Congress, Senate, Committee on Foreign Affairs, Subcommittee on Western Hemisphere Affairs, *Latin America*, 94th Congress, 2d session, 1978, 86.

50. House Subcommittee on Foreign Operations, *Foreign Assistance Appropriations for 1978*, 16.

51. Senate Subcommittee on Western Hemisphere Affairs, *Latin America*, 31-36.

52. House Subcommittee on International Organizations, *Human Rights in Nicaragua*, 157. Emphasis mine.

53. Senate Subcommittee on Western Hemisphere Affairs, *Latin America*, 86.

54. House Subcommittee on Foreign Operations, *Foreign Assistance Appropriations for 1978*, 530.

55. Senate Subcommittee on Western Hemisphere Affairs, *Latin America*, 184-93.

56. See Somoza and Cox, *Nicaragua Betrayed*, 55, and D'Escoto, "Nicaragua," 145.

57. House Subcommittee on Foreign Operations, *Foreign Assistance Appropriations for 1978*, 5-6.

58. Ibid., 583.

59. St. John, "Human Rights," 76. See also Walker, *Land of Sandino*, 35.

60. Cardenal, "Revolution and Peace," 203.

61. Alan Riding, "Nicaragua Drafts the Young for a War on Illiteracy," *New York Times*, 3 June 1980, A2.

62. S. Losev, "A New Life for Nicaragua," *International Affairs* (USSR), 2 (February 1981): 119.

63. Stephan M. Gorman, "Power and Consolidation in the Nicaraguan Regime," *Journal of Latin American Studies*, 13, 1 (1981): 148.

64. Thomas A. Walker, "Nicaragua Consolidates its Revolution," *Current History*, 80, 463, (1981): 89.

65. Warren Hogge, "Nicaragua Poor Get Sidewalks, Buses, and Dialectic," *New York Times*, 2 January 1982, A6.

66. Eldon Kentworthy, "Troubled Nicaragua," *New York Times*, 18 February 1982.

67. U.S. *Congressional Record*, 26 February 1980, p. H1265.

68. Shirley Christian, "Nicaraguan Nemesis," *New Republic*, 26 (May 1981): 16.

69. Cowen, "Nicaragua," 139. Robert Leiken, an early supporter of the Revolution, reported in 1984 that the Literacy Program's "graduates" could frequently not even read their diplomas. See *The New Republic*, 8 October 1984.

70. U.S. Congress, House, Committee on Foreign Affairs, Subcommittee on Interamerican Affairs, *Assessment of Conditions in Central America*, 96th Congress, 2d session, 1980, 46.

71. House Committee on Foreign Affairs, *Special Central American Economic Assistance*, 15.

72. U.S. Congress, House, Committee on Appropriations, Subcommittee on Foreign Operations, *Foreign Assistance and Related Programs Appropriations for 1981*, 96th Congress, 2d session, 1980, 298.

73. U.S. Congress, House, Committee on International Relations, Subcommittee on International Development, *Rethinking U.S. Foreign Policy Toward the Developing World: Nicaragua*, 95th Congress, 2d session, 1978, 11.

74. Senate Committee on Foreign Relations, *S. 2012*, 76.

75. Ibid., 2, 27.

76. House Committee on Foreign Affairs, *Special Central American Economic Assistance*, 80.

77. House Subcommittee on Foreign Operations, *Foreign Assistance Appropriations for 1981*, 291-92.

78. U.S. *Congressional Record*, 26 February 1980, p. H1283.

7

Christian Democracy in Venezuela: The Politics of Accommodation

We saw in Chapters 3 and 5 that, in spite of its early successes in Europe and Latin America, Christian Democracy is declining in importance and may become a marginally influential movement. Even in Italy the challenge of the Communist Party looms large. I suggested that the major reasons for this decline are Christian Democracy's failure to adhere to its original principles, its short-sighted "pragmatism," and its refusal to present a coherent alternative to the statist tendencies of most European and Latin American political parties.

Even in Venezuela, where a Christian Democratic victory in 1968 seemed to herald a new dawn for the movement, the party is in an obvious decline. Since 1968, the party has won only one of Venezuela's four presidential elections. Its partisans were able to take some comfort in the 1988 loss only because it failed to match the devastating results of 1983. Prospects for 1993, when Luis Herrera Campins will be able to run again, are not encouraging. It was he who led the Christian Democrats to their worst loss ever.

ORIGINS OF VENEZUELAN CHRISTIAN DEMOCRACY

The history of Christian Democracy in Venezuela is largely the biography of its founder, Rafael Caldera. Born in the Andean state of Tachira in 1907, Caldera was attracted by the doctrines of Catholic social thought early in his life. He attended university at a time when the

Roman Catholic Church was deeply interested in developing young leaders.

Caldera attended two special conferences in Rome called by the Vatican for this purpose. During the 1934 First Congress of Catholic Youth in Rome, Caldera first studied Catholic social thought and the writings of Jacques Maritain and Emmanuel Mounier in a systematic manner. These writings became the roots of his early Christian Democratic thought.[1]

Caldera later attended a second youth congress in Rome and became acquainted with Eduardo Frei of Chile and Fernando Belaunde Terry of Peru. Cardinal Eugenio Pacelli, Vatican secretary of state who would soon become Pope Pius XII, gave the keynote address. He told the assembled young people of their duty to fight Marxism and to do more to help the poor in their own countries.[2]

Upon returning from this congress, Caldera decided to challenge the complete control that Marxists were exercising over the student movements in Venezuela. He founded the National Student Union (UNE) in 1935, and immediately found an issue in the other student groups' demands for the expulsion of the Society of Jesus.

Caldera's UNE soon became the only Catholic student movement in Venezuela. Caldera himself was a major figure in the student generation that demanded a more open political system after the death of dictator Juan Vicente Gómez in 1935.

The UNE underwent changes and maturation during the López Contreras dictatorship. Moving beyond his Christian student base, Caldera sought to include Venezuelans suspicious of the leftist rhetoric of Rómulo Betancourt, another student leader who founded the social democratic Acción Democratica (AD).[3]

López Contreras fell in 1945, and Venezuela enjoyed a brief interlude of democratic rule known as the Triennio. Betancourt's AD ushered in the democratic change, and Betancourt himself became president. The Christian Democratic movement finally came of age in 1946 when Caldera founded the Christian Democratic Comite de Organización Política Electoral Independiente (Copei). The purpose of this organization was to mobilize support for elections to a constituent assembly, charged with writing a new constitution in the wake of López Contreras' fall from power.[4]

It was during this period that Copei began a long-standing policy of working with rival political parties rather than opposing them in elections. Although the rivalry between the two was bitter, and in spite of seemingly unbridgeable ideological differences, Copei worked with AD from 1945 to 1948. Caldera himself was briefly Betancourt's attorney general.

In 1948, the military returned to power, outlawing every political party except Copei, which technically was not a political party to begin with, but an electoral commission. The army exiled the leaders of AD and of the Democratic Republican Union (URD), another leftist party. Copei moved to fill the vacuum of civilian political leadership by accepting posts in the military government.

Caldera chose the path of neutral cooperation over those of outright collaboration or sullen opposition.[5] His willingness to ignore differences with political rivals reappeared, allowing him to temporarily dominate civilian politics in Venezuela. Caldera and Copei would pay for this noncommittal attitude by being accused of collaboration.

Once again, however, the cooperation did not last. When dictator Marcos Pérez Jiménez voided unfavorable election results in 1952, Copei moved toward outright opposition. Caldera remained in Venezuela and tried to organize domestic opposition to the dictatorship. His first move was to demand opposition from his own party by expelling any Copeyano who took part in the illegitimate Constituent Assembly of Pérez Jiménez.[6]

A number of Copei activists left the country, including Herrera Campins, a second-generation student leader. Taking up residence in Spain, Herrera founded an exile opposition newspaper in 1955. It was during this European exile that many Copei activists became enamored of Christian socialism, through their contacts with European Christian Democrats, who were moving in a leftward direction.[7] Caldera attended the First World Conference of Christian Democratic Movements in Paris in 1956, during which Frei urged his fellow Christian Democrats to embrace the tenets of the left.[8]

These European Christian Democrats were also influential in bringing civilian government back to Venezuela. As the Pérez Jiménez dictatorship began to break down in 1957, due largely to opposition from the Catholic Church, it took revenge upon Caldera because of his alleged links with the Venezuelan hierarchy. Caldera avoided arrest by taking refuge in the Papal Nunciate and then accepting exile in the United States.

While in New York City, Caldera met with Betancourt and Jovito Villaba, the leader of the URD, and arranged to join forces with them against the Pérez Jiménez regime. This crucial meeting was arranged through the New York headquarters of the Christian Democratic Union of Central Europe (CDUCE), a left-leaning Christian Democratic organization.[9]

Caldera's concessions during that meeting determined the future of Copei. He conceded the presidency to Betancourt, in spite of his own popularity within Venezuela, convinced that this was the only way to persuade AD to enter a democratic coalition. Caldera feared that the AD would move toward violent opposition if Betancourt were not courted.

One of Caldera's Copei colleagues deplored this decision, claiming that Caldera might have been elected president if he had tried. Furthermore, the Copei activist argued, uniting with an ideologically incompatible rival was both immoral and bad politics.[10]

Most North American authors conclude that Betancourt was sufficiently popular in Venezuela to allow him to sabotage any democratic system that attempted to exclude him. Caldera was perhaps uncertain of his own appeal to Venezuelan voters, because of his earlier attempt to work with the dictatorship.

If this was the case, Caldera's remedy was an odd one. He tried to counter the stigma of collaboration with one incompatible movement, a rightist dictatorship, with collaboration with an equally incompatible leftist movement. This decision is defensible only if one assumes that the participation of Betancourt was essential to the success of a democratic system. Caldera evidently concluded that this was the case, and made his concessions accordingly.

Still, his actions reflect a lack of confidence in the appeal of his own movement. At a crucial moment, Caldera lost his nerve and opted for an easier path to power than the uncertainty of free elections. Copei became Venezuela's first genuinely loyal opposition, refusing to plot with various factions of the military that were still suspicious of Betancourt.

Opposition was a position to which Copei would become accustomed. Since 1958, it has held the presidency for only ten years. How Copei has dealt with this opposition status, as well as its brief stints in power, points up a number of similarities with other Christian Democratic parties and movements.

ACCOMMODATION WITH STATE POWER

Like most Christian Democratic movements, Copei started as an alternative to the paternalistic parties of the right and left. Its commitment to Catholic social doctrine included that doctrine's distrust of secular state power. By 1958, this distrust was gone and Copei was a strong advocate of increased state power.

Caldera's accommodation with the state began with attempts to use state power to achieve Christian Democratic social goals. Thus Copei adopted what one author calls a "flexible" view of state intervention in the economy. For the Christian Democrats, state intervention is not an end in itself, but rather a means to achieve predetermined social goals. The author states that Copei is likely to use state intervention only when "appropriate."[11] Although he is attempting to paint Copei as a more moderate statist party than AD, the author makes it clear that Copei accepts few restraints on state intervention.

Even in 1946, during Copei's first run for national office, its electoral platform declared that the state had not only the right, but also the obligation to intervene in public life in all cases "in which that intervention may be necessary."[12] Although this document paid lip service to the inviolability of private property, a central tenet of Catholic social thought, it also emphasized that individual interests must bow to the social function of property. The state exists to enforce this.[13]

Christian Democratic social goals also call for state intervention. The departure from orthodox Catholic social thought is striking in some of these examples. Caldera, in conjunction with the Catholic Church, declared the importance of the family to a stable society. But where the Church has emphasized the family as a societal unit to protect individuals from state power, Caldera retained the family emphasis while simultaneously declaring the need for increased state power to protect it.[14]

As the leader of a student movement, Caldera championed the cause of autonomous Catholic education, as well as a recognition of the family's primary role as educator. This principled stand did not last long after 1958. Copei accepted a plank in the 1958 constitution that named the state as primary educator.[15]

Similarly, while the popes wrote of the need for a family wage, and presented it as a moral necessity for employers, Copei demanded that the state provide a family wage, either by requiring employers to pay it or by making up the differences in government subsidies.[16] In the same way, the state should also guarantee employment.[17] Catholic social doctrine demands the ethical treatment of workers. Copei seeks to enforce this by expanding the power of the state to inspect workplaces and punish violators of government regulations.[18]

Catholic social thought demands that government commit itself to man's more complete human development. This has provided an even broader opportunity for Copei to advocate a stronger state. Lorenzo Fernández, a close colleague of Caldera and the party's 1973 presidential candidate, consistently used the phrase "government for man," but used it to mean increased government action in more and more areas of social life, including education, health, housing, employment, family protection, youth groups, and sports.[19]

While Copei's impatience and distrust of the power of large capitalists is, at least superficially, in line with Catholic social thought, its remedy is alien to it. Traditionally, the Catholic Church has advocated societal norms, such as custom and tradition, as well as autonomous communities, such as guilds, to restrain the harmful individualistic tendencies of capitalism.

Christian Democrats, on the other hand, seek to combat the capitalists by attacking independent agencies and increasing the power of the state.

At the very least, they risk creating a capitalist/state dialectic of the type Marx and Engels favored to sharpen class conflict and hasten revolution. They fail to trust society to combat both the capitalists and the state.

PRAGMATISM AND THE PATH TO POWER

Defenders of Copei argue that to accept state power to promote this social justice is merely to be pragmatic. It is difficult in the Venezuelan case to separate pragmatism, meaning the thoughtful tactical compromises that allow government to take place, with opportunism, in which central goals of a movement are sacrificed for short-term gain. The compromises that Copei has made to get to power are an illustration of this difficulty.

As we have seen, Caldera was willing to make common cause with AD after October 1945, in spite of serious ideological differences. Its alternative was to challenge the AD electorally, something Caldera chose not to do, ostensibly for fear that divisions among Venezuelan democrats might tempt the army to stage a coup. Like Maritain, Caldera came to be convinced that there were no enemies on the left. The enemies on the right were more dangerous and fear of the right justified collaboration with anyone on the left.[20]

The failure of the Triennio government only served to reinforce this attitude. Copei concluded after the 1948 coup that compromise, accommodation, and negotiation were Venezuela's key political values, crucial to preventing another military dictatorship.[21] It was these values that Caldera sought to acquire, even at the expense of Christian Democratic ideology. Like the accommodation with statism, Caldera thought that his compromises with AD were all to the service of Copei's goals.

The most immediate result of the 1958 Pact of Punto Fijo, negotiated at Caldera's initiative, was Copei acquiring the Ministries of Agriculture, Development, and Justice in the Betancourt administration. These three ministers used their positions to fill appointed posts throughout the country. They then used these government jobs to increase their grass-roots organizing efforts in new areas of Venezuela. Perhaps because of reluctance to lose these positions, Copei remained a faithful partner throughout Betancourt's five-year term.

Copei even helped AD rehabilitate its anti-Church image. When AD sought to extend state power to Catholic education, Copei worked to mute Catholic opposition, arguing that cooperation with AD was more important than ideological consistency. One expert described the attitude of Copei: "If benefits [to Catholic education] could be secured by working within the system—at a cost obviously lower than that of total confrontation—then perhaps old images of the system and its anti-Catholic bias had to be reconsidered."[22]

Many North American authors, as well as Copei members, defend Caldera's actions in 1958 and even praise him for preventing AD from taking over completely.[23] One Venezuelan author describes the Pact of Punto Fijo as an AD concession to Copei, which Caldera forced upon Betancourt on the strength of Copei's extensive grass-roots organization during the Pérez Jiménez dictatorship.[24] Herrera defended the pact as a political necessity to get democracy in Venezuela started and to hold off rightist challenges.[25]

This opinion is not unanimous, however. German Borregales, a long-time colleague of Caldera and an opponent of the pact, raises serious questions about its necessity. The worst early mistake of Copei, he continued, was deciding not to risk its fate at the polls but instead to enter a coalition that would effectively deprive the Venezuelan people of any choice in the direction of their democratic government.[26] The Copei-AD-URD coalition offered Venezuela only one choice: coalition or continued military rule. While this was one choice that the democrats could not lose, Caldera gave up too much for this chance at a sure thing.

It is difficult to prove or disprove what Borregales says. Copei had an extensive grass-roots organization in 1958, probably more extensive than that of the other parties, whose leaders had been in exile for some years. On the other hand, this exile had increased the stature of Betancourt and Villaba inside Venezuela. Victory for Caldera in an open election was not a certainty. It is difficult to criticize Caldera for acting prudently, under difficult circumstances, to insure a democratic transition in Venezuela.

But the more important question is what Caldera gave up to assure at least a share of power. By allowing Betancourt to lead the coalition, Caldera relegated Copei to second place. In other words, he took a certain second-place position rather than trying for first place. In the process, he also denied to the Venezuelan people a chance to decide for themselves the direction of their new democratic government. The coalition partners, having insulated themselves from accountability, would decide on basic government policies on their own. Whatever benefits Copei might have derived from this arrangement, they came at the cost of truly free elections in Venezuela.

FAILURE TO PRESENT ALTERNATIVES

Copei became "deideologized" after 1969.[27] Its central concern, according to Copei members themselves, was winning elections. Bristling at the suggestion that Copei was, in 1958 or before, a conservative party, most Copei members emphasized their pragmatism and preoccupation with winning elections.[28] A central element of this preoccupation was the refusal to present the citizens of Venezuela with a discernible alternative to AD.

Centralization

The popes, invoking the principle of subsidiarity, favored decentralized governments. Maritain and Mounier both believed that to protect human rights and to promote the individual well-being of man, the powers of the state should be limited and decentralized.[29]

Copei's original base of support, the Andean states of Tachira, Trujillo, and Mérida, were also bases of support for weak central government. Traditionally, Venezuelans with landed wealth have preferred a weak central government while moneyed Venezuelans have preferred sufficient strength to protect the value of their paper holdings. Consistent with its ideological bases and the wishes of its constituents, Copei favored decentralization of administration and strengthening of municipal governments through the Triennio period.[30]

Even during this early period, however, there were signs of erosion on this issue. The 1946 Copei platform, while supporting decentralization, added conditions. Such federalism, it said, must harmonize with the necessities of the republic. Among these necessities was the requirement that the central government be strong enough to oppose "regional oligarchies."[31] Regionalism had suddenly become not an institution to protect individuals, but a threat to the state.

During the 1978 campaign, Herrera attempted to revive and repackage a traditional element of Catholic social thought. This was societal pluralism, or the definition of society as a collection of autonomous groups of citizens. The repackaging of this principle, however, fundamentally changed its meaning.

In his campaign for president, Herrera seemed to be running against the overgrown Venezuelan state by seeking to increase the power of people through civic organizations.[32] The general name given to this emphasis on civic organizations is "communitaria." Herrera explained that since the Christian Democrats rejected both communist and capitalist society, they had to create a third way that would guarantee individual development. Such personal development depended upon respect from the state, and such respect would more likely be forthcoming if the people participated more in government themselves.

Yet for all his talk of the need for communitaria, Herrera refused point blank to be specific about what such a society would look like. He merely repeated that it must be based upon Christian inspiration, must be approached slowly and progressively, and must involve a fundamental change of heart.[33]

For such a reordering of society to work, however, two things are necessary. First, the populace must have civic organizations through which they can communicate with politicians and bureaucrats. This Copei seemed determined to provide. The second requirement, however, is that the state be willing to surrender at least some of its power. For Catholic social thinkers, state power over individuals' economic future is particularly worrisome. Herrera made no change in the power of the Venezuelan state to direct the economic life of the country. In fact, from his days in the Copei youth movement, he used the term communitaria to mean increased state control over the economy.[34] For Herrera, the obstacle to communitaria was not the state, but rather private economic concerns.

Land Reform

As early as 1946, Copei delegates to the Triennio Constituent Assembly agreed with their AD counterparts that large landholdings be parceled out to the peasants who worked them, without regard to productivity.[35] During the coalition government from 1958 to 1963, land reform was under the direction of Victor Giménez Landinez, Christian Democrat and agriculture minister in the Betancourt cabinet.

According to European Christian Democrats, this agrarian reform was the most profound social transformation in Venezuela's history.[36] Yet, as in the Chilean case, it was also a significant departure from earlier Christian Democratic theory. Copei's Giménez did not adhere to the "all proprietors" goal of Catholic social thought. Besides failing to give outright ownership of land to peasants, Copei's land reform program also significantly increased Venezuelan state power.

Caldera himself told the Fifth International Christian Democratic Conference that the state had to play "a decisive role" in agrarian reform, adding, somewhat disingenuously, that this role must not be prejudicial to private enterprise. He added that land reform required the state to provide technical assistance, credits, housing, transportation, and numerous other benefits to rural society.[37]

This represented a substantial state presence in an area hitherto free from it. Rural Venezuela was not only opposed to state economic intervention, it had given birth to Copei specifically to protect itself from increased government encroachment.

Copei-AD Cooperation on Labor

Copei's work among Venezuelan labor was extensive both during and after the Pérez Jiménez dictatorship. Copei even formed its own labor confederation, the Confederation of Autonomous Unions of Venezuela (CODESA).[38]

Nevertheless, as part of the 1958 agreement, Copei sacrificed its chance to make genuine inroads into AD's dominance of organized labor. Copei allowed their labor confederation to join forces with AD's group to form a "united" labor confederation.[39] This effectively prevented the formation of an independent labor confederation.

In return for this concession, Copei received a guarantee that one of its members would become secretary general of the united Venezuelan Workers' Confederation (CTV). In addition, Copei was guaranteed a predetermined number of seats on the CTV Executive Council.[40] AD, for its part, received the presidency of the CTV and a guaranteed majority status on the Executive Council. Today, although the Copei's CODESA still exists, it is a moribund institution with most of its leaders choosing to try to exercise influence in the CTV Executive Council.[41] Thus, Copei reacted to its perceived second-place status in the labor movement by giving up, for the foreseeable future, any chance to improve that position.

Nationalization of Oil

Copei started working within the 1958 to 1963 coalition government immediately to prepare the way for nationalization of Venezuela's oil.[42] Even before, the UNE, while critical of both the United States and the Soviet Union, was always more critical of the United States and, in particular, of American oil companies.[43] Caldera himself, writing in 1962, spoke of the need to retain the services of foreign capital, but he also disparaged the American companies as "robber barons," who would resist "truly constructive enterprise."[44]

In the same article, Caldera rejected "conservative [economic] patterns" and spoke of the need to modernize "worn out systems of production." Thus Copei initiated the "Venezuelan oil for Venezuela" movement in the 1960s that was, in large part, responsible for the eventual 1976 nationalization.[45]

Copei declared that foreign oil companies could continue to operate in Venezuela until such time as the country was prepared to take them over. In this way, Copei repeated AD policy. Such foreign operations had to be consistent with the security of the state, the conservation of oil wealth, and the "appropriate participation of the Nation in the exploitation."[46] Copei also passed laws discouraging the operation of small oil companies and gradually increased state control over the industry.[47]

Dealing with the Guerrilla Threat

Copei also advanced an AD policy of pacification of the Venezuelan countryside. An attempt by Fidel Castro to infiltrate guerrillas into Venezuela in 1963 led to a sharp, but relatively short, period of guerrilla warfare. The AD, under Raul Leoni, pursued an active military pacification policy, tempered with political incentives. The vocal opposition of Copei kept Leoni from making these incentives more attractive to the guerrillas.

Once Caldera came into office, however, his pacification policy was quite lenient. Active fighting had stopped by 1969, and Caldera granted an amnesty to all former guerrillas and prepared for the recognition of Castro's regime. A policy that Copei had criticized while out of power became Copei policy when it was elected. Once again, Venezuelans looking for a difference between their two parties were disappointed.

Electoral Politics

Even during presidential campaigns, when parties usually accentuate the differences between themselves and their opponents, Copei politicians tend to be very vague when asked about the differences between their party and AD. Herrera was asked this question in 1978 and tried to avoid it by expressing surprise that anyone would ask such a question. Pressed, he said that Copei was spiritual, whereas AD was materialistic.[48] He added that Copei, unlike AD, sought a society that emphasizes community over individualistic tendencies.

Since he was running for president when the interview was granted, Herrera quickly turned his answer into a list of campaign promises. His first priority, like that of AD, would be public services. His first task, again like AD, would be organizing the public. What he saw as the poor's submissive attitude toward the state, he would change to "participation."

Participation runs through many of Herrera's campaign speeches. He invariably presented it as a major difference between himself and his AD opponent. This still does not present a genuine alternative. Herrera does not propose to significantly change the role of government; he merely wants people to be more involved with what government does.

Herrera concentrated on attacking not the basic direction of the AD administration, but rather its alleged mismanagement, corruption, and failure to build infrastructure fast enough.[49] Other issues Copei raised, such as public order, personal security, and the problems of the poor, also failed to point up any significant difference between Copei and AD.[50]

In 1988, Copei candidate Eduardo Fernandez tried to run as a fresh alternative to the old business-as-usual politics.[51] He had, after all, defeated Caldera's old guard within Copei for the nomination and he was running against Carlos Andres Pérez, who was trying for a second term. Nevertheless, his "New Look" campaign failed to articulate any differences between himself and Perez. Like Herrera ten years earlier, Fernandez concentrated on AD "scandals."[52]

He spent the first two months of the official campaign talking about AD mismanagement and corruption, avoiding basic issues.[53] This not only cheated the Venezuelan public of a real debate over basic issues, it was also extremely stupid politics. First, the alleged scandals of AD revolved around the personal life of outgoing AD President Jaime Lusinchi, including his well publicized divorce. Fernandez was not running against Lusinchi. Second, Pérez had fought with Lusinchi forces to get the nomination and thus could attack Lusinchi himself. Third, in spite of the scandals, the Lusinchi administration enjoyed a 64 percent approval rating among Venezuelans.[54]

Not given much of a chance against Perez in the first place, Copei was in an excellent position to experiment with a new approach in 1988. Instead, they stayed with the old formulas of imitation of AD. Both promised to deliver land, schools, urban housing projects, and health care.[55] Where Copei did admit difference, they moved to the left. Copei attacked Pérez for being too heavy-handed as chief of internal security during the guerrilla war.[56]

Although Pérez won by a smaller margin than Lusinchi had in 1983, and although Copei made gains in Congress, they still did not come close to significantly challenging AD political dominance. For the first time since 1963, Copei had lost two elections in a row, raising questions about the party's future.

An even more ominous result of the 1988 campaign was the rising tide of apathy and abstention, especially among young people.[57] What used to be a strong area of recruitment for Copei was opting out of electoral politics altogether. As we have seen with older Christian Democratic parties in Europe, young people react negatively to nonideological parties.

ATTEMPTS TO OUTBID THE OPPOSITION

Far from trying to present a coherent alternative to AD, Copei seems frequently preoccupied with pursuing statist policies with even more vigor. When the AD candidate in 1973 said that Copei had merely continued AD policies during the previous five years, Copei responded with indignation, claiming that they had completed even more nationalizations than AD.[58]

Social Spending

One of Copei's goals in imitating AD so faithfully on key issues was to lose the stigma of being Venezuela's "right-wing" party. In this they were successful. They were less successful in selling themselves as Venezuela's left-wing party. The results of the 1973 election showed not only that AD still had that position in the minds of most urban Venezuelans, but also that many rural voters had lost interest in a "moderate" reform party as well. Copei's response to this reverse was to try to lose the tag "moderate" and move to the left of AD. Again, the apparent goal was to prevent a genuine alternative.

Herrera was most eloquent in trying to outbid AD. The party of Betancourt, he explained in 1978, does not try to restructure society, but merely modifies it step by step.[59] Herrera ran as the "president of education" which he promised to use as a tool for uplifting the masses from despair.[60] The method of this uplift was, not surprisingly, more money for education. By promising this, Venezuelan Christian Democrats got into a bidding war with their leftist opposition for the votes of urbanites.

Another example of this was housing. Herrera promised 600,000 new houses during his five-year term, consciously besting an AD promise of 500,000.[61] Had Copei been interested in a genuine alternative, they might have unveiled ways to induce more house building from the private sector, such as changes in the tax code.

Eduardo Fernandez said in 1989 that the state should create mechanisms to preserve the purchasing power of sectors hardest hit by inflation. He also demanded higher tariffs on agricultural products and a multilateral agency to absorb Venezuela's debt. While voicing some support for the debt plan of U.S. Treasury Secretary Nicholas Brady, Fernandez added that debt payments from all Latin American states should stop, at least temporarily. All of these proposals are attempts to outbid AD for labor votes; most involve substantial increases in the economic power of the state.

National Development

Copei moved faster than AD in involving the state in development. It was the Caldera administration that launched the Oriente Development Corporation. Later, Fernandez called for the resurrection of the state-run Agricultural Marketing Corporation, which AD had disbanded.[62]

Copei members also seem keenly disappointed that it was an AD administration that finally nationalized the oil industry. Criticism of the way in which Pérez handled the oil nationalization shows the sort of opposition party that Copei has become. In 1976, Pérez took the final step toward nationalization, and provided compensation to the ousted foreign oil companies in the sum of $1 billion.[63] Although Copei had supported nationalization for years and took important preliminary steps themselves from 1969 to 1974, they refuse to credit Pérez for his 1976 action.

Their criticism comes from a decidedly statist direction. Herrera took Pérez to task for including Article 5 in the nationalization agreement. This allowed the incorporation of oil companies with government participation and private investment from Venezuela or abroad. Herrera worried that this provision would allow private investors (no matter whether domestic or foreign) to take over the oil industry once again.

This must not be allowed, Herrera insisted. The reason for the nationalization in the first place was to insure "community" control of the industry. "The oil industry must be commanded," he said, "basically, by the state."[64] It was Copei, he maintained, that declared Venezuela's economic independence from the United States. It was Copei that took the steps that allowed AD to grandstand on the 1976 nationalization. If Copei had won in 1973, Herrera concluded, the party would have nationalized oil faster than AD.[65]

Foreign Affairs

Copei also moved to the left of AD on the issue of recognition of Cuba. The relationship between Fidel Castro and various Venezuelan presidents is a complex one. Many experts believe that the Cuban Revolution, especially after 1960, helped Betancourt maintain his position in the face of rightist threats. Convinced that overthrowing Betancourt would cause civil war, the army in 1960 concluded that he was at least preferable to the more extreme Cuban leader.

In spite of Betancourt's original enthusiasm for Castro, and his belief that the Cuban Revolution shared an AD-like world view, it was not long before relations began to sour. Most serious, of course, was Castro's attempt to export his version of communist revolution to Venezuela. It was this interference that prompted Betancourt to lead the fight in the Organization of American States to sanction and expel Cuba.

When the Leoni administration began to move toward improved relations with Cuba, Copei resisted fiercely and even threatened to leave the democratic coalition. A second Cuban attempt to support guerrillas allowed Copei to continue its apparent hostility.[66]

Yet once Caldera took office, he moved quickly to improve relations. He legalized the Venezuelan Communist Party and refrained from verbal attacks on Castro.[67] By the end of his term, professional, cultural, and athletic contacts were made, and Castro praised Venezuela for breaking a long-standing agreement with the United States in the wake of OPEC oil price increases.[68] It was Copei's foreign minister that led the fight in the OAS to remove sanctions imposed in the early 1960s. Caldera also moved to improve relations with the Soviet Union.

In 1973, to highlight its difference with AD on this issue, Copei ran Lorenzo Fernandez, who was the architect of the Caldera pacification program and a consistent promoter of amnesty for communist guerrillas, legalization of the Communist Party, and rapprochement with Cuba and the Soviet Union.[69]

The rationale for Copei's leftward movement is difficult to determine. Like their Christian Democratic counterparts in the rest of the continent, they are finding that to be a "moderate" party while at the same time trying to outbid a leftist opposition is impossible. Copei will have to become a revolutionary party if it wishes to remain to the left of AD. How they can do this while retaining their repeated commitments to Catholic social thought is, at best, unclear.

THE COPEYANO RIGHT

Copei had a coherent, democratic right at one time. The Copeyano right was eliminated during the Caldera administration, when they were frozen out of patronage appointments.[70] The process began before 1969, however.

Copei's original documents did contain some conservative-sounding language. They promised to protect private initiative, for example, and to "defend the Venezuelan nation as a real and spiritual unity against Communism."[71] But even here the conservative tenets were watered down. Private initiative was limited by right, by law, by morality, and by the national interest. The defense of Venezuela was not only against communism, but against "any other imperialism" as well.

A controversy with AD during the Triennio convinced Copei that it would have to jettison its right wing. When the Betancourt administration unveiled Decree 321, perceived as a threat to the autonomy of private schools, Copei felt duty-bound to oppose it. In so doing, they found themselves caught up in the ancient Church/state controversy that has plagued Latin American politics since colonial days. Copei's more progressive members found themselves making common cause with rightists. Copei was determined that neither of these things would ever happen again.

This determination formed part of the reason for Copei's conciliatory and mediating attitude after 1958.[72] Their fear of the Venezuelan right, even the democratic right, was strong enough to make Copei's leaders want it removed from their party. Although Copei did not institute a purge, it did ban conservatives from leadership positions. In the words of one observer, conservatives were allowed to join Copei, but not to influence it.[73]

Copei was confident that even this treatment would not cause the right to leave the party in large numbers. Secure in the belief that the right had no other alternatives in Venezuela, Copei moved to make sure no such alternative ever appeared.[74] Leaders like German Borregales, who opposed land reform as unproductive, arbitrary, and confiscatory, were not only removed from leadership, they were attacked and insulted.[75]

The most common form of Copei counteroffensive against a potential conservative foe was to link that foe with the dictatorship of Pérez Jiménez. This happened to Borregales first but Copei repeated the tactic with others. The experience of Pedro Tinoco is instructive. Caldera's first minister of development, Tinoco attempted to run for president in 1973 on a conservative, prodevelopment ticket. Copei successfully linked him with the controversy over Pérez Jiménez' attempt to return from exile. This diluted and distracted from his message and linked Tinoco with the nondemocratic right.[76]

A CONSTITUENCY FOR CHANGE

In 1958, one could reasonably argue that the only right wing in Venezuela was a nondemocratic right. Even as late as 1973 the Venezuelan public overwhelmingly expected the government to solve pressing economic problems.[77] Today the situation is much more complex. If conservatism is defined as a political movement that, among other things, desires less government power overall, and particularly less government intervention in private economic decisions, then there are large numbers of potential conservatives in Venezuela and the political right does not have to choose between dictatorship and obsolescence.

One potential source of conservatism is FEDECAMERAS (Federación de Cámeras de Comercio), an organization dedicated to looking after businesses' political needs. It is one of the most active interest groups in Venezuelan politics. FEDECAMERAS frequently makes its views on economic issues known to people in power. During presidential campaigns both parties are careful to address the group and listen to their ideas on economic policy. These suggestions usually revolve around reducing government power. (The government's power to impose tariffs is a significant exception.) FEDECAMERAS also favors more incentives for the private sector to spur investment.[78]

The official business group does not call for a radical restructuring of Venezuela's economy, however. In fact, their 1989 economic plan was "broadly in line with the initial programme prepared by [President] Pérez's own economic advisors."[79] They favor more privatization, a more freely floating exchange rate, but nothing that goes to the root of Venezuelan statism.

As in most statist economies, Venezuelan opposition to state control has gone underground, becoming part of what economists call the "informal sector." This sector is growing in Venezuela, both in numbers and in productivity. According to a 1986 report from the Central Statistics Office, 42.5 percent of all economically active Venezuelans work in the informal sector. Since 1984, 280,000 newly self-employed people have entered the work force.[80]

During the hard times of 1986 to 1988, when falling oil prices took a toll on the Venezuelan economy, uncontrolled nontraditional exports did very well.[81] As an example, gold mining is largely uncontrolled, with small prospectors, operating without required government permission, accounting for a large part of Venezuelan gold production.[82] By contrast, the Venezuelan state oil company lost hundreds of millions of dollars. Even given the fall in world prices, this is roughly the equivalent of losing money on a golden goose hatchery.

CONCLUSION

Given these economic trends, it is not surprising that many formerly apolitical Venezuelans no longer want to accept the state's economic inefficiency.[83] What is puzzling is why Copei does not recognize these trends and use them to present a clear and discernible alternative to the social democratic formulas of AD. Venezuelan voters have demonstrated that they still perceive AD as the country's leftist party and vote for Copei when they desire a change. In spite of this, Copei has failed to give Venezuelans significant change and has opted instead for imitation and doomed attempts to outbid their leftist rivals.

Now those leftist rivals may be recognizing the opportunity that a growing private sector provides. Pérez was careful to tell businessmen during the 1988 campaign that he favored privatization, a unified foreign exchange rate, and steps to open the economy to foreign investment once again.[84] Pérez is also committed to some form of decentralized state power.

Copei is in danger of allowing AD to capture Copei's traditional stands in favor of individual autonomy, wide distribution of productive private property, and economic liberty. If this occurs, then the Venezuelan version of Christian Democracy will continue on the same route as most of its Latin American counterparts: a brief period of influence, based on clearly articulated, principled stands, followed by the abandonment first of clarity, second of principle. A long decline inevitably follows.

It could be argued that the absence of a strong movement in favor of Liberation Theology in Venezuela is evidence that the Christian Democrats have at least prevented the growth of that more extreme philosophy. However, we have seen that Copei has offered no obstacles to the relatively moderate statism of AD, and in fact, has demanded a larger government role. As such, it would be unlikely to oppose the

Marxist tenets of Liberation Theology. The dearth of this theology in Venezuela, as we shall see in Chapter 9, is due to other factors.

NOTES

1. Ricardo Cambellas Lares, *Copei: Idelogia y Liderazgo* (Caracas: Editorial Ariel, S. A., 1985), 29.
2. Donald L. Herman, *Christian Democracy in Venezuela* (Chapel Hill: University of North Carolina Press, 1980), 10-11.
3. Gehard Cartay Ramirez, *Politica y Partidos Modernos en Venezuela* (Caracas: Ediciones Centauro, 1983), 98.
4. Robert J. Alexander, *Latin American Political Parties* (New York: Praeger Publishers, 1973), 339.
5. Cartay Ramirez, *Politica*, 103.
6. Cambellas Lares, *Copei*, 60.
7. Cecilia M. Valente, *The Political, Economic and Labor Climate in Venezuela* (Philadelphia: University of Pennsylvania Press, 1979), 16.
8. *Christian Democratic Review* (December 1956): 17.
9. *Christian Democratic Review* (January-February 1958): 23.
10. See German Borregales, *Copei Hoy: Una Negacion* (Caracas: Ediciones Garrido, 1968).
11. Cambellas Lares, *Copei*, 46-47.
12. Comite de Organización Politica Electoral Independiente (Copei), "Plataforma Electoral de Copei," in Paciano Padron, ed., *Copei: Documentos Fundamentales* (Caracas: Ediciones Centauro, 1981), 89.
13. Ibid.
14. Miguel Jorrin and John D. Martz, *Latin American Political Thought and Ideology* (Chapel Hill: University of North Carolina Press, 1970), 417.
15. Cartay Ramirez, *Politica*, 97.
16. Ibid., 247.
17. Copei, "Platforma Electoral," 90.
18. Cartay Ramirez, *Politica*, 94.
19. Enrique Baloyra and John D. Martz, *Electoral Mobilization and Public Opinion* (Chapel Hill: University of North Carolina Press, 1976): 135-36.
20. *Christian Democratic Review* (July-August 1961): 13.
21. Valente, *Climate in Venezuela*, 11.
22. Daniel H. Levine, *Conflict and Political Change in Venezuela* (Princeton, NJ: Princeton University Press, 1973), 106.
23. See Herman, *Christian Democracy in Venezuela*.
24. Cartay Ramirez, *Politica*, 107.
25. Alfredo Peña, *Conversaciones con Luis Herrera Campins* (Caracas: Editorial Ateneo de Caracas, 1978), 55.
26. Borregales, *Copei Hoy*, 27.
27. Cambellas Lares, *Copei*, 69.
28. Herman, *Christian Democracy in Venezuela*, 12.
29. Cambellas Lares, *Copei*, 40. See also Jacques Maritain, "Man and the

State," in Joseph W. Evans and Leo R. Ward, *The Social and Political Philosophy of Jacques Maritain* (Notre Dame, IN: University of Notre Dame Press, 1976).

30. Cartay Ramirez, *Politica*, 93.
31. Copei, "Platforma Electoral," 87-88.
32. Herman, *Christian Democracy in Venezuela*, 226.
33. Peña, *Conversaciones*, 93.
34. Borregales, *Copei Hoy*, 250.
35. Herman, *Christian Democracy in Venezuela*, 29.
36. *Christian Democratic Review* (July-August 1961): 13.
37. *Christian Democratic Review* (March 1960): 16.
38. Valente, *Climate in Venezuela*, 185-86.
39. Alexander, 350.
40. Valente, 183.
41. Ibid., 187.
42. Alexander, *Latin American Political Parties*, 349.
43. Herman, *Christian Democracy in Venezuela*, 13.
44. Rafael Caldera, "The Christian Democratic Idea," *America*, 7 (April 1962): 14.
45. Edward Williams, *Latin American Christian Democratic Parties* (Knoxville, TN: University of Tennessee Press, 1967), 262.
46. Cartay Ramirez, *Politica*, 248.
47. Herman, *Christian Democracy in Venezuela*, 151-54.
48. Peña, *Coversaciones*, 53.
49. Valente, *Climate in Venezuela*, 26.
50. Donald L. Herman, "The Christian Democratic Party," in Howard Penniman, ed., *Venezuela at the Polls: The National Elections of 1978* (Washington, DC: American Enterprise Institute, 1980), 141,
51. Merrill Collett, "The Next Liberator? Pérez Approach to Latin Debt Worries U.S. Bankers," *Atlantic* (February 1989): 32.
52. *Andean Report* (19 May 1988): 6.
53. *Andean Report* (28 July 1988): 7.
54. *Andean Report* (19 May 1988): 6.
55. William McCord, "Venezuela's Determined Democracy," *New Leader* (10 February 1986): 6.
56. Stephen Ellner, "Politics of the Probable: No Savior in Sight," *Commonweal* (18 November 1988): 614.
57. "How to Be a Democrat," *Economist* (10 December 1988): 44.
58. Herman, *Christian Democracy in Venezuela*, 136.
59. Peña, *Coversaciones*, 54.
60. Herman, "The Christian Democratic Party," in Penniman, *Venezuela*, 144.
61. Ibid., 146.
62. Caracas, *El Universal*, 26 February 1989, 15 (*Foreign Broadcast Information Service*, hereinafter FBIS, 29 March 1989, 38-40).
63. *New York Times*, 30 November 1978, 11.
64. Peña, *Coversaciones*, 59.
65. Ibid.
66. Charles Ameringer, "The Foreign Policy of Venezuelan Democracy," in

John D. Martz, ed., *Venezuela: The Democratic Experience* (New York: Praeger Publishers, 1977), 345.

67. Ibid., 350.

68. Herman, *Christian Democracy in Venezuela*, 189.

69. *New York Times*, 27 April 1973, A8.

70. Baloyra and Martz, *Electoral Mobilization*, 134.

71. Copei, "Platforma Electoral," 101.

72. Levine, *Conflict and Political Change in Venezuela*, 92.

73. *Christian Democratic Review* (August-September 1960): 15.

74. *Christian Democratic Review* (January-February 1958): 21.

75. Borregales, *Copei Hoy*, 28.

76. Baloyra and Martz, *Electoral Mobilization*, 78.

77. Ibid., 54.

78. Caracas, Venezuela de Television, Canal 8, 1600 GMT, 18 May 1988. (FBIS 20 May 1988, 14).

79. *Andean Report* (2 March 1989): 2.

80. *Andean Report* (9 October 1986): 3.

81. Judith Ewell, "Debt and Politics in Venezuela," *Current History* (March 1989): 122-23.

82. *Andean Report* (6 October 1988): 7.

83. *Economist* (23 January 1988): 36.

84. *Andean Report* (28 July 1988): 7.

8

Christian Democracy in Nicaragua: The Limits of Accommodation

The wave of Christian Democratic foundings that swept Latin America in the 1950s touched Nicaragua as well. Even the long Somoza dictatorship could not discourage Christian-oriented, politically active Nicaraguans from searching for a nonrevolutionary alternative to continued despotism. For a time, the Nicaraguan Social Christian Party (PSC) led the most consistent and principled opposition to the Somoza family.

Yet by 1978, the PSC was no longer the single voice for change in Nicaragua, or even the loudest. It was one of several parties vying for second place behind the dominant anti-Somoza group, the Sandinista Front for National Liberation (FSLN). By that time, the PSC was no longer even Nicaragua's only Christian Democratic party. Dissident Social Christians founded the Popular Social Christian Party (PPSC) in 1976.

As we saw in Chapter 6, the FSLN's major role in the revolt against Anastasio Somoza was to radicalize formerly moderate centers of opposition. The PSC did nothing to hinder that role. Thus, the PSC lost its chance to become the dominant anti-Somoza party for the same reasons that Christian Democratic parties have lost opportunities for political success elsewhere. First, the PSC accepted too many of the basic assumptions of its main political rivals. Second, the party fell prey to the same short-sighted opportunism that has plagued Christian Democracy all over Latin America. Third, they followed a policy of accommodation with a hegemonic political movement that failed to show any serious commitment to political pluralism.

Because of these errors of judgement and of ideology, the PSC became one of several Nicaraguan parties that tried to retain a separate identity in the face of the FSLN's ultimately successful determination to guide Nicaragua's destiny on its own. The PPSC, for its part, committed the same errors as the older Christian Democratic party, except to a larger degree. Its place in Nicaraguan politics is even more marginal. For this reason, this chapter will deal exclusively with the PSC.

ORIGINS OF NICARAGUAN CHRISTIAN DEMOCRACY

Origins of the PSC

Nicaraguan politics, through most of the twentieth century, has been the struggle for power between the traditional Liberal and Conservative Parties. As we saw in Chapter 6, the Conservative Party represented the interests of Nicaragua's landed elite. The Conservatives favored a weak central government and a strong role for the Catholic Church. The Liberals represented Nicaragua's moneyed elite. More cosmopolitan in their outlook, and influenced by positivism, this party favored a strong centralized government and a subordinate role for the Church. This same political split was visible in many Latin American countries before World War II.

By the middle of the twentieth century, both parties had become ossified, defensive, and completely unresponsive to any but the Nicaraguan elite. After 1934, the complete dominance of Somoza's Liberal Party only made the ruling elite more remote. Reacting to this, a group of university students formed the National Union of Popular Action (UNAP), a Catholic study group. Among its leaders were Reinaldo Tefel, Rodrigo Victor Tinoco, and Pedro Joaquin Chamorro.

UNAP was not primarily political in nature, although the students' examination of the social encyclicals of the Catholic Church soon led them to demand changes in the political system. They had become sufficiently well known to government circles in 1956 to suffer harassment and then disbanding in the wake of Anastasio Somoza, Sr.'s assassination. To have undergone such repression became a mark of honor among Nicaragua's political opposition.

After UNAP was put out of business, two of its members, Eduardo Rivas Gasteazoro and Orlando Robleto Gallo, founded the Nicaraguan Social Christian Party (PSC) in 1957. Like UNAP, the initial function of the PSC was to study and discuss the papal encyclicals, as well as the ideology of European social Christianity. The works of Jacques Maritain were particularly important to the young Nicaraguans.[1] Their first social projects were literacy centers and health centers, for which they solicited private contributions. In the realm of politics, they lobbied for lower taxes for workers.[2]

Splits in the movement were visible almost from the beginning. As the examples above show, the first efforts of the PSC were not directed toward greater state intervention in the economic or social life of Nicaraguans. Yet some party members favored this, especially Chamorro, a strong advocate of reformist state intervention.[3] There were also splits over the attitude to take toward the Nicaraguan Roman Catholic hierarchy, which was not yet ready to openly oppose Somoza.

The most important early split in Nicaraguan Christian Democracy came over the question of accommodation with political rivals. Although the movement was founded out of disgust with the two traditional parties, by 1957 many PSC members wanted to enter the Conservative Party, get control of it, and transform it into a Social Christian "People's" party.[4]

The effort lasted five years. In 1963, the PSC members had dislodged almost all of the old guard Conservative leaders and had replaced them with their own, mostly PSC members loyal to Reinaldo Tefel. One such PSC member was Fernando Aguero, who had risen to prominence through the PSC. At a crucial moment, however, Aguero turned his back on his Social Christian colleagues and joined forces with old guard Conservatives to purge the upstarts from Conservative ranks.[5]

Thus the PSC's first experiment in political co-optation ended in failure. Its one good result was the number of defections from the Conservative Party that temporarily swelled PSC ranks.[6] But the cost was high. Rather than oppose both traditional parties, and brand the Conservatives collaborators in the Somocist system, the PSC tried a short cut to political power. In the process, they accepted the Conservatives as a legitimate opposition party and lost an opportunity to claim that mantle for themselves.

The true costs of the Conservative adventure became clearer in 1967, when Luis Somoza allowed elections. Having lost valuable time and effort in their doomed attempt at co-optation, the PSC found itself without the money or organization to make a serious try for power in 1967.

Compounding the error, the PSC leadership made an agreement to stay off the ballot and support the Conservative Party in return for promises from their old nemesis Aguero. These were soon broken and the PSC found themselves with one senator and one deputy.[7] These concessions, inconsequential to Somoza and the Conservative Party, had the effect of tying the PSC to Somoza's government and helping to legitimize that government.

While Senator Rivas and Deputy Robleto toiled in obscurity, the PSC went back to its student roots, winning control of student government in León and Managua Universities in 1968.[8] They also formed a labor branch, which expanded into a Christian Democratic Labor Confederation in 1972.

DEVELOPMENT OF PSC IDEOLOGY

Background

One of the most interesting figures in Nicaraguan Social Christian Democracy is Reinaldo Tefel, one of the founders of UNAP. It is through Tefel's life and experiences that two of the major difficulties of Nicaraguan Christian Democracy are illustrated: its failure to distinguish between Catholic social thought and the more radical strictures of Liberation Theology; and its failure to avoid the tempting course of statism, which has done so much to corrode Christian Democratic theory.

Tefel received a Catholic education, going to a Christian Brothers' high school in Nicaragua and later attending Jesuit-run Fordham University in New York. His education in Catholic social thought began with Maritain and Emmanuel Mounier, then moved to Fyodor Dostoyevsky and Pierre Teilhard deChardin.[9] It was through the latter that he became enamored of Liberation Theology.

Tefel entered the Conservative Party with other PSC members in the late 1950s and became the dominant PSC voice in party leadership struggles. His most influential years were 1962 and 1963, just before Aguero's duplicity caused the entire experiment to fail.[10] During this period the Conservative Party was almost completely under his control.

The years of PSC/Conservative collaboration also saw a bizarre episode in Tefel's life, which is instructive to later Christian Democratic actions. In 1959 Tefel and Chamorro broke from the PSC, and did so in dramatic fashion. Visiting the newly installed Fidel Castro in Havana, the two Nicaraguans requested aid from Castro and Che Guevara to overthrow the Somoza dynasty militarily. The result was an inept "invasion" which failed immediately and led to Tefel's temporary imprisonment.

What is instructive about this episode was the willingness of Tefel and Chamorro to recruit outside assistance, even outside military assistance, for their political aims. Their choice of Castro was also instructive. It recalls Maritain's belief that there are no enemies on the left, and in fact, that communists are invaluable partners in dismantling a right-wing regime. The PSC would make these same miscalculations again.

Tefel and Liberation Theology

Tefel's movement from Catholic social thought to Liberation Theology is well marked. It began with a disgust with what he saw as the collaborationist attitude of the Nicaraguan Church. Tefel said in 1964: "A usurious priest or a handkisser of tyrants . . . does more damage to Christianity than the most extreme religious persecution."[11] Tefel evidently linked traditional Catholic social thought with the unsatisfactory behavior of some Nicaraguan clergy. He concluded, on the basis of this questionable connection, that traditional Catholic social thought was insufficient for the political ends he desired. In fact, if Catholic social thought was what his "handkissers" were practicing, it was positively harmful. Tefel's attitude is reminiscent of Miguel D'Escoto's. Like D'Escoto, he adopted the more radical Liberation Theology.

Outside of the Conservative Party, the PSC continued to move toward Liberation Theology. In the mid–1960s the party founded the Institute for Human Promotion (INPRHU). This group, funded by progressive Catholics motivated by a concern over Liberation Theology, concentrated on literacy programs for Nicaragua's rural poor.[12] According to Geraldine Macias, an ex-Maryknoll nun who was well acquainted with the PSC leadership, INPRHU used Paulo Freire's teaching methods and imitated his politics.[13]

Like Freire, INPRHU did not limit its literacy classes to spelling and grammar. Political orientation was a large part of the lessons, and INPRHU followed up its literacy efforts with rural organization. Its members struggled to "raise the consciousness" of the rural poor and develop political organizations to challenge the Somoza dictatorship.[14] So openly political were the literacy efforts that many Catholic priests and nuns refused to take part.[15]

INPRHU's effort was to try to oppose Liberation Theology by imitating it. In Tefel's words, the purpose of INPRHU was "to prepare the agrarian worker and small landholder for syndical struggle, cooperative work and Agrarian Reform."[16] The PSC evidently hoped to raise the consciousness of the rural masses and then motivate those radicalized peasants to accept a moderate, Christian Democratic path to political improvement. Had Nicaragua lacked more radical political movements, this effort might have been successful.

As it was, the newly "conscientized" peasants soon became enamored of the more radical solutions of the FSLN and soon forsook the PSC as the very type of bourgeois reformers against whom Freire's pedagogy is directed. The FSLN, for its part, allowed the PSC to organize the rural masses and prepare them for later radicalization. The PSC, oblivious to the danger, provided their main political and philosophical rivals not only with philosophically compatible peasants, but also with the organizational structure to allow the FSLN to put that compatibility to use.

Tefel and Statism

One of the temptations that has been most alluring to Latin American Christian Democratic movements has been to use state power to achieve their ends. The Nicaraguan party has not been immune to this. As in their acceptance of some of the tenets of Liberation Theology, Tefel's intellectual leadership was key.

Tefel's intellectual acceptance of increased state power came from his experience as a sociologist studying the effects of poverty on slum dwellers outside Managua. He recorded his impressions of slum life-styles in *El Infierno de los Pobres* (1972). In this volume, Tefel blames what he calls the "internal disintegration" of marginal men and women on their low participation in base organizations.[17]

One by one, Tefel examines private organizations that could, or should, fulfill the role of organizing poor people into politically active groups that can effectively demand their economic rights. Private, nongovernmental neighborhood groups, he thinks, cannot solve the problem of integration. After an initial burst of enthusiasm, such groups become centers of paternalistic action by a small number of committed directors.[18]

Another fault of private community groups is their lack of coordination, which occasionally results in rival groups actually working against each other. At times private activists do brilliant work, he concedes, but they never act in an organized and planned way that reaches to the heart of the problem of economic marginality.[19]

Church groups are similarly unsatisfactory. Not only is the practice of Catholicism fairly low, especially among poor men, but a considerable part of the marginal population believed that the Catholic Church did not care about them. Tefel is quick to link this dissatisfaction with the nonradical nature of the Nicaraguan Church in 1972, but he offers no evidence, save one anecdote of a parish priest preaching on the need for patience from the poor and charity from the rich.[20] This perceived Catholic paternalism, like that of private community groups, is insufficient for the task at hand.

Nicaragua's two traditional political parties also lacked base organizations at the time that Tefel wrote.[21] The political activism of party members, even in those rare cases in which such activism is directed toward the poor, is distinguished by its "petty bourgeois" attitude. Tefel accuses middle-class reformers of "clinging to a romantic notion of the 19th century." He does not explain what he means.[22]

Tefel sees only one way out of this cycle of paternalism, dependency, and internal disintegration. The state must create community centers, in large numbers. These centers must be authorized and funded to tackle the daunting problems of the barrios without having to depend upon middle- and upper-class charity. He rejects even the notion that marginals might form their own organizations. His survey data show a significant drop in what he calls "social solidarity" once newly arrived migrants to Managua attained the first rung of the economic ladder.[23]

Tefel evidently did not consider it significant that many were attaining this rung without government assistance.

Statism as PSC Ideology

Tefel, as influential as he was in the PSC, was not the only Nicaraguan Social Christian that jettisoned the Catholic distrust of state power and instead learned to live with it. The party's first manifesto, consisting of ten basic reforms, shows the extent to which his colleagues also accepted a growing state role in the economic and social life of Nicaraguans.[24]

The manifesto begins innocently enough, demanding the orientation of executive and legislative power toward the common good, and not toward the good of one party, class, or dynasty (point 2). It even adheres to the Catholic goal of decentralized power by calling for the direct election of mayors (point 4).

The reconciliation with the state begins here. Although Nicaraguans should be able to elect their mayors, there should be, according to the manifesto, a "consolidation of municipal autonomy under the coordination and supervision of the State." While it is normal for political manifestoes to contain nuanced language, such an outright contradiction as "autonomy under supervision" is unusual. It shows, at the very least, that the drafters were unaware of the dangers to municipal autonomy that they accepted.

State power should also be increased to advance democratization in Nicaragua. Each person should be compelled to spend part of the year in military service, or some other community action, all under a national development plan (point 5). The goal of this seems to be to achieve a stronger democratic spirit through greater involvement and participation. As such, it is consistent with Catholic social thought. By making it compulsory, however, the PSC highlights its basic lack of trust in Nicaraguans' ability to democratize themselves.

Point 6 of the manifesto deals with education, the one area where Catholic social thought makes its strongest demands for autonomy from state power. In the first sentence, the PSC ascribes to the state the responsibility to improve immediately Nicaraguan education. The government should undertake a permanent literacy campaign, in coordination with land reform.

The drafters then add, incongruously, that none of this increase in state power should interfere with the "primordial right of parents to the education of their children." Again, the most favorable reading of this contradiction is to assume that the PSC did not realize the dangers to parental autonomy that increased state power represented. It is also possible that in their zeal to redirect state power to their own ends, they ignored its potential dangers.

Economic and social matters in the manifesto also call for increased state power. In the area of labor (point 7), the state should provide a family wage and an annual paid vacation. Cities should be planned and social services improved. In the countryside, the PSC favors agrarian reform in which the state guarantees a title to land, and then provides technical assistance, loans, marketing mechanisms, and a system of co-operatives, agrarian leagues, and community groups.

Nicaragua's economy should also be subject to state planning and harmonious with the goal of Central American and Latin American integration. Interestingly, the PSC rejects the one existing mechanism for economic integration, Central America's Common Market. This the manifesto calls capitalistic, and recommends its replacement with a "popular and Social Christian" Common Market.

As we have seen before, the PSC's acceptance of state power, at least at the beginning, was motivated by a desire to use state power to achieve Christian Democratic goals. The party originally favored worker-ownership, then wanted the state to undertake ownership instead.[25] Similarly, they originally favored strengthening autonomous social units, then insisted that the government create such units. The pattern is a familiar one.

As the Sandinista rebellion approached, the PSC had already accepted its commitment to radical theology and to the increase of state power. The PSC was reformist only in its tactics; its goals were revolutionary. When the Sandinistas promised revolutionary tactics to achieve many of the same goals, Nicaraguans perceived the PSC as ineffectual and lacking the courage of its convictions. Under these circumstances, it was unable to present a coherent alternative.

COLLABORATION WITH SANDINISMO

The Broad Opposition Front

For much of the Sandinista Revolution, the PSC did not even try to distinguish itself from the FSLN. On the contrary, its every effort seemed bent at imitating the FSLN and riding its coattails to power. Only after the FSLN became the dominant political opposition did the PSC attempt to break away. By then, it was too late.

Like most democratically oriented Nicaraguans, PSC members were increasingly disgusted with the venal and heavy-handed tactics of Anastasio Somoza as he attempted to retain power in the mid-1970s. In an apparent effort to separate their opposition from that of the radical FSLN, the PSC led a number of other opposition political parties into forming the Broad Opposition Front (FAO) in 1977.

This front was briefly able to stay ahead of the anti-Somoza movement, especially after the death of Pedro Chamorro in January 1978. As we saw in Chapter 6, Nicaragua's bourgeois opposition staged a lock-out over this outrage. Both Chamorro's assassination and the reaction to it by the "moderate" FAO convinced many Nicaraguans, as well as many foreigners, that Somoza's days were numbered.[26]

For a rival political movement, however, the FAO was surprisingly friendly with the FSLN. Some of the leaders of the FAO, including Reinaldo Tefel, the PSC representative, joined with FSLN members to form the Group of Twelve, another purportedly "moderate" opposition bloc.[27] Like the PSC's earlier attempt to penetrate the Conservative Party, the formation of the Twelve had the effect of legitimizing the very political movement that the PSC was trying to supplant. The FSLN was the only member of the Twelve to gain stature from joining.

The FSLN representatives left the Twelve in January 1979, convinced that the United States was working to make the Twelve and the FAO ineffective. After this, the FSLN would become, at least in the minds of Latin American and North American policymakers, the dominant anti-Somoza group. In spite of this chilling sign of the FSLN's desire for political hegemony, PSC president Roger Miranda sought to keep the FAO together by declaring his full support for the now-shrunken FAO on 5 January 1979.[28]

Early Stages of the Sandinista Revolution

I discussed the events of the Sandinista Revolution in Chapter 6. Suffice to say now that the PSC remained a junior partner, bordering on the superfluous, throughout the last months of the Somoza dynasty. Either the PSC failed to realize the challenge of Sandinismo or its members were sufficiently close to the FSLN philosophically that the potential political dominance of this movement did not bother them particularly. There is convincing evidence for the latter conclusion.

Once again, Tefel is the key. Tefel became a firm supporter of Sandinismo, declaring in 1986 that "there can be no true democracy without Socialism, in Nicaragua in particular or in Latin America in general."[29] By that time Tefel had become the minister of social security and welfare. At an earlier stage of the Sandinista regime, Tefel was in charge of peasant relocations, including the relocation of the Native Americans on the Atlantic Coast.[30] For no other abuse of human rights have the Sandinistas been so widely condemned.

In fairness to him, Tefel was not the only PSC member that allowed his enthusiasm for the FSLN to run over. In October 1979, during the first flush of revolutionary victory, Guillermo Cordoba Rivas, PSC representative to the Council of State, stated baldly that the PSC was not frightened by structural changes. "Our political program," he added, "includes [such changes] in their most radical and necessary form."[31] Regarding the Sandinista Front, the PSC must "strengthen its presence inside the revolution and not outside so that our position as assistants and watchmen of the revolutionary process will be felt." That the FSLN desired any assistance or watching was accepted without question.

At the early stage of the Revolution, the Sandinistas seemed to accept the bourgeois opposition as equal partners by allowing two moderate reformers on the five-person junta and a balance of Sandinista and non-Sandinista representatives on the Council of State. The PSC was offered and accepted a seat on this latter body. Significantly, they failed to relinquish it even after the Sandinistas increased membership to ensure themselves a permanent majority.[32] The goal of collaboration remained paramount.

Although the PSC was denied much of a voice in affairs of state, the FSLN did allow the PSC to raise money for them. In the spring of 1980, PSC fund-raising delegations visited Italy, Belgium, France, and Spain, all countries with active Christian Democratic parties. So committed were the PSC delegates to putting the best face on the Sandinista Revolution that PSC president Adan Fletes refused to answer questions about Sandinista human rights violations before a meeting of the Italian DC.[33]

By June, the lobbying bore fruit. The PSC got a commitment of money from various European countries to assist the Nicaraguan Revolution.[34] Just as religious representatives of the new regime had persuaded the U.S. Congress to provide substantial financial aid, the pleas of their fellow Christian Democrats were sufficient to get the Europeans to help too.

These fund-raising efforts continued even after the March 1982 state of emergency did away with most political freedoms in Nicaragua. In June of that year Fletes sent a note to Mariano Rumor, president of the International Christian Democratic Union, asking that a favorable attitude be adopted with regard to financial aid to the Sandinistas. The PSC's disagreement over the state of emergency, he added, should not be a factor in the international body's decision.[35]

The 1984 Electoral Process

The announcement of general elections for president, vice president, and National Assembly in 1984 provided Nicaragua's civil opposition an opportunity to demand full political liberties and the chance to wage a legitimate campaign. Both at home and abroad, the elections were perceived as a test of the Sandinistas' sincerity.

The electoral process in 1984 also tested the opposition. In contrast to their demands during the Somoza years, which usually began with demands for Somoza's resignation and exile, the PSC demands on the

FSLN were surprisingly mild. During meetings to arrange an accord among Nicaragua's political parties, the PSC called for the restoration of civil liberties, nonpartisan neighborhood organizations, and proportional access to state media. They added a vague demand that the Sandinistas reexamine the verdicts of the Sandinista "Popular Tribunals," which dealt out revolutionary justice to "enemies of the revolution."[36]

PSC opposition to the FSLN's political dominance seemed to increase with the formation, with PSC backing, of the Democratic Coordinator in 1981. This group originally consisted of opposition members of the Council of State, but expanded after the 1984 elections were scheduled.[37] PSC president Fletes became the chief spokesman of the coordinator at this time and would remain so until it named Arturo Cruz its presidential candidate.

Under PSC leadership until late in the electoral process, the demands of the coordinator were surprisingly moderate. Only after Cruz's assumption of leadership did the coordinator's demands become more stringent. They included, for example, a demand for dialogue with the armed opposition, repeal of the state of emergency, and the separation of the state from the FSLN party apparatus.[38]

Many observers, including a delegation from the Latin American Studies Association, believe that it was American pressure that made the coordinator include these "killer" demands, purportedly in the hope of depriving the Sandinista election of legitimacy.[39] This begs the question. Why should the PSC-led coordinator have needed outside pressure to demand what are really minimal standards of respect for a political opposition? It is not unreasonable to demand that an electoral campaign exclude state control of the media, undue restrictions on political gatherings, and a commitment that the ruling party prepare to surrender power. A series of political demands based upon Catholic social thought would have been far more stringent.

The PSC membership did gain the coordinator a modicum of international respect that might otherwise have been lacking. Venezuelan President Luis Herrera Campins, of the Social Christian Party, paid for trips by coordinator members to other Latin American countries to represent its ideology and aims.[40] Other than accepting this cosmetic assistance, the PSC did nothing to take advantage of the opportunity that the 1984 electoral process provided. What should have been principled demands for political respect and a change in the basic direction of Sandinismo turned out to be half-hearted pleas for marginal changes, made with an almost apologetic attitude.

PSC Constitutional Influence

There are also Christian Democratic contributions to Sandinista constitutional documents. The first of these was the Sandinista Statute of

Rights and Freedoms, proclaimed in late 1979. The FSLN promised land reform, for example, that restricted private ownership of land to the right to use and to receive the fruits of "something not belonging to oneself."[41] Repeating the pattern of Christian Democratic land reform, Nicaraguans were not given outright title to land. They also could neither sell their plots nor even let them lie fallow.

Nicaragua's 1987 constitution includes various economic and social rights, first demanded by Christian Democrats all over Latin America and now standard features of all totalitarian constitutions.[42] Property, according to this constitution, is "subordinated to the higher interests of the nation and must fulfil a social function." Besides the prohibition against sale of land "titles," the constitution also prohibits transfer or subdivision.[43]

Far from presenting obstacles to these increases in state power, PSC doctrine demands them. This points up the inadequacy of the PSC's perception of government power. As many observers have pointed out, the power given to the ruling party by the Sandinista Constitution is not out of line with other Latin American examples.[44] This is exactly the point. By investing a government with so much power, one becomes dependent on the good will of that government not to abuse it. Catholic social thought, based on the theological position of imperfect man, assumes no such good will and demands limitations on government power. Christian Democrats, perhaps because they are more trusting of man, once he assumes a position in government, do not have the same fear.

The PSC and the Contras

The PSC has always been careful not to question the basic direction of the Sandinista Revolution. This pattern was, until the 1990 elections, repeated with regard to the single most important issue in Nicaragua: the armed rebellion against Sandinista rule, aided and abetted by the United States. The PSC position on what the Sandinistas call the "counterrevolution," and its perpetrators, the "contras," has differed only in degree from the Sandinista position.

Many commentators dismiss the Democratic Coordinator as a creation of the Reagan administration and the political arm of the armed rebellion. The actual situation is more complex. In January 1982, when the contra menace first became visible, Adan Fletes was among the first to condemn the armed revolt. Speaking in Managua, Fletes took issue with Alfonso Robelo, who had said that the path of civic opposition to the FSLN was exhausted. Fletes insisted that there were still numerous private organizations alive and functioning, adding that it was the duty of all Nicaraguans to cooperate in the face of the contra threat.[45]

Later that same year, the Fourth Directorio of the PSC rejected Marxism-Leninism at the same time that it rejected "those who claim that the force of arms is the only path for reestablishing a just peace and attaining democracy in the country."[46] There is scant praise here for the FSLN, but the PSC statement served the Sandinista priority of delegitimizing the contras.

PSC leadership also criticized American aid to the contras when the *New York Times* and *Newsweek* first reported such aid in November 1982. As it had earlier, the PSC took the opportunity to exhort all Nicaraguans to "be motivated to build national unity."[47] In an interview with the Chilean magazine *Cosas* 11 months later, Fletes again denied that his party supported "armed groups operating from abroad."[48] This characterization of the contras itself serves the Sandinistas, since it matches their insistence that the contras are foreign invaders. Fletes still maintained in 1983 that a civic solution was possible.

Less than three months later, Fletes again condemned the contras, and in even stronger terms. Commenting on an ongoing U.S. Senate debate over funding for the rebels, Fletes publicly regretted that such a debate was taking place, saying that the Senate had no business aiding "the counterrevolutionary groups that murder the Nicaraguan people."[49] That the contras themselves were Nicaraguan was irrelevant, both to the PSC and the FSLN.

While the PSC, as part of the Democratic Coordinator, did call for "dialogue" with the rebels in 1984, it continued to oppose U.S. support for them. Erick Ramirez, elected PSC president in September 1985, spoke out against a $100 million aid package for the contras, and denied that he had ever advised the ruling party to talk to them.[50]

Finally, in July 1987, a seminar of seven Nicaraguan opposition parties, including the PSC, convened in Madrid. The concluding document rejected what it called the Sandinista-contra "dialectica" and also rejected any further U.S. aid to the contras.[51] While their final resolutions were filled with criticism for the ruling party, they aligned with them on the crucial question of funding for their armed opposition. In the light of this alignment, the Sandinistas were probably able to bear their criticism with equanimity.

SANDINISTA REPRESSION OF THE PSC

Attitudes before the Triumph

One might think that as a result of their constant efforts, the Sandinistas would accept the PSC as valuable partners in revolution. One might even expect the PSC to be the subject of milder repression than other opposition movements in Nicaragua because of their essential congruence with the Sandinistas on so many important issues. Such has not been the case. The Sandinistas' attitude toward their bourgeois partners in general, and the PSC in particular, has been consistently deprecating and contemptuous.

Carlos Fonseca, a founder of the FSLN and martyr to its cause, wrote about the usefulness of rival philosophies in a 1964 pamphlet: "I welcome the popular essence of the distinct ideologies of Marxism, of Liberalism, of Social Christianity."[52] He added, however, that the welcome extended only as long as they were useful to the triumph of Sandinismo.

Social Christianity could serve this end by promoting "progressive" religious beliefs and redirecting Christians' perception of their doctrine in a revolutionary way. But for the Social Christians, Fonseca said, Christianity might have become a monopoly of conservative and counterrevolutionary forces.[53] In other words, Fonseca was glad that the Social Christians kept the Catholic Church from becoming a genuine alternative to revolutionary action.

As the Sandinistas gained confidence in their own ability to overthrow Somoza, their patience with their Social Christian partners became strained. A Sandinista manifesto, published in 1978, showed how the Sandinistas perceived the role of the PSC. It said: "The anti-somocista struggle has counted on . . . the newly rich people of the PSC who have been begging Somoza for the legalization of their party."[54]

The Sandinistas also dismissed as "bourgeois" PSC organizations, including those that the Sandinistas had used to broaden their own base of support.[55] A faction of the Sandinistas went into the FAO to convince its less radical members of their good intentions. Such a partnership would allow the FSLN to "win material and political support from certain liberal forces," including the PSC.[56]

Jaime Wheelock, one of the nine Sandinista commandantes who wielded real power after the Revolution, used even harsher language than Fonseca to describe the PSC. Both the Democratic Union for Liberation (UDEL) and the FAO, formed under PSC leadership, he said, were efforts to sustain "Somocismo without Somoza." The PSC was part of the bourgeoisie that tried to strip the FSLN of its rightful place as vanguard of the Nicaraguan revolution.[57]

For the Sandinistas, there were two struggles going on in 1979. The first was against Somoza. The second was against the bourgeoisie that aspired to continue its political hegemony, only without Somoza. The FSLN goal was not the "outright destruction" of the dominant classes, but their "autotransformation into the process of national liberation."[58] In this regard, the bourgeois PSC, accepting much of the FSLN's program, if not its tactics, was invaluable.

Nor was the direction of the PSC left entirely to chance. To insure that the Social Christians continued to accept the Liberationist Sandinista line, the FSLN infiltrated its own members into the PSC. This is confirmed by an FSLN official, who said in 1979: "Some comrades in our organization some years ago were working within the PSC. You have to be very careful with the PSC, as it is not a very reliable ally."[59]

The FSLN also used Social Christian factionalism, in part promoted by the FSLN itself, as a reason for dismissing the PSC as a legitimate political opposition. Carlos Tunnerman, then Sandinista ambassador to the U.S., said in 1988 that the civic opposition is insignificant because of its divisions. "There is almost no opposition party," he said, "that does not have one, two or three factions."[60]

After the Triumph: Repression

Once coming to power, the diversity and freedom of expression that the Sandinistas had championed under Somoza gave way to demands for strict adherence to the Sandinista party line. Besides various legal weapons, such as the suspension of the PSC's charter as a political party, the Sandinistas also used less gentle tactics.

After the proclamation of a state of emergency in March 1982, the government used bands of roughs to break up meetings of opposition political parties, as well as of free labor unions and church groups.[61] In 1982, PSC headquarters in Managua was the most frequent target of the "Divine Mobs" (Turbas Divinas), as Interior Minister Tomas Borge calls them.[62] The pretexts for attacks on the PSC are sometimes flimsy. In March 1981, for example, the Sandinista official newspaper *Barricada* attacked the PSC's José Esteban Gonzalez for speaking of the growing unrest among the Nicaraguan Native Americans while he was on a visit to Caracas. Gonzales's view, the paper said, coincided with that of U.S. Secretary of State Alexander Haig.[63] The threat in this juxtaposition is thinly veiled.

In 1985, Erick Ramirez was welcomed to his new job as president of the PSC by being arrested and held for a few days. During his incarceration, he was interrogated by Lenin Cerna of the Interior Ministry. Ramirez was forced to wear prisoner's clothing for that interrogation.[64] It was soon afterward that he so emphatically opposed additional contra aid.

Ramirez, who seems to have taken a more militant posture vis à vis the Sandinistas than his predecessor, has been arrested since then, once for leading a demonstration of the mothers of political prisoners.[65] In 1988 Ramirez was arrested again, this time for leading a march on the National Assembly to demand repeal of that body's media regulation law.[66] The Sandinistas also prevented Ramirez and his fellow PSC leaders from meeting the Christian Democratic president of Guatemala on a 1987 visit to Managua.[67]

The Sandinistas have also linked the PSC with the contras, in spite of the latter's frequent condemnations of the armed rebels. The PSC's new demand, along with the other coordinator members, that the government talk to the contras provided an excuse for this tactic, but it started long before the PSC made that demand. When PSC leader Salomon García was arrested in 1981, Radio Sandino linked him with the contras in León.[68] We have already seen Gonzalez linked with Haig, the contras' creator in the eyes of the Sandinistas, simply for highlighting the plight of the Miskito Indians.

The PSC in the 1990 Election

Somewhat belatedly, the PSC attempted to put more distance between themselves and the Sandinistas. Especially under Erick Ramirez, the party has sought a more openly critical position. In 1986 Ramirez staged a short protest march of 3,000 PSC supporters after a meeting with Christian Democratic representatives from Italy, Belgium, West Germany, Venezuela, Guatemala, Honduras, and Costa Rica. Flamio Piccoli, president of the International Christian Democratic Union, was also present.[69]

Ramirez has also broken a long moratorium on communication with the armed resistance. He met with contra representatives in January 1989 to try to form a united opposition front and to develop a single set of electoral proposals to put before the ruling party.[70] Ramirez had evidently concluded that as long as he was going to be accused of contra links in any event, he may as well try to gain some advantage from them.

As the civil war in Nicaragua intensified in the late 1980s, the Sandinistas began to search for political solutions to the crisis, while maintaining military pressure on the contras. Working with the other Central American presidents, Daniel Ortega agreed to hold internationally sponsored elections in return for a commitment to disband the armed resistance. These elections, held in February 1990, provided the Sandinistas' opposition with an opportunity to reach the voters.

The PSC made the least of this opportunity. For many of Nicaragua's opposition leaders, the central questions of the electoral process were first, whether to take part, and second, whether to run independently or to form an anti-Sandinista coalition. For the PSC the central question seemed to be whether or not the Supreme Electoral Council would recognize non-PSC Christian Democratic parties.

A reading of the Nicaraguan press during the initial phases of the campaign is enlightening. News stories about the various factions of the Christian Democrats (there were three major splits) always identified the party not by title, but by the name of the leader. This shows that personalities had become far more important to the Christian Democrats than ideology. During the one opportunity of the Sandinista era to present a clear ideological alternative, the PSC fought a meaningless and vituperative campaign against other Christian Democrats.

As many of the Sandinistas' opponents coalesced into the UNO (Union Nacional Opositora) party, the PSC faced the choice of joining or running on their own. They eventually decided on the latter. This was not because they had any serious disagreements with the UNO leadership. Indeed, the PSC was quite critical of the FSLN during the campaign. Rather, the PSC remained alone for surprisingly parochial reasons, given the stakes involved.

While the PSC was part of the Democratic Coordinating Board, UNO's precursor, they quit when the board decided to include the Social Christian Democratic Party under Agustin Jarquin. Erick Ramirez, head of the PSC, later stated that the PSC would participate in the UNO coalition only if he were included on the ticket with Violeta Chamorro.[71] It is also possible that the PSC ran alone to atone for its 1960s and 1970s collaboration.[72] If this is the case, it is odd that the PSC should reject collaboration at the one point when it would have led them to political power.

The UNO partners, for their part, accused the PSC of de facto collaboration with the Sandinistas. Arguing that the opposition's only chance for victory lay in uniting against the ruling party, they concluded that the PSC's independence would take votes from UNO and make an FSLN victory more likely. Perhaps the PSC was unable to escape its history; even the act of intransigence appears collaborationist.

The PSC ran a bad third in 1990, receiving less than 1 percent of the presidential vote and less than 2 percent of the Assembly vote. The party did reasonably well only along the North Atlantic coast, due to a short-lived collaboration with a Miskito Indian organization. They have one deputy in the National Assembly.

CONCLUSION

The elections showed signs of a wide break with the ruling party, although even here, the PSC still did not directly challenge the basic direction of the FSLN. More significant is the PSC's developing attitude toward the Catholic hierarchy. As Sandinista repression grew worse, the PSC sought to ally itself more closely with the bishops.

During his interrogation by Cerna, for example, Ramirez told his captors that his party identified itself with the Catholic Church and supported Cardinal Miguel Obando y Bravo. In October 1988, the PSC again expressed its "full solidarity with Obando y Bravo and with the Catholic Church."[73] Ironically, the PSC is moving closer to the Church at the same time that the Nicaraguan hierarchy is rejecting the Social Christian model of political activism and rediscovering the principles of Catholic social thought. This process will be the subject of Chapter 10.

NOTES

1. Enrique Alvarado Martinez, *El Pensamiento Politico Nicaraguense* (Managua: Artes Graficas, 1968), 54.

2. Thomas W. Walker, *The Christian Democratic Movement in Nicaragua* (Tucson, University of Arizona Press, 1970), 31-33.

3. John A. Booth, *The End and the Beginning: The Nicaraguan Revolution* (Boulder, CO: Westview Press, 1985), 107.

4. Edward J. Williams, *Latin American Christian Democratic Parties* (Knoxville: University of Tennessee Press, 1967), 20.

5. Booth, *End and the Beginning*, 107.

6. Ibid., 100.

7. Walker, *Christian Democratic Movement*, 41.

8. Booth, *End and the Beginning*, 107.

9. Jerome Nilssen, "Admitting to Ambivalence about the Nicaraguan Revolution," *Christian Century* (17 December 1986): 1158.

10. Alvarado, *Pensamiento*, 55.

11. Walker, *Christian Democratic Movement*, 20.

12. Thomas W. Walker, ed., *Nicaragua in Revolution* (New York: Praeger Publishers, 1982), 52.

13. U.S. Congress, Senate, Committee on the Judiciary, Subcommittee on Security and Terrorism, *Marxism and Revolutionary Christianity in Central America*, 98th Congress, 1st session, October 18–19, 1983, 118-19.

14. Thomas W. Walker, *Nicaragua: The Land of Sandino*, 2d ed. (Boulder, CO: Westview Press, 1986), 102.

15. Senate Subcommittee on Security, *Marxism and Revolutionary Christianity*, 119.

16. Walker, *Christian Democratic Movement*, 48.

17. Reinaldo Antonio Tefel, *El Infierno de los Pobres: Diagnostico Sociologico de los Barrios Marginales de Managua* (Managua: Ediciones el Pez y el Serpiente, 1972), 17.

18. Ibid., 156.

19. Ibid., 168.

20. Ibid., 136.

21. Ibid., 159.

22. Ibid., 167.

23. Ibid., 130.

24. Reprinted as an appendix in Alvarado, *Pensamiento*.

25. Walker, *Christian Democratic Movement*, 21.

26. Henri Weber, *The Sandinist Revolution* (London: Verso Editions, 1981), 41.

27. Ibid., 43.

28. Panama City, ACAN, 0242 GMT, 5 January 1979 (*Foreign Broadcast Information Service*, hereinafter FBIS, 8 January 1979, P14).

29. Nilssen, "Admitting to Ambivalence," 1158.

30. Humberto Belli, *Breaking Faith: The Sandinista Revolution and Its Impact on Freedom and Christian Faith in Nicaragua* (Westchester, IL: Crossway Books, 1985), 128.

31. Managua, *La Prensa*, 4 October 1979, 2 (FBIS 12 October 1979, P9–10).

32. George Black, *Triumph of the People: The Sandinista Revolution in Nicaragua* (London: Zed Press, 1981), 244.

33. Managua, *La Prensa*, 30 March 1980, 4 (FBIS 4 April 1980, P12).

34. Radio Mundial, 1200 GMT, 23 June 1980 (FBIS 26 June 1980, P22).

35. Radio Sandino, 1200 GMT, 21 June 1982 (FBIS 23 June 1982, P9–10).

36. José Luis Coraggio, *Nicaragua: Revolución y Democracia* (Mexico City, DF, Editorial Linea, 1985), 116-19.

37. Booth, *End and the Beginning*, 194.

38. Peter Rosset and John Vandermeer, *Nicaragua: Unfinished Revolution* (New York: Grove Press, 1986), 68.

39. Ibid., 106.

40. Joseph E. Cassidy, "Voices of the Opposition: Perspectives on Nicaragua-II," *Commonweal* (22 April 1983): 242.

41. *Time* (17 October 1983): 37.

42. Andrew Reding, "Nicaragua's New Constitution," *World Policy Journal*, 4, 2 (Spring 1987): 263.

43. Ibid., 270-71.

44. Ibid., 271.

45. Radio Sandino, 1200 GMT, 21 June 1982 (FBIS 23 June 1982).

46. ACAN, 2338 GMT, 26 October 1982 (FBIS 29 October 1982, P7–8).

47. ACAN, 2206 GMT, 4 November 1982 (FBIS 9 November 1982, P20).

48. Santiago, *Cosas*, 6 October 1983, 47 (FBIS 14 October 1983, P36–38).

49. Radio Sandino, 1200 GMT, 7 January 1984 (FBIS 9 January 1984, P15).

50. Radio Sandino, 1200 GMT, 8 March 1986 (FBIS 13 March 1986, P12).

51. Madrid, EFE 2038 GMT, 24 July 1987 (FBIS 31 July 1987, I1–2).

52. Carlos Fonseca Amador, *Obras*, vol. 1 (Managua: Editorial Nueva Nicaragua, 1982), 235-36.

53. Ibid.

54. Quoted in Anastasio Somoza and Jack Cox, *Nicaragua Betrayed* (Boston: Western Islands Publishers, 1980), 161.

55. Belli, *Breaking Faith*, 15.

56. Weber, *The Sandinist Rovolution*, 55.

57. "Speeches by Sandinista Leaders," in *Nicaragua: The Sandinista People's Revolution* (New York: Pathfinder Press, 1985), 131.

58. Coraggio, *Revolución y Democracia*, 36-37.

59. Black, *Triumph of the People*, 139.

60. Radio Sandino, 1930 GMT, 19 December 1988 (FBIS 21 December 1988, 34-35) .

61. *Time* (17 October 1983).

62. Cassidy, "Voices of the Opposition," 242.

63. *Barricada*, 21 March 1981, 12 (FBIS 7 April 1981, P17).

64. ACAN, 048 GMT, 21 October 1985 (FBIS 22 October 1985, P17–18).

65. ACAN, 1423 GMT, 23 January 1987 (FBIS 27 January 1987, P1).

66. Paris, AFP 1840 GMT, 2 June 1988 (FBIS 9 June 1988, 12).

67. ACAN, 1837 GMT, 29 March 1987 (FBIS 1 April 1987, P16).

68. Managua, Radio Corporacion, 2300 GMT, 1 June 1981 (FBIS 4 June 1981, P19).

69. San José, Radio Reloj, 1200 GMT, 29 September 1986 (FBIS 1 October 1986, P3).

70. Radio Corporacion, 0400 GMT, 10 January 1989 (FBIS 11 January 1989, 35-36).

71. *Barricada*, 14 August 1989, 1 (FBIS 17 August 1989, 15-16).

72. See Latin American Studies Association Commission to Observe the 1990 Nicaraguan Election, *Electoral Democracy Under International Pressure* (Pittsburgh: LASA, 1990), 17-18.

73. Radio Noticias, 1130 GMT, 19 October 1988 (FBIS 20 October 1988, 17).

9

Liberation Theology in Venezuela: Catholic Social Thought Dominant

Liberation Theology is almost nonexistent in Venezuela. Deane William Ferm's book on the subject mentions only two authors of any significance from Venezuela and neither of these two are significant contributors to the movement. They are not even mentioned in a number of texts on Liberation Theology.

Even if Venezuelan Liberation Theology boasted more prestigious figures, I think that their influence in Venezuela would still be slight. As this chapter will show, the Venezuelan Bishops' Conference, unlike many of its counterparts in Latin America, has taken the offensive against Liberation Theology, forestalling its rise. Unlike Christian Democrats in much of Latin America, the Venezuelan bishops have not shorn themselves of the intellectual bases for principled opposition to Marxism. Significantly, they base their opposition to Liberation Theology on Catholic social thought, as interpreted by the Holy See.

A WEAK MOVEMENT

The major thinkers of Liberation Theology in Venezuela are Antonio Pérez Esclarin and Otto Maduro. Pérez Esclarin is best known for his contention that Christianity would benefit from a healthy dose of atheism. Atheism for him was preferable to idolatry, the sin that Pérez Esclarin asserted the modern Catholic Church was committing.

The "Christian" world, Pérez Esclarin stated, had become the most inhuman and exploitative part of the world. The reason for this is the

Christian embrace of capitalism.[1] Religion in the modern world has become, for many, a cultural act only, with the "believers" more concerned with appearances than with true faith. Genuine faith, Pérez Esclarin continued, consisted of acting to liberate the downtrodden. As examples, he suggested hungry Indians, lowly proletarians, alienated and lonely bureaucrats, and dedicated revolutionaries.

These unfortunates are left out by the official Church, which Pérez Esclarin described as leading "a grimy existence, often allied to oppressive power structures." He deplored the supposed openness of the Church to all classes, which leads to "Christians with Cadillacs receiv[ing] the same fraternal communion as hungry, barefooted Christians do."

Humanistic atheism, he wrote, would "tend to emphasize faith in human beings rather than the denial of God." Atheism, for its part, worships the "full humanity" of human beings, and can serve to revitalize and purify Christian faith, according to Pérez Esclarin. It points the way to "justice in practice," presumably by allowing more extreme actions in the cause of "liberation" than would be permitted to someone trying to follow the strictures of traditional Christianity. Faithful to the Marxist background of Liberation Theology, Pérez Esclarin believed that only those who act on behalf of Liberation, whether Christians or atheists, are with God. Pérez Esclarin took his own advice, noting in a "Personal Epilogue" that he hurriedly finished writing the book and left academe to "live out its contents with the oppressed."

The other Venezuelan liberationist of prominence is Otto Maduro. Unlike many liberationists, Maduro is both an open and an avowed Marxist. His works express a determination to reinterpret Marx in a Latin American context. An essential part of that context is the Catholic Church. Thus, any social or political philosophy that attempts to respond to the Latin American reality must take Catholicism into account.[2]

Maduro defined religion in a sociological manner that is quite compatible with the inductive reasoning and economic determinism of Karl Marx. Religion, for Maduro, is a "structure of discourse and practices common to a social group and referred to some forces which believers consider as foregoing and superior to their natural and social being, before which believers express feeling a certain dependence and consider themselves obliged to maintain a certain behavior with their kind."

Maduro believed, inductively, that the "social function of a religion will vary according to the needs of a particular society."[3] Each Latin American country must develop a "Latin American praxis of the socialist self-liberation of the oppressed." Thus for Maduro, it seems that the only fixed rule is that there are no fixed rules. Praxis, theology, tactics, all seem to depend upon circumstances. Perhaps for this reason, his Venezuelan-based theology has not spread beyond Venezuela.

Father Francis Wuytack of Louvain University in Belgium attempted to mix religion and politics in the Caracas slums in the 1960s, only to be expelled from the country, by the Christian Democrats, in 1970. Eighty-eight Caracas priests and nuns signed a petition of support and demonstrated against his expulsion. The words of Wuytack's supporters are spoken in the language of Liberation Theology. "For the people," the petition read, "the pretty words of Medellín and [Pope] Paul VI are not enough."[4] The Venezuelan hierarchy did nothing to prevent his departure.

One of the most visible signs of a flourishing Liberationist movement is a large number of Christian Base Communities, or CEBs. Even a sympathetic observer admits that Venezuela has only a few CEBs, which he describes as "Venezuela's only echo of Medellín, of Puebla, of Liberation Theology."[5] Another author makes only passing reference to CEBs founded in Venezuela by U.S. Father Ralph Rogowski.[6]

Among the hierarchy, sympathy to Liberationist tenets is more difficult to find. A 1968 episcopal document comes close to endorsing Pierre Teilhard deChardin's belief in Christian evolutionary progress to the this-worldly perfection of the Omega point.[7] As we will see later, however, the remainder of that document disputes Liberation Theology almost point for point.

Other than this, the only signs of leftist, to say nothing of radical, thought among senior Venezuelan clerics are: first, a 1981 statement by Caracas bishop José Rincon Bonilla that Venezuela should "review" its policy of aiding the Christian Democratic government of El Salvador, pending investigation of the "death squads";[8] second, a 1983 statement by Maracaibo bishop Domingo Roa that the Church/state situation in Nicaragua was "improving."[9]

It might be argued that the fact that Venezuela is a democracy, unlike many other Latin American countries until very recently, explains the dearth of liberationists' success. Yet Colombia and Chile have long traditions of democratic rule, and a large and influential Liberationist clergy. In addition, Venezuelan radical religious, and their external supporters, dispute that Venezuela is a genuine democracy.[10]

BACKGROUND OF THE VENEZUELAN HIERARCHY

In spite of its comparative wealth, Venezuela has more in common with its Latin American neighbors than it has in contrast. It has a wide gulf between rich and poor, an alienated intellectual class, slums around the capital and other large cities, and serious rural poverty. None of these provide a variable creditable with the prevention of a strong Liberationist movement. So why does Venezuela lack Liberation Theology? The answer lies with the hierarchy. In their history and present attitudes, the Venezuelan Episcopal Conference has preempted Liberation Theology, not through the Christian Democratic strategy of half-hearted imitation, but by adhering more closely than any other Latin American Church to the teachings of traditional Catholic social thought. The roots of this fidelity lie in the history of Catholicism in Venezuela.

The Venezuelan Church has never been allowed to become a dominant force in domestic politics, even during colonial times. Since independence, various influences have combined to prevent the Venezuelan Church from consolidating an independent base of political power. The revolutionary government of Gran Colombia, which consisted of what is now Venezuela, Colombia, and Ecuador, claimed extensive powers over the Church after independence in 1824. Gran Colombia's Congress could create new dioceses, call episcopal synods, grant or refuse permission for new monasteries, nominate new bishops, and regulate tithing.[11]

In the successor state of Venezuela, the anti-Bolivarian conservative oligarchy also failed to offer the Church any special protection or privilege in the new constitution. In fact, several bishops were exiled from Venezuela for refusing to take a required oath of fealty to the government; no exemption for clergy existed.[12]

When the liberals replaced the conservatives in the 1830s, outright persecution replaced the hands-off approach. Religious feast days were suppressed in 1837, and all monasteries for men were closed. Convents for women were outlawed sometime later. To soften this repression, the liberals offered official protection and government funding to what remained of the Church.[13] This was a transparent attempt to render Catholicism a strictly private matter and, at the same time, subordinate an impotent Church to secular control.

In 1862, Venezuela was ready to sign a concordat with Rome. The Church, for its part, demanded a recognition of its rights to autonomy and independence, especially in the areas of education and proselytization, and to economic independence through government incomes, the amount of which would be set in the concordat and not subject to unilateral change. The Venezuelan government retained the right to nominate bishops and to approve the creation of new dioceses.[14]

This concordat would never come into effect, however. Soon after its signing, dictator José Antonio Paez was overthrown, and in 1872, Guzman Blanco attempted to eliminate ecclesiastical independence. Even the residual Church rights of registering births and marriages disappeared. Guzman also tried to allow priests to marry, presumably to increase their dependence on government income.

The Venezuelan Church would remain impecunious until the 1930s. Until the 1950s, the Venezuelan Church was "weak and complacent," with no social activism except encouraging private works of charity. At the same time, however, the Church used the benign neglect of the Juan Vicente Gómez and Marcos Pérez Jiménez dictatorships to build a "vigorous system of elite Catholic schools."[15]

This school system would provide for the Church's reentry into Venezuelan politics, albeit an involuntary one. During the 1945 to 1948 Triennio, the Church became embroiled in a bitter dispute with Acción Democratica (AD) over the question of government regulation of the Catholic schools. One expert on the Venezuelan Church sees this conflict as an attempt by the Venezuelan Church to retain its secure, if minor, position of earlier years.[16] As we saw in Chapter 7, however, this question reflected the deeper determination of the Venezuelan Church to maintain its independence, at the very time that the Christian Democrats were sacrificing their independence to AD.

THE VENEZUELAN HIERARCHY AND CATHOLIC SOCIAL THOUGHT

Withdrawal from Politics

Since the restoration of democratic rule in Venezuela in 1958, and the coincident end of AD's attempt to severely restrict Church independence, Venezuela's Catholic hierarchy has played a marginal role in the everyday politics of the nation. It is during this modern period that the close adherence of the Venezuelan Church to Catholic social thought is most obvious. Indeed, the fact that it has not played a larger political role is part of this adherence. According to Catholic social thought, the political role of the Church should be limited to protecting its own independence and condemning governmental violations of the Natural Law.

Also evident from the statements and actions of the Venezuelan Church is a determination to follow the lead of the Vatican, and especially Pope John Paul II, in addressing social questions in general and Liberation Theology in particular. On the question of ecclesiastical involvement in politics, for example, John Paul II has said that priests are "pastors, not politicians."[17] The Venezuelan Church has imitated this attitude.

As we have seen, the Venezuelan Church has never had to defend what other Latin American Churches would consider their traditional privileges. Thus, the Venezuelan Church was freed from the role of status quo defender.[18] It could look at Venezuela's frequent changes in government with equanimity, so long as its independence was respected.[19] With the appearance of the Christian Democratic Copei, which promised to protect the Church from the more serious assaults of AD, the Church could afford to withdraw from politics even more.[20] Activism, for many Venezuelan churchmen, would merely be a revival of cleri-calism, which would require a permanent entry into a polarized Church/anti-Church political situation.[21]

In short, the Venezuelan Church was a Thomistic Church, uninter-ested in the rough and tumble of politics and able to accommodate itself to almost any regime. As such, the Venezuelan Church is very different from the Bourbonic Churches of much of Latin America, where the hierarchy was tied so closely to a ruling elite that it saw its destiny intimately connected to the success of that elite. Such "kept" Churches are the prime targets of the Liberationists.

Venezuelan Bishop Ovidio Pérez Morales, whom Daniel Levine de-scribes as one of the more "liberal" clerics, stated his opposition to exercising political power in an interview with Daniel Levine. He said: "Efforts in the struggle for power can compromise the genuineness of [a bishop's] witness, which, although it might seem less effective polit-ically, may nevertheless be more in accord with the attitude of service and poverty of the Gospel."[22]

Yet the Church cannot withdraw from politics altogether, since it has a "prophetic" mission. This mission, which requires the Church to speak out against violations of the Natural Law, leads almost inevitably to political conflict. Thus, as the 1970s and 1980s progressed, and Vene-zuela's state-run oil company failed to eliminate poverty and injustice, the Church spoke more frequently on the need for social justice. Its attitude, however, remains very cautious.

Church as a Source of Unity

This reluctance to enter the partisan political arena is born of Catholic political practice. Catholic clerics believe that they have a responsibility to make the Church act as a source of unity for society. By this Catholics mean that anyone in society is eligible for membership in the Church and for eternal salvation through its mission. In a society sharply divided by politics or economics, this role is even more important. Opponents of a political regime, for example, should not feel that the Church has so obviously and irrevocably taken sides that the Sacraments are no longer open to them.

The Vatican views support for some theologies of Liberation as par-tisan political activity and condemns it. In 1984, Cardinal John Ratzinger, head of the Vatican Sacred Congregation for the Faith, wrote what re-mains the Church's most authoritative response to Liberation Theology. According to Ratzinger, the selective offering of Christian love, based on class, which is what the Liberationists demand, means that love is withheld from certain classes. Such an exclusion, according to Ratzinger, is a denial of true Christian love and ignores Christ's command to love one's enemies.[23]

The Venezuelan bishops repeat this emphasis on the Church as a focal point of unity.[24] Archbishop Luis Eduardo Henriquez told the delegates at Medellín: "The Church is not a closed group, and tends toward the universal communication of her program, ever seeking to become incarnate in the world and its culture."[25] Bishop Pérez Morales repeated this attitude when he wrote that the Church cannot be Marxist or anti-Marxist. Its ministry must be for everyone.[26]

The Role of the Laity

Also related to the Venezuelan Church's reluctance to enter politics is the traditional belief that such worldly concerns are the province of the laity. The Vatican has devoted a great deal of attention to the role of the laity in recent years, reaffirming its traditional stance.[27]

In Venezuela, the Church is even uncomfortable with its related groups, such as Catholic Action, taking increasingly political stands, to the detriment of their primarily religious function.[28] For the bishops, laypeople have the primary responsibility for direct social and political action. The role of the Church is to inspire such direct action, and perhaps define what sorts of actions are acceptable. Venezuelan clerics insist that while their role of "activation" of the laity is appropriate, "activism" is out of bounds.[29]

Criticism of Capitalism

Limiting its role to activation of the laity does not mean that the Church must keep silent on political or social issues, however. Just as the papal authors of Catholic social thought were critical of capitalism, so too the Venezuelan Episcopal conference expresses its skepticism about this economic and social system. Its criticism of capitalism is more significant in its emphases and direction, however, than in its mere existence. It shows another aspect of the Venezuelan commitment to Catholic social thought.

Ratzinger says that the crushing poverty of the Third World is intolerable, and that the shocking national and international inequalities of wealth are not acceptable. He blames these problems, significantly, on a lack of equity and solidarity in international transactions.[30] Ratzinger even accepts the argument that structures that conceal poverty are, themselves, forms of violence.[31]

The Venezuelan Church takes its lead from Rome. The episcopal Commission on Justice and Peace published a lengthy, paragraph by paragraph study of Pope Paul VI's encyclical *Populorum Progressio* in 1968.

In that study the commission quoted the Medellín final document with approval, saying that capitalism has failed to feed the world or to distribute goods. The reason for these failures is the capitalist system of values.[32]

Yet the criticism of capitalism in this document is specific. The authors emphasize that raising money and investing it are not aspects of capitalism that deserve condemnation. Rather, making profit the prime mover of economic relationships and subordinating man to profit is what they criticize.[33]

In another context, the Venezuelan bishops make it clear that they criticize capitalism not in itself but for its side effects, especially consumerism and the development of unhealthy competition for private gain.[34] More specifically, Pérez Morales's 1976 Christmas message deplored oil-rich Venezuela's "delirium of spendthrift wealth." Capitalism was not the problem, but rather the "spreading philosophy of easy money, social climbing and opportunism."[35]

Capitalism is not sinful per se, but it can be misused. The Justice and Peace commission, for example, says that there are many acceptable systems of private property. What makes a system acceptable is its placing of things at the service of man, rather than the other way around.[36] Private property as a social institution can do either. Individuals determine whether or not to sin. The Marxists, the commission says, are wrong; structures are not inherently good or bad.

Unproductive speculation and keeping money outside the country in foreign bank accounts are two sins that property owners might commit.[37] People in the Third World, for their part, might sin by rejecting opportunities to learn from the First World. The First World, for its part, sins by keeping tariff walls too high for Third World products to cross. Such selfishness hurts agricultural sectors hardest.[38]

Listing these sins is significant not only because it implies that some capitalistic activities are moral, but also because it shows that emphasis that the commission placed on productive economic activity directed toward national economic independence. Such emphasis on economic improvements that actually benefit people in the short term is completely absent from Liberation Theology. In the case of tariffs, the commission actually calls for more capitalism, and less regulation.

Primacy of Individual Morality

If capitalism has an inherent flaw, it is that it tempts people to put their own immediate, private economic gain above higher concerns. Like any other temptation, however, this one can be resisted. In fact, the faithful must resist the temptation; if they do not, then the sin is theirs and not the capitalist system's. For Catholics, economic systems are incapable of sin.

As Paul VI wrote in *Populorum Progressio*, "If the functioning of an economic system imperils human dignity, that system is unjust." This statement implies that systems themselves are neutral; how they are applied by individuals is important. Cardinal Ratzinger states this conclusion even more baldly, writing that all forms of slavery are rooted in the slavery of sin.[39] True Liberation, therefore, will be marked by the gift of the Holy Spirit and the conversion of individual hearts. Citing the Sermon on the Mount, Ratzinger insists that conversion and renewal must occur in the depths of individuals.[40]

Echoing this statement, a Venezuelan bishop told Daniel Levine: "Real liberation begins with one's own self. Changing [social and economic] structures is not so easy. But that each of us manages to liberate himself from his egoism, his envy, his immorality, that *is* possible and must be done."[41]

This emphasis on individual guilt or innocence protects the Venezuelan bishops from the facile group or class redemption or condemnation that marks Liberation Theology. It also avoids the Marxist inductive method of determining moral principles. For both Marxists and Liberationists, truth is to be found in the needs that each social situation requires. This can only be determined by studying specific sets of circumstances.

Catholics, on the other hand, must begin with moral principles, whose applicability extends to all places and circumstances, and proceed to social actions consistent with these moral principles. By refusing to indict whole classes en masse, the Venezuelan bishops retain a clear and compelling intellectual and spiritual basis for resisting the easy solutions of Liberation Theology.

Democracy

Because individual morality, and individuals themselves, are important, the Venezuelan bishops have developed, since the Pérez Jiménez dictatorship, a strong commitment to democracy. The Church was instrumental in deposing Pérez Jiménez, despite the statement of Copei's Rafael Caldera to the *New York Times* in late 1957: "It is impossible that the Church will come out against Pérez Jiménez."[42]

Nevertheless, on 1 May 1957, the Church did just that. A pastoral letter from Monsignor Rafael Arias, prelate of Venezuela, stated the Church's outright opposition to any attempt by Pérez Jiménez to maintain himself in power.[43] The letter also emphasized that Venezuela's economic problems were the cause for the Church's opposition. In good Thomistic style, Arias measured the conditions in Venezuela against acceptable moral values and found the current conditions wanting. An immense mass of Venezuelans, he said, "are living in conditions that cannot be called human." Unemployment, low wages, the lack of a family wage, and general abuse of the working class stripped the Pérez Jiménez dictatorship of its legitimacy.[44]

Venezuelan clerics constantly repeated the substance of the letter in sermons, and the Catholic Labor Youth organization publicized it as well.[45] Soon after its publication, Monsignor Arias was called into the interior minister's office and ordered to explain this "unfriendly act." He not only refused an explanation, but also refused to refrain from future criticism.

After the pastoral letter, Father José Hernandez Chapellin, editor of *La Religion*, published critical editorials and started a clandestine collaboration with the civilian opposition.[46] Father Hernandez also allowed the opposition use of the cathedral press, which, among other things, allowed opponents of the regime to spread the word about a general strike in January 1958.[47] It was this strike that sparked Pérez Jiménez's departure. Less than one month later, the bishops published a letter in which they praised democracy as the system of government "best adapted to human nature itself."[48]

Here again, the Venezuelan Church acted in concert with the Vatican. When Copei's Caldera was finally arrested by Pérez Jiménez in January 1957, the Vatican embassy in Caracas offered him refuge and negotiated a deal through which he could go into exile. It was during this Vatican-sponsored exile that he met in New York with Romulo Betancourt of AD and the two made their fateful decision to collaborate.

The weakness of the Pérez Jiménez dictatorship, the availability of lay actors such as Caldera and Betancourt, the support from the Vatican, and the almost universal revilement of Pérez Jiménez by late 1957 all had an effect on the Church's willingness to involve itself in the political dispute.

What is more significant, however, is that this involvement very carefully adhered to the traditional Catholic rules for revolutionary activity. The most important of these are significant violations of the Natural Law and the requirement that any activity directed toward the overthrow of a government must have a reasonable chance for success. Thus even the Venezuelan Church's reluctance to challenge Pérez Jiménez before the factors were in place to see him peacefully out of power is an expression of commitment to Catholic social thought.

Independent Social Institutions

To many, the Church's support for the military coup in 1948 and the democratic coup in 1958 represents inconsistency. Seen from the vantage point of Catholic social thought, however, the two attitudes are compatible. By the end of the Triennio, especially after Betancourt tried to diminish the independence of private schools, the Church could reasonably see the democratic movement of Betancourt as a threat to independent social institutions and embrace a military that promised respect for those institutions. By 1958, it was the military that threatened societal independence and the Copei-AD-URD coalition that seemed best suited to protect it.

The key is the Church's commitment to private institutions, independent of government, that serve as a buffer between helpless individuals and the power of the state. Such institutions are absolutely necessary to the maintenance of freedom and human dignity, according to Catholic social thought. The Venezuelan Church shares this preoccupation with the promotion of independent institutions.

The 1957 May Day letter, for example, was primarily a reflection on the rights of workers and the responsibility of the Catholic faithful to protect these rights.[49] This is reminiscent of Pope Leo XIII's emphasis in *Rerum Novarum*. Most important among the rights of workers is their right to organize independent and freely chosen labor unions.[50]

It was the apparent determination of Pérez Jiménez to prevent workers from exercising these rights that led to the Church's opposition. By threatening the right to unionize, Pérez Jiménez was threatening liberty and the Church decided that it had to take a stand.[51] Besides criticizing Pérez Jiménez, the Church hierarchy also sponsored Catholic Workers Circles, which trained union leaders in Catholic doctrine, public speaking, and organization.

Significantly, the Church was interested in setting up a union system which would be independent of government at the same time that the Christian Democrats were rushing to force government to sponsor and subsidize their unions. While Caldera followed the path of expediency on this issue, the Church followed the path of principle. Not surprisingly, the graduates of the Catholic Social Circles shunned the Copei union federation.[52]

Labor unions were not the only protected societal groups, however. Pérez Morales wrote that the family was the fundamental unit of society, and the one in need of greatest protection from government power.[53] Similarly, free and autonomous Catholic schools are also necessary to protect society from the state's "ideological power."[54] The defense of certain types of private property is part of this general defense of societal and individual autonomy as well. Property, as a source of livelihood outside of state control, is an integral part of liberty, according to Catholic social thought.[55]

Because it favors the extension of property rights to all classes, the Venezuelan Justice and Peace Commission rejects Christian Democratic-style land reform and favors colonization programs that would put new land under cultivation. Significantly, the commission favors using private initiative to get such colonization programs started. For example, the state could raise taxes on unused land, making it uneconomic and providing incentive to cultivate, rather than simply coercing landowners through the use of government confiscation.[56]

Once land is colonized, free collectives are a concrete method of reintroducing communal property rights. For a collective to be a moral enterprise, it must be made up of a group of individuals who freely decide to possess and use the land in common. Ceding the land reform initiative to the state, the commission warns, means ceding land ownership to the state as well. This endangers the liberty of groups and of individuals.[57]

Expropriation of land should occur, according to the Venezuelan bishops, only under specific circumstances. If land has been "abandoned" by its owners, or if the concentration of land in too few hands has demonstrably produced misery in the population, or unduly prejudiced national policy, then there is a legitimate cause for expropriation.[58]

In general, state intervention should consist of incentives more often than coercion, and also should be directed toward the strengthening of intermediate organizations to a point where state intervention is no longer necessary.[59] For the Venezuelan Catholic Church, in contrast to both the Liberationists and the Christian Democrats, removing the state from society is as important as inserting it.

Statism

Thus, the Venezuelan Church, unlike the Christian Democrats, would regard expansion of state power with fear and loathing, in all cases. This closely follows the strictures of Catholic social thought, especially in its earlier expressions. In fact, the Venezuelan Church at times seems more fearful of state power than either John XXIII or Paul VI. While *Populorum Progressio* exhorted Catholics to reject liberalism and err on the side of too much state intervention, the Commission on Justice and Peace adds that the "invisible hand" of Adam Smith must be replaced by the "equally invisible" hand of the state.[60]

For the state to assume greater power in the economic sphere is not necessarily good, according to the commission. The state can be inhuman and it can ignore man's spiritual nature. More important, the state is much stronger than any private group.[61] State action, if it must exist, must be in harmony with the continued existence of private enterprise and intermediate associations. Otherwise, the danger of totalitarianism looms. While the state can coerce its own employees, it should play an indicative, and not an imperative, role with regard to private citizens.[62]

The Christian Democratic solution of "State capitalism" is, for the commission, dangerous.

This insistence on societal pluralism is directly related to the traditional Catholic view of man. To orthodox Catholics, man is inherently drawn to God, thanks to Christ's redemptive sacrifice, but is still imperfect. As such, any governmental structure he creates will be imperfect. Political power, wielded by weak imperfect men, is a dangerous thing. While political power cannot be destroyed, for man cannot live in anarchy, it must be checked, divided, and limited. Man's temptation to abuse power is great; the opportunities to do so must be small.

Cooperation With Marxism

Liberation Theology also runs up against the Venezuelan Catholic Church's determination not to collaborate with communism in any way, per the instructions of Pius XI. Marxism and Christianity are incompatible, according to Ratzinger, because Marxists put their ideology first and the truth second. It is "illusory and dangerous," he continues, to ignore the radical bonds of various strands of Marxist thought. While he acknowledges that Marx has many interpreters, insofar as all of these interpreters are Marxists, they all have Marxist errors in common.[63]

Thus, the Catholic Church not only opposes Marxist collaboration, but it knows why it is opposing it. From Leo XIII to John Paul II, the Church has offered coherent reasons for its opposition, and not mere paranoia or prejudice. In his interviews with Venezuelan bishops, Levine learned that their reluctance to work with Marxism is part of their larger determination to avoid identification with any particular political direction or party. Such identification would make non-Marxists reluctant to come to them for the Sacraments or for pastoral guidance.[64]

Venezuelan bishops with more pastoral experience are more willing than some of their colleagues to enter a dialogue with Marxists, which is consistent with their image of the Church as a source of unity.[65] Yet they approach such dialogue skeptical that any good will come from it. They also fear being used by the Marxists. Significantly, the more highly educated bishops are the most likely to reject both dialogue and collaboration with Marxists.[66] All of Venezuela's "highly educated" bishops studied at the Vatican, and their exposure to Vatican thought on Marxism is undoubtedly a factor.

The attempt by Venezuelan communists to violently overthrow the newly democratic government in 1963 cost them dearly in popular support. This lack of support, and a general fear of communism, is present in the hierarchy as well. Cardinal José Humberto Quintero predicted in a 1962 pastoral letter that communists had infiltrated Venezuelan society at all levels and were resorting to violence to touch off a civil war.[67]

Quintero expressed a knowledgeable criticism of communist guerrilla warfare when he said in that letter: "It is impossible that a doctrine be considered rational and beneficial which instead of working for betterment of needy classes aggravates the situation because it destroys sources of employment and hinders the establishment of new ones by implanting in the minds of potential investors and employees distrust, fear and discouragement."[68] This brief statement completely undercuts the legitimacy of violence, as suggested by the Liberationists and shows again the traditional Catholic preoccupation with incremental and immediate improvement.

For the "liberal" Pérez Morales, dialogue with Marxism can be useful only to the extent that Marxists are willing to become less dogmatic. Given this willingness, Christians can walk with Marxists with their eyes open, seeing what Marxism has to teach them.[69] History has shown us, he continues, that Marxism has some impressive accomplishments, but that among these are greater oppression and totalitarianism.[70]

In a document believed to have been drafted by Pérez Morales, the Venezuelan bishops stated baldly that Marxism contradicts Christian faith because it is atheistic, materialistic, and "based on hate."[71] This directly contradicts Jacques Maritain's estimate of Marxism and thus it is not surprising that the Venezuelan bishops reach a different conclusion on the issue of collaboration.

In directly confronting Liberation Theology, the Venezuelan bishops imitate the spirit of the Ratzinger letter by saying that there are many forms of Liberation Theology, and that as long as they follow the Magisterium of the Church and do not renounce any fundamental dimensions of the Christian message, they may lead to genuine Liberation.[72]

In 1982, Monsignor Roa of Maracaibo, then head of the Venezuelan Episcopal Conference, warned his brethren that much of the armed violence in Latin America was born of "heresies with a mixture of religion and politics." The Popular Church of many Latin American countries, he continued, "is like a political party, rather than an answer to faith as taught by the Catholic doctrine."[73] Acknowledging the need for rapid and deep social changes in Latin America, he emphasized that there must be no violence and no messianism."[74]

Violence

Ratzinger emphasizes the need to avoid violence in his document on Liberation Theology, saying that the legitimate aspirations for justice must avoid being used by ideologies that hide or pervert the meaning of justice. Such ideologies, he adds, propose ways of action that mean violence, contrary to "any ethic which is respectful of persons."[75]

The Commission on Justice and Peace dealt at length with the problem of violence in its reflection on *Populorum Progressio*. In paragraph 30 of that document, Paul VI wrote that the structural violence of poverty screams to the heavens and makes violence an attractive temptation. The commission suggests interpreting the pope's words with caution, reminding readers that the criterion for violence is the impossibility to continue living under the structural violence without surrendering human dignity.[76]

Moreover, Catholic social thought requires that would-be revolutionaries be certain that their actions will not result in something worse. In addition, recourse to violence involves two enormous practical difficulties. First, violence destroys rational thinking. The irrationality of violence may be useful in the overthrow of a bad system, but it will not help to build a system which is respectful of human dignity.[77]

Second, recourse to violence requires violent men; men to whom violence is a profession. Such men will necessarily poison efforts to build a just system. Violence is not a hobby of otherwise moral men, the commission points out. It can easily fly out of control. The commission asks aspiring revolutionaries if they are prepared to assume risks for others.[78]

Here again we see the precepts of traditional Catholicism. Just as acquiring a government job does not confer perfection onto an otherwise flawed human being, neither does dedicated effort on behalf of a good cause. If state power in the hands of imperfect people is a danger, violence is a greater one. This danger can be overcome only under dire circumstances and only under the direction of a well-developed conscience. To combat structural violence, the commission suggests development. Responding to the impatience of the Liberationists, who ask: "Will such development occur in time?" the Commission responds that it must. There is no other choice.[79]

CONCLUSION

What this study of the Venezuelan Church reveals is not a group of hopelessly ignorant, unsophisticated clerics nostalgic for the thirteenth century, but a reasonable, thoughtful hierarchy that opposes Marxism, opposes statism, and bases this opposition on a coherent philosophical and theological system. The value of this system is evident not only in Venezuela, where Liberation Theology has never been allowed to take hold, but even more so in Nicaragua. As we shall see in the next chapter, the Nicaraguan bishops have responded to the rise of Liberation Theology by rediscovering the very principles of Catholic social thought that their Venezuelan counterparts never forgot.

NOTES

1. Antonio Pérez Esclarin, *Atheism and Liberation*, trans. John Drury (Maryknoll, NY: Orbis Books, 1978), 195-97.

2. Deane William Ferm, *Third World Liberation Theologies: An Introductory Survey* (Maryknoll, NY: Orbis Books, 1986), 50.

3. Ibid.

4. Daniel H. Levine, *Religion and Politics in Latin America: The Catholic Church in Venezuela and Colombia* (Princeton, NJ: Princeton University Press, 1981), 197.

5. Joaquin Marta Sosa, *Iglesia y Crisis de Fe: El Caso Venezolano* (Caracas: Secedo, 1985), 119.

6. Edward L. Cleary, *Crisis and Change: The Church in Latin America Today* (Maryknoll, NY: Orbis Books, 1985), 114.

7. Comision Venezolana de Justicia y Paz, *Justicia y Paz: El Subdesarrollo Latinoamericano a la Luz de Populorum Progressio* (Caracas: Curia de Venezuela, 1968), 2.

8. Paris, AFP, 2358 GMT, 27 August 1981 (Quoted in *Foreign Broadcast Information Service*, hereinafter FBIS, 2 September 1981, L1).

9. Managua, Radio Sandino, 1200 GMT, 30 November 1983 (FBIS 2 December 1983, P16).

10. Marta Sosa, *Iglesia y Crisis de Fe*, 107.

11. J. Lloyd Mecham, *Church and State in Latin America: A History of Politico-Ecclesiastical Relations* (Chapel Hill: University of North Carolina Press, 1934), 112.

12. Ibid., 123.

13. Ibid., 127.

14. Ibid., 128.

15. Levine, *Religion and Politics*, 75-76.

16. Ibid., 77.

17. See John Paul II, "Addresses in Zaire and Brazil," in Quentin L. Quade, ed., *The Pope and Revolution: John Paul II Confronts Liberation Theology* (Washington, DC: Ethics and Public Policy Center, 1982).

18. Robert J. Alexander, *The Venezuelan Democratic Revolution: A Profile of the Regime of Romulo Betancourt* (New Brunswick, NJ: Rutgers University Press, 1964), 15.

19. Glen L. Kolb, *Democracy and Dictatorship in Venezuela, 1945–1958* (Hartford: Connecticut College Monograph 10, 1974), 123.

20. Levine, *Religion and Politics*, 79.

21. Ibid., 179.

22. Ibid., 80.

23. Sacred Congregation for the Doctrine of the Faith, *Instruction on Certain Aspects of the "Theology of Liberation,"* official Vatican translation (Boston: Daughters of St. Paul, 1984), 24.

24. Levine, *Religion and Politics*, 178.

25. Ibid., 81.

26. Ovidio Pérez Morales, *10 Problemas Retan a un Obispo* (Caracas: Ediciones Paulinas, 1978), 126.

27. See the Apostolic Exhortation of Pope John Paul II, *Christifideles Laici* (On the Role of the Laity), official Vatican translation (Boston: Daughters of St. Paul, 1988).

28. Cleary, *Crisis and Change*, 85.

29. Levine, *Religion and Politics*, 178.

30. Sacred Congregation for the Doctrine of the Faith, *Instruction*, 5-6.

31. Ibid., 31.

32. Comision Venezolana, *Justicia y Paz*, 126.

33. Ibid., 120.

34. Agostino Bono, "The Venezuelan Hierarchy and Presidential Politics," *America* (1 December 1973): 421-22.

35. *New York Times*, 25 December 1976, A26.

36. Comision Venezolana, *Justicia y Paz*, 110.

37. Ibid., 115.

38. Ibid., 316.

39. Sacred Congregation for the Doctrine of the Faith, *Instruction*, 9.

40. Ibid., 10-11.

41. Levine, *Religion and Politics*, 177.

42. *New York Times*, 12 November 1957, A32.

43. *New York Times*, 4 August 1957, A22.

44. Helena Plaza, *El 23 de Enero de 1958 y el Proceso de Consolidacion de la Democratica Representativa en Venezuela* (Caracas: Garbizer and Todtmann Editores, 1978), 74.

45. *New York Times*, A22.

46. Enrique A. Balaroya, "Public Opinion about Military Coups and Democratic Consolidation in Venezuela," in Donald L. Herman, ed., *Democracy in Latin America: Colombia and Venezuela* (New York: Praeger Publishers, 1988), 205.

47. Kolb, *Democracy and Dictatorship*, 168.

48. Levine, *Religion and Politics*, 78.

49. Plaza, *El 23 de Enero*, 77.

50. Ibid., 74.

51. Alexander, *Venezuelan Democratic Revolution*, 48.

52. Ibid., 235.

53. Pérez Morales, *10 Problemas*, 134.

54. Ibid., 183.

55. See John XXIII, *Mater et Magistra* (Mother and Teacher), offical Vatican translation (Boston: Daughters of St. Paul), para. 109.

56. Comision Venezolana, *Justicia y Paz*, 114.

57. Ibid., 111.

58. Ibid., 113.

59. Ibid., 146.

60. Ibid., 170.

61. Ibid., 225.

62. Ibid., 172-73.

63. Sacred Congregation for the Doctrine of the Faith, *Instruction*, 17-19.

64. Levine, *Religion and Politics*, 184.

65. Ibid., 187.

66. Ibid., 186.

67. *New York Times*, 17 September 1962, A9.

68. *Christian Century* (10 April 1963): 478.

69. Pérez Morales, *10 Problemas*, 126-27.

70. Ibid., 131.

71. Bono, "Venezuelan Hierarchy," 422.

72. Pérez Morales, *10 Problemas*, 117. Compare to Sacred Congregation for the Doctrine of the Faith, *Instruction*, 8-12.

73. Paris, AFP, 1403 GMT, 5 January 1982 (FBIS 8 January 1982, L1).

74. Ibid.

75. Sacred Congregation for the Doctrine of the Faith, *Instruction*, 7.

76. Comision Venezolana, *Justicia y Paz*, 151.

77. Ibid., 154.

78. Ibid., 155.

79. Ibid.

10

Church and State in Nicaragua: Catholic Social Thought Resurgent

Nowhere in Latin America are the results of injecting Liberation Theology into the art of government clearer than in Sandinista Nicaragua, where Liberation Theology became virtually an official religion under the Sandinistas. As we saw in Chapter 6, the orthodox Catholic Church in Nicaragua, personified by the Episcopal Conference, accepted in large degree the precepts of Liberation Theology. In addition, the Catholic hierarchy was supportive of the coalition that opposed Anastasio Somoza and even celebrated the dictator's departure. After the Triumph, church and state in Nicaragua enjoyed a brief honeymoon.

Within two years of the Sandinista Revolution, however, relations between the Church and the government began to sour. By 1984, Sandinista junta coordinator Daniel Ortega and Archbishop Miguel Obando y Bravo had become bitter enemies. They remain so to this day. In this chapter I shall trace the process of alienation between the Church and state and argue that the nature of the Sandinista regime, and the Church's understanding of its temporal mission, made this falling out inevitable.

As the rift between the Church and state has widened, the Episcopal Conference has rejected not only its earlier support for Liberation Theology, but has also found little use for the more "moderate" Christian Democracy. To combat the political hegemony of the Sandinistas, the Nicaraguan bishops have copied their Venezuelan counterparts and have adhered more closely to traditional Catholic social thought.

BACKGROUND—SOMOZA'S FALL AND THE HONEYMOON

Obando and Somoza

The relationship between the Somoza family and the Roman Catholic hierarchy of Nicaragua was generally friendly until 1968. In that year, Monsignor Miguel Obando y Bravo became the first native Nicaraguan to achieve a hierarchical post in his own country. Anastasio Somoza tried immediately to tie the young and untested prelate to his regime, as he had done so successfully with his predecessors.

Obando soon indicated, however, that the days of friendliness were over. He returned a luxury car that Somoza tried to provide for his use in 1970. When Somoza refused to accept it, Obando sold the car, using the proceeds for Managua charities.[1] In 1972 Obando withheld his blessing from a Somoza-created "coalition" government, having judged that this coalition existed only to provide cover for continued dictatorship. The bishops issued a pastoral letter, itself a new form of episcopal communication, which called for a "whole new order" in Nicaraguan politics and economics.

In December, Obando refused to join a relief commission Somoza created to deal with the Managua earthquake. Somoza himself attributes this to Obando's hunger for power.[2] It is more likely that Obando recognized the opportunities for personal enrichment that the international earthquake aid would provide Somoza and did not wish to legitimize potential graft.

In 1977, the bishops issued a letter that criticized Somoza for creating a "state of terror" in Nicaragua through the routine use of torture and execution of political prisoners.[3] In 1974 and 1978, Obando mediated hostage crises between the government and the Sandinista Front. This, Obando would remind the Sandinistas later, saved the lives of many of Nicaragua's future rulers.[4]

In August 1978 a new pastoral letter embraced many of the same goals that Christian Democrats supported all over Latin America, including national health service, land reform, and more government control over the national economy.[5] Finally, in June 1979, the bishops smoothed the way for the Sandinista takeover by issuing their landmark pastoral letter in which they concluded that the conditions for just insurrection existed in Nicaragua and that it was "not possible to deny [the Sandinistas] moral legitimacy in the face of a blatant and prolonged tyranny."[6]

After the Triumph—The Early Days

Like most Nicaraguans, the Catholic bishops hoped that the fall of Somoza would herald a new dawn of freedom in Nicaragua. To aid that process, the Church praised the new government, acknowledging the leading role that the Sandinista Front (FSLN) played in the broad coalition that brought Somoza down. Early problems, such as the junta's demand that the Catholic radio station be put at their disposal, were smoothed over. In August 1979, Bishop Julian Barni of Matagalpa told the press that minor difficulties between church and state had been "cleared up."[7]

Bishop Antonio Vega, who would become a fierce critic of the regime, said that a pastoral letter issued in August 1979 warning of the dangers of dictatorship should not be construed as criticism of the regime. Obando, for his part, recalled that the "previous regime shut itself off from the Church." He added: "I believe that things are now moving along well."[8]

The November 1979 Pastoral Letter

The height of this era of good feelings came on 17 November 1979 when the bishops published their first major reflection on the Sandinista regime. In this pastoral letter, the bishops acknowledged the importance of "Christian participation in the revolution," a reference to the importance of Liberation Theology. In addition, the letter also emphasized the "dramatic conversion of our Church," a tacit Act of Contrition for the Nicaraguan Church's previous coziness with the Somozas. The mention of "conversion" could also refer to the hierarchy's own embrace of Liberation Theology.

The bishops also embraced specific aspects of Liberation Theology. They called the Revolution a "broad and profoundly liberating action," mimicking Sandinista slogans.[9] Revolutionary creativity, the letter continued, "opens broad and fruitful avenues to the commitment of all those interested in struggling against an unjust and oppressive system and in constructing a new man." The letter recognized "the dramatic fact of class struggle that should lead to a just transformation of structures." Among the agents of this transformation would be the Christian Base Communities (CEBs); the bishops acknowledged their "authentic Christian and pastoral character."

The letter also praised specific Sandinista policies, such as "nationalization to recover the country's wealth, the first steps of agrarian reform, and so forth." The Church backed the national literacy campaign, believing it would "dignify our people's spirit and enable them to participate more responsibly in the revolutionary process." The bishops acknowledged some areas of friction, but said that the solution lay in dialogue and active popular participation "through people's democratic organizations that already exist and those that will be created through a national dialogue."

The bishops also found words of praise for socialism. They attempted to distinguish between "bad socialism" and "good socialism." The former, they said, takes away from man his character as a free protagonist in his own history. It also gives arbitrary power to those in authority, takes away the right to public religious expression, and denies to parents the right to educate their children.

Good socialism, on the other hand, means a national, planned economy, nationalization of assets and resources, reduction of the gap in pay for manual and nonmanual labor, and greater participation by the worker in his own product. Good socialism should also increasingly share power with "organized people," and do away with class struggle if this means class hatred. This description of "good socialism" is remarkably similar to the Christian Democrats'.

For the Church, there were to be no special privileges. The bishops stated that there would be no Church/state trouble as long as the Church was able to preach and "conduct activities that permit the faithful to live out the moral commitment of their faith in their private, family and social lives."

The only critical statement was a brief acknowledgement that the Revolution was prone to error, since "no process in history is of absolute human purity." This approximation of traditional Catholic view of man as an imperfect creature makes it all the more surprising that the rest of the letter was so positive. In other words, the Catholic bishops gave a great deal of legitimacy to an institution that they admitted would remain impure.

Although Church/state relations deteriorated almost immediately after this letter was published, the bishops indicated on several occasions that they did not wish to burn the bridges between themselves and the ruling junta. In January 1981, for example, Obando told the Venezuelan press that Church/state relations in Nicaragua were "normal." He said that the Sandinistas, unlike Somoza, did not intervene in Church tasks and did not interfere with religious education.[10]

In May 1982 Obando discouraged the growing opposition to the Sandinista regime by quashing rumors that he was to join a government in exile. Obando concluded that the time for such an extreme step had not yet come.[11] Even as late as 1984, the bishops of Esteli, Matagalpa, and Bluefields condemned an attack by anti-Sandinista guerrillas during which 30 telephone workers were killed.[12]

Nevertheless, the ruling Sandinistas soon made it clear that any honeymoon between themselves and Nicaragua's Catholic hierarchy would last only so long as the latter toed the Sandinista line very faithfully. As early as May 1981, when friction between church and state was just beginning, Ortega told the official Sandinista newspaper that "when [the bishops] announce the coming of Christ, they are really announcing the arrival of the counterrevolution." Ortega followed this extraordinary statement with a history of hierarchical support for the Somozas and for U.S. imperialism.[13] Although his history stopped short of the current hierarchy, his message was clear: in Nicaragua, one is wholly with the Revolution or wholly with Somoza.

GROWING OPPOSITION FROM THE CATHOLIC CHURCH

Beginning in 1982, relations between the Sandinista rulers and the Roman Catholic hierarchy deteriorated rapidly. The major issues of contention between the two were: government policy toward the Liberationist and unofficial Popular Church, the presence in the Sandinista junta of five Catholic priests, censorship of Church publications and broadcasts, the Sandinista draft, and the question of dialogue with the armed opposition.

Each of these issues refers to an elementary area of contention between traditional Catholic political theory and the claims of absolutist states. As Church opposition to the Sandinistas solidified, the hierarchy rediscovered the traditional Catholic theory on statism, autonomous social institutions, an independent Church, individual morality, authority of bishops, and the Church as a focus of societal unity. Through this rediscovery, the bishops would reject not only Liberation Theology, but much of Christian Democratic theory as well.

Statism

At the beginning of the Sandinista revolution, the hierarchy favored the use of the state to achieve social goals, much like the Christian Democrats we saw in Chapters 3, 5, 7, and 8. Given the confidence that the hierarchy placed in the Sandinista junta, an energetic state probably did not seem excessive. Moreover, the prolonged misuse of state power for personal gain under the Somoza regime no doubt persuaded the hierarchy that it was time this power be directed toward the common good.

But the bishops were not writing in a vacuum, in which only Nicaraguan experiences were applicable. On the contrary, they had centuries of Roman Catholic fear of misdirected state power from which to draw. This should have taught them that any all-powerful centralized state, no matter how well-meaning its leaders, is a danger to autonomous society.

The hierarchy's first indication that they had trusted the Sandinista state with too much power came in the substance of the Sandinista literacy campaign of 1980. I described this campaign in detail in Chapter

6, so suffice it to say now that shortly after the Revolution the bishops warned that although raising the consciousness of the people through politicized reading lessons was acceptable, such consciousness raising should avoid "massification." As the full impact of the literacy campaign became clear, the Church withdrew its sponsorship. Obando told the Organization of American States (OAS) in 1986 that the literacy campaign was designed foremost to indoctrinate and organize the people and only last to teach them to read and write.[14] Obando's concern over the campaign's goal of organization reflects a growing skepticism with Christian Democracy's emphasis on state-led organization.

In October 1980, the bishops warned that the Sandinistas were consolidating too much power. They reminded their faithful, and perhaps themselves, that political power can always be turned against a defenseless population.[15] Later, the bishops would deplore the fact that the Sandinistas' assumption of responsibility for education, development, and welfare was leaving less scope for religious charitable activity.[16] In 1983 the bishops initiated a series of social welfare programs aimed at diminishing the impact of similar government efforts. Put differently, the Nicaraguan bishops set themselves to undoing what Christian Democrats in the rest of Latin America are still demanding.

The Church's opposition to the Sandinista conscription law must be seen in this larger context of the hierarchy's increasing concern over the growing power of the state and its effect on autonomous societal institutions. On 29 August 1983, the bishops released a pastoral letter condemning the new Sandinista draft law. The reason for their opposition was the orientation of the Sandinista army. The Sandinista army was a party army, meaning that its first loyalty, by oath, was not to the Nicaraguan nation but rather to the FSLN. The hierarchy condemned this politicization of the army, insisting that this institution remain committed to the nation as a whole, and not just to the fortunes of a single political party.[17]

Autonomous Social Institutions

As we have seen, traditional Catholic social thought emphasizes free and autonomous social institutions, such as families, labor unions, professional organizations, churches, and private schools, among others. Such institutions allow individuals to band together to protect themselves against the power of the state, since it is always harder to compel an organized group than it is to compel an individual. Nicaragua's bishops, as they lost their original enthusiasm for statism, would rediscover the importance of such institutions.

Like the Venezuelan hierarchy, in their effort to forestall the rise of Liberation Theology, the Nicaraguan bishops, seeking to counter Liberation Theology, closely follow the lead of the Vatican. Pope John Paul II frequently stresses the need for independent educational facilities. He even devoted one of his major addresses in Nicaragua to the right of parents to decide upon the content of their children's education and to the importance of freedom for confessional schools.

The task of the hierarchy, however, was not only to recognize the importance of autonomous organizations, but to help to build them. Perhaps because of the legacy of statism under Somoza, Nicaragua in 1979 was a country with few strong societal institutions. It lacked great universities, long established clubs or philanthropic groups, and thriving civic institutions.[18] An exception was education, especially on the primary and secondary level.

The issue of independent schools in Nicaragua was brought into sharp focus by the August 1982 incident in which Bismark Carballo, chief spokesman for the Episcopal Conference, was lured into a house with a female Sandinista, then forced to strip and exit the house, where Sandinista press cameramen were waiting in a convenient semicircle.[19]

Among the widespread expressions of outrage over this crude attempt at character assassination was a student strike at the Catholic schools of Masaya diocese several days later. The Sandinistas arrested the director of the private Salesian academy in Masaya, Spanish priest José Morataya Escudero. The government accused Morataya of inciting the "rebellion." The priest's answer to his accusers is instructive. He admitted that he and his students did rebel, "as we did against Somoza."[20]

The Sandinistas then took over the school altogether, purportedly for the purpose of finishing out the school year. The action can be seen as part of a broader attack on Catholic education, since the Salesian academy was also the largest Catholic school in the area. Moreover, the original order for the school's closure included instructions for the Educational and Culture Ministries to turn the school into a Sandinista education center.[21]

The school was eventually returned to the order, but only under stringent conditions. Morataya Escudero had his visa revoked and had to return to Spain. The Catholic hierarchy was allowed to name a new director, but had to promise that the new Salesian principal would "obey the law."[22] This attack on the school's autonomy can also be seen as a veiled attack on Obando, since he is a Salesian priest himself.

In a 24 August 1982 pastoral letter, the hierarchy protested: "The main and leading educators, who are the parents, have been apparently left out [of educational decisions]."[23] The bishops reasserted the need for education which is open to transcendent values and which is above the "narrow, materialistic ideologies that ignore or deny the existence of God."

Parents must retain the right to freely choose their children's education, the bishops insisted, since this "contributes to the freedom of conscience . . . and to the advance of culture itself." They went on to oppose "any school monopoly, which is contrary to the natural rights of humans." The pastoral letter concludes with another expression of fidelity to the political thought of the pope. Quoting the recently published *Familiaris Consortio,* the bishops said: "If ideologies contrary to the Christian faith are taught in the schools, the family, together with other families and, if possible, through some kind of family association, must with all their strength and wisdom help youths not to stray from the faith."

Protecting the role of parenthood from state interference was also why the Church reacted strongly to a Sandinista plan to have the state take over the distribution of Christmas gifts to children in 1980. Under the plan, which Sandinista officials defended as a way of preventing Christmas commercialism, children would receive their Christmas gifts from the state, through Sandinista-led neighborhood organizations. To further secularize the holiday, Nicaraguans were requested to perform "voluntary" field work on government farms during the December coffee harvest.[24] This plan, especially its paternalistic overtones, caused the hierarchy to refer to the Sandinista junta as the "New Pharaoh."

The Church has also defended the independence and autonomy of the indigenous Miskito Indian population, especially after the substance of the hierarchy's charges about mistreatment of this minority was confirmed by Amnesty International.[25] In a letter on their forced relocation, the bishops said that the human rights of individuals take precedence even over the need for national defense. This need, they added, had not been proven.[26]

The Nicaraguan hierarchy has defended other societal institutions as well. Speaking at a workers' conference just after the Sandinista takeover, Obando told the assembled workers that the labor union "is an irreplaceable force that must guarantee its autonomy and defend the rights and freedoms of the workers."[27]

Even the highly vaunted economic advances of the Sandinista regime do not excuse extensive growth in state power. Refuting this Christian Democratic argument, Obando said in 1985 that the government "makes people pay for social advances with losses and drawbacks in another achievement, which is liberty."[28] In a Managua homily he said that freedom was the most precious asset that God granted to mankind. (This phrase got by the government censors of Radio Catolica, and the Sandinistas closed the station for 24 hours.)[29]

Religion as a Strictly Private Matter

The government responded to much of this Church-led agitation with attacks on the religious nature of the Catholic hierarchy's opposition.

The Sandinistas' public Communique on Religion of October 1980 promised that "the profession of a religious faith would be an inalienable right and is guaranteed by the revolutionary government." Christians supported by their faith, the communique went on, "can serve the needs of the people and the revolution."[30]

A subsequent paragraph of the communique indicated what sort of religious profession was allowed. "All those in agreement with our objectives," the comandantes said, "and who meet the personal requirements demanded by our organization are free to participate as members in our ranks, regardless of their religious faith."

Religion, then, can only support commitment to the Sandinista cause; it cannot detract from it. The communique, after promising freedom of religion, threatens to "defend the people and the Revolution" from any religious-based opposition.[31] Near the end of the communique the language is even clearer: "Once away from political aspects, Christian members . . . have the right to express their beliefs." The Communique concludes: "For our Revolutionary state, religion is a personal matter." As we saw in Chapter 1, this is exactly the way Marx and Engels sought to neutralize religion; to restrict religion to private (and silent) prayers and to prevent any connection between religious faith and everyday life.

When the Sandinistas have encountered opposition from the Church, they have insisted that such opposition does not represent a confrontation between the Revolution and religion, at least religion as defined by the October 1980 communique. Opposition to the Revolution, no matter how clearly based on religious principles, is a political matter. Thus the Sandinistas insist that there is no restriction on religious freedom in Nicaragua. Rather, they oppose political activities masquerading as expressions of religious belief.[32]

An example of this attitude is the fate of a Catholic Church publication called *La Iglesia*. The Catholic hierarchy produced this eight-page newsletter in 1986, after all other forms of communication between the Church and its faithful had been censored by the government. Most of the eight pages dealt with strictly religious matters, such as the Gospel readings for the next two weeks, and a pastoral message from Obando.

The newsletter also contained an editorial that repeated the hierarchy's opposition to conscripting Nicaraguan youth into a Sandinista army. For this reason, the government declared the entire publication illegal and moved to collect every last copy. The government declared that this heavy-handed action did not constitute religious intolerance, since *La Iglesia* was not a religious, but rather a political publication. "The attitude of the curia's spokesman [Bismark Carballo] represents a clear and open challenge to the authority of any Constitutional government and is absolutely intolerable."[33]

The Sandinistas repeated this restriction of religion to the strictly private in their 1987 constitution. Private religious freedom is guaranteed, but the preamble is directed only to those Christians who "have committed themselves to and become part of the struggle for the liberation of the oppressed."[34] Sandinista educational regulations allow the Catholic Church to influence only religion classes, further divorcing religion from the rest of life.[35]

Not surprisingly, the Sandinistas soon opened to question even the strictly private religious practice and the moral authority of the bishops in religious matters. In September 1980, Interior Minister Tomas Borge criticized Catholics who "go around beating their chests with a little medal, going to Communion frequently, praying to the Virgin."[36] An editorial in the progovernment *El Nuevo Diario* in 1981 stated: "[The bishops] can give the last word with moral authority and good judgement only after they have listened to the rest of the Church, the government, and the people."[37]

An Independent Church

What is really at stake here is the legitimacy of antigovernmental, or even nongovernmental, expressions of moral or political authority. For the Sandinistas, the state defines what is the proper sphere of the Church and the Church obeys, much like any other agency of the government would obey a directive. In this way, and through the severe restrictions that the government has tried to place on religious activity, the Sandinistas attempt to restrict the Catholic Church to those activities that the Liberationists say are proof that the hierarchy does not care about the people.

This policy is consistent with the stated goal of the Sandinista government with regard to the Catholic Church. The record of a lengthy meeting of Sandinista leaders, called the "72-Hour Document," demands a policy of dividing the Catholic Church. The authenticity of this document is confirmed by high-level Sandinista defectors. It reads in part: "With the Catholic Church and the Protestant Churches, we should strengthen relations on a diplomatic level, maintaining, generally, a careful policy which seeks to neutralize as much as possible conservative positions, and to strengthen our ties with priests sympathetic to the Revolution, while at the same time, stimulating the Revolutionary sectors of the Church."

The Liberationists have insisted for years that the Church is only interested in the next world, in devotional and petitionary prayer, in private charity, and in the personal reception of the Sacraments. Under the Sandinista restrictions, the Church would be limited to no more than these activities, at best. Thus the Liberationists' *raison d'être* would remain intact and they could continue to portray the traditional hierarchy as the enemies of the people.

The Nicaraguan hierarchy has fought consistently, however, for its autonomous and independent role in society. The bishops responded to the 1980 communique on religion by saying that the Church was being denied a role in society and being made merely "an appendage of the state."[38] Even in the November 1979 pastoral letter, the bishops warned that their support did not mean unquestioning obedience to any new ideology. The mildness of this warning is reflected in the bishops' confidence that government mechanisms will effectively receive any complaints that might arise against the revolutionary process.

In August 1982 a pastoral letter complained that the government had launched a "systematic campaign to discredit the faith and reduce respect for ecclesiastical authority."[39] In so doing, the government could also threaten the independent moral voice of the Church.

During the 1984 election campaign in Nicaragua, the bishops were often asked if they had a preference among the parties vying for office. Obando told the media that the Nicaraguan Church would "instruct Christians to vote for those who will give the Church ample leeway to carry out its evangelical mission."[40] The issue of Church autonomy had become serious enough for the hierarchy to abandon its traditional reluctance to get involved in electoral politics.

By 1986, attacks on the Catholic Church took a more serious turn, as the Sandinista government began drafting Catholic seminarians into the army. Again, the Church's opposition to conscription to fill the ranks of a party army appeared. But more important was the apparent Sandinista intention to target seminaries, presumably to make young men reluctant to enter them and thus deprive the Church of its life's blood.

The Sandinistas also issued threats to foreign priests who stayed loyal to the bishops.[41] In a July 1986 pastoral letter, addressed "to all the Episcopal Conferences of the World," the Nicaraguan bishops complained that priests who were faithful to the bishops were constantly visited by State Security, "with the intention of separating them from their Bishops." Since 1979, the letter went on, 2 nuns and 26 priests had been expelled. Replacements had to wait months for entry visas, and residence visas were almost unattainable. Even the quintessentially apolitical Mother Theresa could not obtain one until after Fidel Castro had received her.[42]

In October 1985 the government took over the Social Pastoral Department of the Archdiocese of Managua, citing the new state of emergency law. This action not only halted much of the Church's social action, but even slowed down strictly pastoral functions such as Baptisms, by denying to the Bishops the official stationery necessary to document that all-important Sacrament.[43] To the deeply religious people of Nicaragua, this was the equivalent of holding their children's salvation hostage to the Church/state dispute. At the very least, it calls into question the Sandinista commitment to allowing private religious observance.

The most brazen attack on the Catholic Church in Nicaragua came in the spring of 1986 when, within a few days, the government prohibited Bismark Carballo from reentering the country after a visit to the United States, and physically expelled Bishop Vega from Nicaragua. Both were accused of encouraging aid to the rebels, after they refused to take sides in the civil war. This action by the government even attracted the notice of Pope John Paul II, who was visiting Medellin, Colombia, at the time. The pope denounced the Vega expulsion, saying: "This almost unbelievable incident has deeply saddened me. This is because it makes me recall dark times ... in which actions were carried out against the Church."[44]

In a 1986 article for the *Washington Post*, titled: "The Sandinistas Have Bound and Gagged Us," Obando summarized government actions against him. His column in *La Prensa* was halted. Curia offices were first seized, then officially confiscated. His televised Mass was censored. Sermons had to be delivered to the Interior Ministry days before delivery.[45] The Sandinistas repeatedly offered the Church a choice between submission or extinction.

One commentator stated the root of Obando's problems with the government succinctly: "Obando believes that true social regeneration must have a religious base. As such, he is a natural anti-Sandinista."[46] Any Nicaraguan who believed that social regeneration could come from any nongovernmental part of society would be equally opposed by the Sandinista government; for radical statists like the Sandinistas, such regeneration must come from the government.

A 1984 statement by Carlos Tunnerman, Sandinista ambassador to the United States, highlights the similarity between the Sandinistas and traditional absolutists. Commenting on Church-state relations in the aftermath of the 1984 Easter pastoral letter, which was very critical of the Sandinistas, Tunnerman expressed his surprise that the bishops could consider his government anti-religious. After all, he argued, the Sandinista government provided subsidies to 20 religious schools.

The Church as a Source of Unity

The controversy over the five priests who held government positions in Sandinista Nicaragua becomes more intelligible if seen in the light of the conflict over an independent Church.[47] According to Roman Catholic canon law, which guides the bishops in this controversy, priests may hold political positions only under extraordinary circumstances. Thus, during the immediate postrevolution period, the bishops allowed the five to retain their vital government posts.

When the Sandinista junta replaced itself with a permanent Council of State, the government seemed to indicate that the extraordinary circumstances were over. The five priests refused to leave their posts, however, prompting the bishops to compare them to the priests who accepted powerful and lucrative positions from feudal governments during the Middle Ages.[48] Their criticism of the priests sharpened after the publication of the religious communique, when the bishops implied that the priests were "naive tools" of the government.[49]

For the bishops, the government priests were violating the unitive mission of the Church by taking sides in a partisan political system. For the pope, this was important enough to dedicate a pastoral letter to the bishops of Nicaragua in which he reiterated the Thomistic view of the Church dedicated to the common good, and especially to the unity of believers.

"The Church," the pope said, "especially in a divided society, . . . must be strong enough to overcome divisive forces to which it is subjected."[50] "Nicaragua's Christian congregation," he went on, ought not to be "hopelessly divided by fortuitous options stemming from systems, trends, parties or organizations." Addressing the priests themselves, the pope concluded: "It is not in the role of politicians, but as priests, that the people want to have you near."

Political positions are better filled by laymen who do not have a spiritual mission.[51] The bishops reminded the priests that their primary functions were spiritual, asking if those opposed to the Sandinistas would feel comfortable coming to Miguel D'Escoto or Ernesto Cardenal for Confession or Confirmation. Consistent with this insistence that priests be open to everyone, the bishops have assigned revolutionary priests to more conservative middle-class parishes.[52]

The priests defended themselves by pointing to the important work that they were doing and insisted that working with the Sandinista government was, in itself, a spiritual mission. Such supplementary missions, according to one of their defenders, are common in the Third World, and often "the only way to witness Christian love."[53]

Other defenders of the priests see the conflict as class based, with the official Church refusing to see the class differences within the Church itself.[54] Any honest comparison of the lifestyles of Miguel D'Escoto and Obando y Bravo, however, would invalidate this perspective. Moreover, Obando is more popular with poor Nicaraguans than with the middle and upper class, who perhaps still resent his early embrace of the Sandinistas.[55]

The controversy raged for months, and eventually involved the Vatican secretary of state. Finally, on 15 July 1981, the five priests agreed not to perform their priestly functions to retain their government posts.[56]

Since 1981, Fernando Cardenal and Edgar Paralles have left the Society of Jesus in order to retain their political posts.

The root of the controversy remains the proper relationship between priests and secular power. The five priests insist that their involvement with the revolutionary government is "symbolic of the Church's renunciation of its past alliances with ruling elites."[57] This argument is valid only if one pretends that the Sandinistas themselves are not a ruling elite. In fact, the Sandinista priests, as well as nongovernmental supporters of Nicaraguan Liberation Theology, are repeating the ancient Catholic error of tying themselves to a secular regime, with, perhaps, the best of motives.

Unity within the Church was the theme of Pope John Paul II's visit to Nicaragua in March 1983. At a Mass in Managua's main square, the Holy Father chose the Genesis story of the Tower of Babel for his First Reading, and followed with the Gospel story of the Good Shepherd.[58] The Sandinistas used the visit to highlight division within the Church and to attempt to alienate the Nicaraguan people from the pope, himself the symbol of unity in the Catholic Church.

The details of the papal visit are well known, although frequently ignored. Sandinista television recorded the disruptions of the pope's Managua Mass, and clearly showed the Sandinista leadership provoking the "spontaneous" demonstrations. Technical enhancements, such as turning off the pope's microphone and providing government demonstrators with loudspeakers, also pointed to official sponsorship.[59]

Interruptions of the pope's Homily began after he called for obedience to the bishops and spoke of the importance of Church unity. True to form, the junta insisted that the pope's call for unity was not religious, but a political statement. Recalling the 1980 communique, the government said that when the pope ceased to speak of private matters, he crossed the forbidden line into politics.[60]

The Popular Church is another threat to Church unity and to the unitive function that the Church must perform. John Paul II spoke of the Popular Church in his June 1982 pastoral letter, recalling that the title "Popular Church" was found by the Puebla conferees as "not too fortunate" a name.[61] It is a title that generally conceals another reality.

Elaborating, the pope said that the "Popular Church" usually means a "Church born more markedly from the alleged values of a sector of the population than from God's free and gratuitous initiative." It is marked by earthly ideologies and placed at the service of their demands. In short, the Popular Church repeats the oft-criticized behavior of the official Church. As the latter is accused of placing too much emphasis on the next life in heaven, the Popular Church places its emphasis on the next, and presumably perfect, earthly society. The needs of present-day society are sacrificed just as readily.

Asked about the Popular Church as it existed in Nicaragua in 1987, Obando replied that a group of Liberationist priests had identified itself with the government. "I would say," he added, "that they are part of the structure itself.... They do not have a large number of people at the base levels, but they do enjoy a great deal of governmental publicity, especially abroad." Again, this is consistent with the policy stated in the 72-Hour Document. Obando added in another interview that priests "who work for Marxism are well-treated in publications, magazines and books, and have access to every media organization without difficulty."[62]

Individual Morality as the Source of Change

Like the Venezuelan bishops, the Nicaraguan hierarchy does not reject the need for change, even radical change, in existing political and social relationships. Faithful to Catholic social thought, however, they insist upon the importance of individual morality as the source of change. In their pastoral letters of August 1978 and November 1979, before disillusionment with the Sandinistas, the bishops paid lip service to the need for a profound change of individual hearts and for individual conversions.

By 1981, Obando was openly concerned about the effect the Revolution would have on individuals. He warned that worshipping the Revolution was the same as adoring "sex, wealth, or [man's] own mind and being." The Revolution was a temptation for man to forget his own fallibility. In the 1984 pastoral, the tone of the bishops changed. Part I of the letter was entitled: "Sin, the Root of All Evil." The bishops recalled that sin entered the world when man desired to worship himself, and "become like gods."

The cure, the bishops continue, is conversion, which must start with individual human hearts. Only then will attitudes marked by sin, and social structures caused by sin, start to disappear. Conversion must be seen not as an event, but as a process, because even after redemption, man can abuse his freedom and persist in sinful activity. One of the most serious temptations is materialism, which "reduces man to merely material categories devoid of spiritual content and leaves the individual subject to material forces that are called the dialectic of history."

Note that by 1984, the bishops identified the Sandinistas' philosophy as materialistic and had evidently given up on reforming or redirecting the Sandinistas' anti-Christian attitudes. Rather, the bishops concluded that materialism itself was a hopelessly wrong understanding of the world, and they expressed grave doubt that anything good could come from it.

Materialism is a reflection of individual sin. The bishops in 1984 attributed the horrid situation of wartime Nicaragua to personal sin, the root of death, fear, divided families, and such social evils as materialistic and atheistic education.[63] Later, Obando would reiterate that "war is born in the heart of the sinner." Peace, on the other hand, means the "growth of man as an individual, as a citizen of the nation."[64]

To defend their call for talks with the armed opposition, the bishops again referred to the need for conversion and the importance of individuals. Reconciliation, which for the bishops was Nicaragua's highest political need, could be achieved only if man converted himself. As Vega explained: "By conversion we mean the reunification of man with God, not a dependency on any earthly power that seeks absolute and total power."[65]

Conversion is important for the members of the Popular Church as well. Obando criticized this Church's promotion of class hatred, saying in a 1987 homily: "It is not possible to liberate others when the liberators themselves are not free inside, free from the slavery of ideologies, the tyranny of fads, false idols, the urge to dominate and possess, and suffocating egoism."[66]

CRITICISM OF MARXISM

When the five government priests issued their refusal to leave their government posts, they said: "We declare our unbreakable commitment to the Popular Sandinista Revolution, in loyalty to our people, which is the same as saying, in loyalty to the will of God."[67] They added in an official response: "We believe in the poor, who will build a more just fatherland and will help us save ourselves."[68] These statements summarize much of what the bishops find objectionable about Marxism, although they are not Marxist statements per se. Nevertheless, the inductive search for God, starting with the people and forsaking revealed truth, leads to a number of other errors.

One commentator expressed impatience with the bishops' criticism of both Somocismo and Marxism before the revolution. For the bishops, both philosophies excuse violence. For the commentator, Marxist violence was different because it was a response to the structural violence of Somozist "capitalism."[69] The Marxist/Liberationist idea of structural violence is inconsistent with the Catholic idea of individual guilt or innocence and thus the bishops reject it.

Again, the Nicaraguan bishops follow the lead of the Vatican. Pope John Paul II condemns violence even if it is directed at the achievement of a new social order. Marxist violence, based on the struggle of classes, "only leads to new forms of slavery," according to John Paul II.[70]

Even during their period of greatest trust in the Sandinistas, the bishops worried about the class struggle. At first, they hoped to use class struggle to advance justice but at the same time to make the conflict "more humane and promoted with a true social peace." The bishops offered no clues about how to reconcile these opposites.[71]

Eventually, they found it to be impossible. Explicit warnings about Marxism became more frequent as the Sandinista government more closely resembled other Marxist states. In 1982, Obando said that after two years of hope and trust in the Sandinistas, their Revolution was "drifting toward Marxism according to the Cuban model."[72] In 1984, Obando made himself clearer. Denying that Nicaragua was a "second Cuba," he said that "different circumstances exist which distinguish Nicaragua from Cuba. Nicaragua is not an island; it has borders."[73] If this geographic difference was the only one that Obando could think of, the political similarity must have been nearly complete.

Criticism of Liberation Theology

The bishops' embrace of Liberation Theology in the late 1970s did much to legitimize the theology and put it at the service of the Sandinistas. Since 1982, the bishops have sought to separate themselves from the new theology embracing, as we have seen, the traditional tenets of Catholic social thought.

Bishop Bosco Vivas, auxiliary bishop of Managua and then secretary of the Episcopal Conference, wrote on Liberation Theology in 1984, saying: "This theology interprets the liberation of man as a class truggle." Liberation Theologians, he added, are "loyal followers of Marxist dialogue and [they] ignore the Church's teachings and the hierarchy."[74]

Following the Vatican policy of distinguishing between good and bad Liberation Theologies, Obando said in Guatemala: "We must guard against class hatred" by applying Liberation Theology "without resorting to Marxism-Leninism, because one can indeed work for the poor under the guidelines of the Puebla document."[75]

REVIVAL OF TRADITIONAL DEVOTIONS

Perhaps the clearest indication of the rejection of Liberation Theology by the bishops of Nicaragua is their recent embrace of traditional Latin American forms of worship, especially devotion to the Blessed Virgin and the veneration of the saints. Both of these practices originally came from the faithful during the Middle Ages, and are routinely criticized by Liberation Theologians. In Sandinista Nicaragua, attendance at Marian devotions has become a symbol of opposition to the official Theology of Liberation.

The bishops have supported the people's devotion. In a series of well-attended open-air Masses in 1982, the bishops consecrated Nicaragua to the protection of the Virgin Mary. These Masses were also the first signs of a strong religious revival among the middle class.[76] Even after his expulsion in 1986, Bishop Vega emphasized the importance of traditional devotion. His first Mass in Honduras was at the Shrine of the Virgin of Suyapa.[77]

The pro-Sandinista November 1979 pastoral letter invoked Mary the Revolutionary, accepting the Liberationist interpretation of the Magnificat. By contrast the Easter 1984 letter invoked "the Holy Virgin, who assumed her painful function as co-redeemer with exemplary integrity."[78] This is the traditional Mary; Mary the revolutionary is gone.

Devotion to patron saints is also on the rise in Nicaragua. Obando has taken to using Feast Day Masses to make important statements, such as his condemnation of the government's attempt "to extinguish our devotion of the Holy Virgin" in 1984. The occasion was a Mass on the Feast of Saint Michael the Archangel, who cast the Devil out of Heaven.[79] When Popular Church members occupied a church in Ocotal to protest the anti-government stand of the bishop of Esteli, they were forced out by 5,000 faithful who wanted to celebrate the feast day of the church's patron saint.[80]

CONCLUSION

At the start of the Sandinista Revolution, the Nicaraguan hierarchy collaborated with a radical Marxist movement, hoping either to moderate that movement or to redirect its efforts toward desirable goals. In the process, they gave the Sandinistas national and international legitimacy that would have been unthinkable without the hierarchy's approval.

As the Sandinistas consolidated their power, the Nicaraguan bishops rejected their earlier flirtation with Liberation Theology, and rejected many of the accommodationist tactics of the Christian Democrats as well. Instead, they insisted on the rights of the Church according to traditional Catholic social thought. A major element of this social theory is the insistence on protection for independent social groupings, including the Church itself.

Eventually, it was this insistence on legal opposition that would overthrow the Sandinistas. When Sandinista President Daniel Ortega began meeting with the other Central American presidents to try to find a political solution to the Nicaraguan civil war, his position at the talks depended on his success in presenting Sandinista Nicaragua as a genuinely pluralistic society. The health of the Roman Catholic Church became a widely accepted barometer of this pluralism.

While the Church was allowed to exist, other societal groupings as well, including opposition political parties and *La Prensa*, the independent newspaper, could also survive. It was these parties and this newspaper that would finally insist upon genuinely free and open elections, overseen by international observers, and would use these elections to end Sandinista domination of Nicaragua.

The influence of the Church in these elections cannot be overestimated. On election morning, for example, Obando appeared on the cover of *La Prensa* blessing Violeta Chamorro. In all of the speeches that Obando and his colleagues gave prior to the balloting, they spoke of the importance of an independent Church, of freedom of religion, and of societal pluralism. The clear implication was that only the UNO opposition coalition would allow a society based on Catholic social thought.

The Nicaraguan bishops are returning to the principles of Catholic social thought and to strict adherence to the political ideas of the Holy See. As the world approaches the centennial of *Rerum Novarum*, the watershed expression of Catholic social thought, there is no greater proof of its enduring value.

NOTES

1. Andrew Bradstock, *Saints and Sandinistas: The Catholic Church in Nicaragua and its Response to the Revolution* (London: Epworth Press, 1987), 24.

2. See Anastasio Somoza and Jack Cox, *Nicaragua Betrayed* (Boston: Western Islands Publishers, 1980).

3. Bradstock, *Saints and Sandinistas*, 25.

4. Stephen Kinzer, "Nicaragua's Combative Archbishop," *New York Times Magazine*, (18 November 1984): 107.

5. Laura Nuzzi O'Shaughnessy and Luis H. Serra, *The Church and Revolution in Nicaragua* (Athens: Ohio University Center for International Studies, Latin America Series 11, 1986), 7.

6. Paris, AFP, 1639 GMT, 3 June 1979 (Quoted in *Foreign Broadcast Information Service*, hereinafter FBIS, 4 June 1979, P9).

7. Panama City, ACAN, 2134 GMT, 10 August 1979 (FBIS 13 August 1979, P12).

8. Ibid.

9. FBIS 27 November 1979, P8-P14.

10. Paris, AFP, 0208 GMT, 13 January 1981 (FBIS 23 January 1981, P26).

11. Managua, *La Prensa*, 2 May 1982, 1, 12 (FBIS 14 May 1982, P10).

12. Dennis Gilbert, *Sandinistas: The Party and the Church* (Oxford, Basil Blackwell, 1988), 146.

13. Managua, *Barricada*, 25 May 1981, 12 (FBIS 1 June 1981, P20–21).

14. Radio Sandino, 1200 GMT, 24 January 1986 (FBIS 27 January 1986, P15).

15. Nuzzi O'Shaughnessy and Serra, *Church and Revolution*, 26.

16. Bradstock, *Saints and Sandinistas*, 40.

17. Michael Dodson, "The Politics of Religion in Revolutionary Nicaragua," *Annals of the American Academy of Political and Social Science*, 483 (January 1986): 46.

18. Kinzer, "Nicaragua's Combative Archbishop," 95.

19. This account of the Carballo incident was related by Miguel Bolanos Hunter, a defector from the Sandinista Interior Ministry, which was responsible for the attack. His account is corroborated by other sources as well.

20. ACAN, 2112 GMT, 17 August 1982 (FBIS 18 August 1982, P10).

21. Buenos Aires, LATIN, 2037 GMT, 19 August 1982 (FBIS 20 August 1982, P17).

22. ACAN, 2154 GMT, 27 August 1982 (FBIS 30 August 1982, P16).

23. FBIS 8 September 1982, P12.

24. Managua Domestic Service, 0107 GMT, 27 September 1980 (FBIS 29 September 1980, P11).

25. Bradstock, *Saints and Sandinistas*, 52.

26. Nuzzi O'Shaughnessy and Serra, *Church and Revolution*, 21.

27. ACAN, 0306 GMT, 20 September 1979 (FBIS 25 September 1979, P9).

28. AFP, 2137 GMT, 4 April 1985 (FBIS 8 April 1985, P10).

29. Madrid, EFE, 1940 GMT, 30 November 1985 (FBIS 3 December 1985, P23).

30. Radio Sandino, 0300 GMT, 8 October 1980 (FBIS 9 October 1980, P8).

31. Gilbert, *Sandinistas*, 137.

32. Sandinista Television, 0200 GMT, 19 August 1982 (FBIS 20 August 1982, P16–17).

33. Managua International Service, 0247 GMT, 17 October 1985 (FBIS 18 October 1985, P12).

34. Joseph E. Mulligan, "Religion and the Nicaraguan Constitution," *Christian Century* (29 April 1987): 398.

35. Gilbert, *Sandinistas*, 140.

36. Radio Sandino, 0300 GMT, 23 September 1980 (FBIS 24 September 1980, P7) .

37. *El Nuevo Diario*, 11 June 1981, 2 (FBIS 19 June 1981, P11).

38. Dodson, "Politics of Religion," 44.

39. Voice of Sandino, 0000 GMT, 10 August 1982 (FBIS 13 August 1982, P13).

40. ACAN, 1747 GMT, 14 March 1984 (FBIS 15 March 1984, P12).

41. San José Radio Impacto, 1830 GMT, 29 October 1985 (FBIS 5 November 1985, P14).

42. ACAN, 0240, GMT, 9 July 1986 (FBIS 9 July 1986, P9).

43. ACAN, 0225 GMT, 26 October 1985 (FBIS 29 October 1985, P15).

44. AFP, 1953 GMT, 5 July 1986 (FBIS 7 July 1986, P9).

45. *The Washington Post*, 12 May 1986.

46. Kiuzer, "Nicaragua's Combative Archbishop," 100.

47. The five priests were: Father Miguel D'Escoto, Maryknoll priest and foreign minister; Father Ernesto Cardenal, minister of culture; Father Fernando Cardenal, first coordinator of the Literacy Campaign and later education minister; Father Edgar Paralles, ambassador to the OAS; and Father Alvaro Argüello, Counil of State member.

48. Bradstock, *Saints of Sandinistas*, 61.

49. Teofilo Cabestero, *Ministers of God, Ministers of the People: Testimonies of Faith from Nicaragua* (Maryknoll, NY: Orbis Books, 1983), 3.

50. FBIS 18 August 1982, P13-P16.

51. Managua, Radio Reloj, 0100 GMT, 16 May 1980 (FBIS 16 May 1980, P14).

52. Gilbert, *Sandinistas*, 140.

53. Cabestero, *Ministers of God*, 2.

54. Bradstock, *Saints and Sandinistas*, 28.

55. Kinzer, "Nicaragua's Combative Archbishop," 103.

56. Cabestero, *Ministers of God*, 6.

57. Bradstock, *Saints and Sandinistas*, 64.

58. Ibid., 67.

59. ACAN, 1220 GMT, 5 March 1983 (FBIS 7 March 1983, P25). This version of the events surrounding the pope's Mass also draws from a Venezuelan television report that used Sandinista videotape. The tape was widely available in the United States.

60. Managua Domestic Service, 0300 GMT, 9 March 1983 (FBIS 10 March 1983, P9).

61. FBIS 18 August 1982, P13–16.

62. Asuncion, *Hoy*, 13 March 1987, 6–7 (FBIS 27 March 1987, P9–10).

63. FBIS 9 May 1984, P13–17.

64. AFP, 2229 GMT, 16 April 1987 (FBIS 23 April 1987, P11).

65. ACAN, 1822 GMT, 2 May 1984 (FBIS 3 May 1984, P14).

66. AFP, 2229 GMT, 16 April 1987 (FBIS 23 April 1987, P11).

67. Nuzzi O'Shaughnessy and Serra, *Church and Revolution*, 19.

68. Radio Sandino, 0300 GMT, 9 June 1981 (FBIS 10 June 1981, P8).

69. Cesar Jerez, *The Church and the Nicaraguan Revolution* (London: Catholic Institute for International Relations, 1984), 13.

70. Bradstock, *Saints and Sandinistas*, 65.

71. ACAN, 0306 GMT, 20 September 1979 (FBIS 25 September 1979, P9).

72. Radio Reloj, 1730 GMT, 20 June 1981 (FBIS 22 June 1981, P17).

73. Tegucigalpa, Television Hondurena, 0130 GMT, 21 March 1984 (FBIS 22 March 1984, P17).

74. *La Prensa*, 16 December 1984, 1, 10 (FBIS 20 December 1984, P14).

75. ACAN, 1950 GMT, 9 May 1986 (FBIS 12 May 1986, P8).

76. Dodson, "Politics of Religion," 47.

77. Tegucigalpa, Cadena Audio Video, 1130 GMT, 14 July 1986 (FBIS 16 July 1986, P5).

78. FBIS 9 May 1984, P13-P17.

79. Kinzer, "Nicaragua's Combative Archbishop," 75.

80. Henry Houser, "Religious Pluralism in Revolutionary Nicaragua," *Christian Century* (20 April 1988): 406.

Selected Bibliography

BOOKS

Alexander, Robert J. *Latin American Political Parties*. New York: Praeger Publishers, 1973.

————, ed. *Political Parties of the Americas: Canada, Latin America and the West Indies*. Westport, CT: Greenwood Press, 1982.

Alvarado Martinez, Enrique. *El Pensamiento Politico Nicaraguense*. Managua: Artes Graficas, 1968.

Alves, Rubem. *A Theology of Human Hope*. St. Meinard, IN: Abbey Press, 1969.

Assmann, Hugo. *Theology for a Nomad Church*. Maryknoll, NY: Orbis Books, 1976.

Baloyra, Enrique A., and Martz, John D. *Electoral Mobilization and Public Opinion*. Chapel Hill: University of North Carolina Press, 1976.

Boff, Leonardo. *Jesus Christ Liberator: A Critical Christology for Our Time*. Maryknoll, NY: Orbis Books, 1972.

Borregales, German. *Copei Hoy: Una Negación*. Caracas: Ediciones Garrido, 1968.

Braham, Randolph L., ed. *Documents on Major European Governments*. New York: Alfred A. Knopf, 1966.

Cabestrero, Teofilo. *Ministers of God, Ministers of the People: Testimonies of Faith From Nicaragua*. Maryknoll, NY: Orbis Books, 1983.

Caldera, Rafael. *El Bloque Latinoamericano*. Caracas: Oficina Central de Informacion, 1970.

Cambellas Lares, Ricardo. *Copei: Ideologia y Liderazgo*. Caracas: Editorial Ariel, S. A., 1985.

Cartay Ramirez, Gerhard. *Politica y Partidos Modernos en Venezuela*. Caracas: Ediciones centauro, 1983.

Cleary, Edward L. *Crisis and Change: The Church in Latin America Today*. Maryknoll, NY: Orbis Books, 1985.

Comision Venezolana de Justicia y Paz. *Justicia y Paz: El Subdesarrollo Latinoamericano a la Luz de Populorum Progressio*. Caracas: Curia de Venezuela, 1968.

Conference of Latin American Bishops. *Los Obispos Latinoamericanos Entre Medellin y Puebla: Documentos Episcopales*. San Salvador: UCA Editores, 1978.

Cooper, John W. *A Theology of Freedom: The Legacy of Jacques Maritain and Reinhold Niebuhr*. Macon, GA: Mercer University Press, 1985.

Davis, Harold Eugene. *Latin American Thought: A Historical Introduction*. Baton Rouge: Louisiana State University Press, 1972.

Dussel, Enrique. *Caminos de Liberación Latinoamericana*. Buenos Aires: Latinoamericanos Libros, 1972.

────. *History and the Theology of Liberation: A Latin American Perspective*. Maryknoll, NY: Orbis Books, 1976.

Eagleston, John, ed. *Christians and Socialism: Documentation of the Christians for Socialism Movement in Latin America*. Maryknoll, NY: Orbis Books, 1975.

────, and Schrarper, Philip, eds. *Puebla and Beyond: Documentation and Commentary*. Maryknoll, NY: Orbis Books, 1979.

Einaudi, Mario, and Goguel, François. *Christian Democracy in Italy and France*. Notre Dame, IN: University of Notre Dame Press, 1952.

Evans, Joseph W., and Ward, Leo R. *The Social and Political Philosophy of Jacques Maritain*. Notre Dame, IN: University of Notre Dame Press, 1976.

Ferm, Deane William. *Third World Liberation Theologies: An Introductory Survey*. Maryknoll, NY: Orbis Books, 1986.

Fleet, Michael. *The Rise and Fall of Chilean Christian Democracy*. Princeton, NJ: Princeton University Press, 1985.

Frei Montalva, Eduardo. *Latin America: The Hopeful Option*. Maryknoll, NY: Orbis Books, 1978.

────. *The Mandate of History and Chile's Future*. Translated by Miguel D'Escoto Brockmann. Athens: Ohio University Center for International Studies, Papers in International Studies, Latin America Series 1, 1977.

Freire, Paulo. *Pedagogy of the Oppressed*. New York: Seabury Press, 1970.

Fremantle, Anne. *The Papal Encyclicals in Their Historical Context*. New York: Mentor Omega, 1963.

Galtung, Johan. *A Structural Theory of Revolutions*. Rotterdam: Rotterdam University Press, 1974.

Gross, Leonard. *The Last, Best Hope: Eduardo Frei and Chilean Democracy*. New York: Random House, 1967.

Gutierrez, Gustavo. *The Power of the Poor in History*. Maryknoll, NY: Orbis Books, 1983.

────. *A Theology of Liberation*. Maryknoll, NY: Orbis Books, 1973.

Hagopian, Mark N. *Ideals and Ideologies of Modern Politics*. New York: Longman Press, 1985.

Herman, Donald L. *Christian Democracy in Venezuela*. Chapel Hill: University of North Carolina Press, 1980.

────, ed. *Democracy in Latin America: Colombia and Venezuela*. New York: Praeger Publishers, 1988.

Irving, R. E. M. *Christian Democracy in France*. London: George Allen and Unwin, 1973.

Jerez, Cesar. *The Church and the Nicaraguan Revolution*. London: Catholic Institute for International Relations, 1984.

Jorrin, Miguel, and Martz, John D. *Latin American Political Thought and Ideology*. Chapel Hill: University of North Carolina Press, 1970.

Kirchner, Emil J. *Liberal Parties in Western Europe*. Cambridge: Cambridge University Press, 1988.

Landsberger, Henry A., ed. *The Church and Social Change in Latin America*. South Bend, IN: Unversity of Notre Dame Press, 1970.

Levine, Daniel H. *Conflict and Political Change in Venezuela*. Princeton, NJ: Princeton University Press, 1973.

———. *Religion and Politics in Latin America: The Catholic Church in Venezuela and Colombia*. Princeton, NJ: Princeton University Press, 1981.

Ling, Trevor. *Karl Marx and Religion in Europe and India*. London: Macmillan, 1980.

Lukes, Steven. *Marxism and Morality*. Oxford: Clarendon Press, 1985.

Maritain, Jacques. *Christianity and Democracy*. San Francisco: Ignatius Press, 1986.

———. *Reflections on America*. New York: Charles Scribner's Sons, 1958.

Marta Sosa, Joaquin. *Iglesia y Crisis de Fe: El Caso Venezolano*. Caracas: Sedeco, 1985.

Martz, John D., ed. *Venezuela: The Democratic Experience*. New York: Praeger Publishers, 1977.

Marx, Karl. *Capital: A Critical Analysis of Capitalist Production*. London: William Glashier, 1920.

———. *Critique of Hegel's "Philosophy of Right."* Cambridge: Cambridge University Press, 1970.

McKown, Delos B. *The Classical Marxist Critique of Religion: Marx, Engels, Lenin, Kautsky*. The Hague: Martinus Nijhoff, 1975.

McLellan, David, ed. *Karl Marx: Selected Writings*. Oxford: Oxford University Press, 1977.

Mecham, J. Lloyd. *Church and State in Latin America: A History of Politico-Ecclesiastical Relations*. Chapel Hill: University of North Carolina Press, 1934.

Miranda, José Porfirio. *Marx and the Bible: A Critique of the Theology of Oppression*. Maryknoll, NY: Orbis Books, 1974.

Mondragon, Rafael, and Decker Molina, Carlos. *Participacion Popular en Nicaragua*. Mexico, DF: Claves Latinoamericanos, 1986.

Moreno Valencia, Fernando. *Cristianismo y Marxismo en la Teologia de la liberacíon*. Santiago de Chile: Editorial Salesiana, 1976 .

Morgan, Roger and Silvestri, Stephano. *Moderates and Conservatives in Western Europe: Political Parties, the European Community and the Atlantic Alliance*. London: Heinemann, 1982.

Newell, William Lloyd. *The Secular Magi: Marx, Freud and Nietzsche on Religion*. New York: Pilgrim Press, 1986.

Niebuhr, Reinhold, ed. *Karl Marx and Friedrich Engels on Religion*. New York: Schocken Books, 1964.

Norman, Edward. *Christianity and World Order*. Oxford: Oxford University Press, 1979.

Nuzzi O'Shaughnessy, Laura, and Serra, Luis H. *The Church and Revolution in Nicaragua*. Athens: Ohio University Center for International Studies, Monographs in International Studies, Latin America Series 11, 1986.

Padron, Patricio, ed. *Copei: Documentos Fundamentales, 1946*. Caracas: Ediciones Centauro, 1981.

Peña, Alfredo. *Conversaciones con Luis Herrera Campins*. Caracas: Editorial Ateneo de Caracas, 1978.

Pérez Esclarin, Antonio. *Atheism and Liberation*. Translated by John Drury. Maryknoll, NY: Orbis Books, 1978.

Pérez Morales, Ovidio. *10 Problemas Retan a un Obispo*. Caracas: Ediciones Paulinas, 1978.

Plaza, Helena. *El 23 de Enero de 1958 y el Proceso de Consolidacion de la Democracia Representativa en Venezuela*. Caracas: Garbizer and Todtmann Editores, 1978.

Quade, Quentin L., ed. *The Pope and Revolution: John Paul II Confronts Liberation Theology*. Washington, DC: Ethics and Public Policy Center, 1982.

Schall, James V. *Liberation Theology in Latin America*. San Francisco: Ignatius Press, 1982.

Schodt, David W. *Ecuador: An Andean Enigma*. Boulder, CO: Westview Press, 1987.

Segundo, Juan Luis. *The Hidden Motives of Pastoral Action*. Maryknoll, NY: Orbis Books, 1978.

———. *The Liberation of Theology*. Maryknoll, NY: Orbis Books, 1976.

Smith, Brooke Williams. *Jacques Maritain: Antimodern or Ultramodern?* New York: Elsevier, 1976.

Sobrino, Jon. *Christology at the Crossroads*. Maryknoll, NY: Orbis Books, 1978.

Somoza, Anastasio, and Cox, Jack. *Nicaragua Betrayed*. Boston: Western Islands Publishers, 1980.

Tefel, Reinaldo. *El Infierno de los Pobres: Diagnostico Sociologico de los Barrios Marginales de Managua*. Managua: Ediciones el Pez y el Serpiente, 1972.

Vallier, Ivan. *Catholicism, Social Control and Modernization in Latin America*. Englewood Cliffs, NJ: Prentice Hall, 1970.

Walker, Thomas W. *The Christian Democratic Movement in Nicaragua*. Tucson: University of Arizona Press, 1970.

———, ed. *Nicaragua in Revolution*. New York: Praeger Publishers, 1982.

———. *Nicaragua: The Land of Sandino*. Boulder, CO: Westview Press, 1981.

Weber, Henri. *Nicaragua: The Sandinist Revolution*. London: Verso Editions, 1981.

Williams, Edward J. *Latin American Christian Democratic Parties*. Knoxville: University of Tennessee Press, 1967.

Zuckerman, Alan. *The Politics of Faction: Christian Democratic Rule in Italy*. New Haven, CT: Yale University Press, 1979.

ARTICLES

Andean Report. Various issues.

Burtchall, James Tunstead. "How Authentically Christian is Liberation Theology?" *Review of Politics* 50, 2 (1988): 264-81.

Caldera, Rafael. "The Christian Democratic Idea." *America*, 7 (April 1962): 14-15.

Cardenal, Ernesto. "Revolution and Peace: The Nicaraguan Road." *Journal of Peace Research*, 18, 2 (1981): 201-7.

Christian Democratic Review. Various issues from the late 1950s and early 1960s.

Cowen, Wayne H. "Nicaragua: The Revolution Takes Hold." *Christianity and Crisis*, 40, 8 (May 1980): 137-40.

Cox, Harvey, and Sand, Faith Annette. "What Happened at Puebla?" *Christianity and Crisis*, 39, 4 (1979): 57-60.

D'Escoto Brockmann, Miguel. "Nicaragua and the World." *Christianity and Crisis*, 40, 8 (May 1980): 141-45.

Dodson, Michael. "The Politics of Religion in Revolutionary Nicaragua." *Annals of the American Academy of Political and Social Sciences*, 483, (January 1986): 36-49.

Ewell, Judith. "Debt and Politics in Venezuela." *Current History* (March 1989): 122–125.

Falcoff, Mark. "Eduardo Frei Montalva, 1911–1982." *Review of Politics*, 44, 3 (1982): 323-27.

Frei Montalva, Eduardo. "The Second Latin American Revolution." *Foreign Affairs*, 50, 1 (1971): 83-96.

Gorman, Stephen. "Power and Consolidation in the Nicaraguan Regime." *Journal of Latin American Studies*, 13, 1 (1981): 133-49.

Irving, R. E. M. "Christian Democracy in Post-War Europe: Conservatism Writ Large or Distinctive Political Phenomenon?" *Western European Politics*, 2, 1 (1979): 53-68.

Losev, S. "A New Life for Nicaragua." *International Affairs* (USSR), 2 (February 1981): 114-20.

Martz, John D. "The Crisis of Venezuelan Democracy." *Current History*, 83, 490 (1984).

———. "Ecuador: The Right Takes Command." *Current History*, 84, 499 (1985): 69-72, 84-85.

———. "Instability in Ecuador." *Current History*, 87, 525 (1988): 17–20, 37-38.

Pearson, Neil J. "Nicaragua in Crisis." *Current History*, 76, 446 (1979): 78-80, 84, 86.

Pridham, Geoffrey. "The Italian Christian Democrats After Moro: Crisis or Compromise?" *Western European Politics*, 2, 1 (1979): 69-88.

Reding, Andrew. "Nicaragua's New Constitution." *World Policy Journal*, 4, 2 (Spring 1987): 257-94.

Roberts, W. Dayton. "Where Has Liberation Theology Gone Wrong?" *Christianity Today*, XXIII, 24 (1979): 26-28.

Rodriguez, Carlos [pseud.]. "The Frei Alternative." *Monthly Review*, 28, 5 (1976): 52-55.

Rupp, E. Gordon. "Thomas Munzer: Prophet of Radical Christianity." *Bulletin of the John Rylands Library*. 48, 2 (Spring 1966): 467-87.

Schall, James V. "Central America and Politicized Religion." *World Affairs*, 144, 2 (1981): 126-49.

Sontag, Heinz, and de la Cruz, Rafael. "The State and Industrialization in Venezuela." *Latin American Perspective*, 12, 4 (1985).

Syzmanski, Albert. "The Rise and Decline of the Christian Democratic Party in Chile: An Analysis of the 1961 and 1965 Congressional Elections." *Social and Economic Studies*, 24, 4 (1975): 458-80.

PAPAL DOCUMENTS

All of the following are official Vatican translations.

John XXIII. *Mater et Magistra* (Mother and Teacher). Boston: Daughters of St. Paul, 1961.

———. *Pacem in Terris* (Peace on Earth). Boston: Daughters of St. Paul, 1968.

John Paul II. *Christifideles Laici* (On the Role of the Laity). Boston: Daughters of St. Paul, 1988.

———. *Laborem Exercens* (On Human Labor). Boston: Daughters of St. Paul, 1981.

———. *Sollicitudo Rei Socialis* (On Social Concern). Boston: Daughters of St. Paul, 1987.

Leo XIII. *Rerum Novarum* (On the Condition of the Working Classes). Boston: Daughters of St. Paul, 1891.

Paul VI. *Populorum Progressio* (On the Development of Peoples). Boston: Daughters of St. Paul, 1968.

Pius XI. *Quadragessimo Anno* (On Social Reconstruction). Boston: Daughters of St. Paul, 1931.

———. *Divini Redemptoris* (On Atheistic Communism). Boston: Daughters of St. Paul, 1937.

Sacred Congregation for the Doctrine of the Faith. *Instruction on Certain Aspects of the "Theology of Liberation."* Boston: Daughters of St. Paul, 1984.

PUBLIC DOCUMENTS

Foreign Broadcast Information Service. Latin America Daily Report.

U.S. Congress. House. Committee on Appropriations. Subcommittee on Foreign Operations and Related Agencies. *Foreign Assistance and Related Agencies Appropriations for 1978*. 95th Congress, 1st session, 1977.

U.S. Congress. House. Committee on Foreign Affairs. *United States Post-Disaster Assistance to Nicaragua*. Report of a Staff Survey Mission to Nicaragua. 93rd Congress, 2nd session, 1974.

U.S. Congress. House. Committee on International Relations. Subcommittee on International Organizations. *Human Rights in Nicaragua, Guatemala and El Salvador: Implications for U.S. Policy*. 94th Congress, 2nd session, 1976.

U.S. Congress. House. Committee on Merchant Marine and Fisheries. Subcommittee on the Panama Canal. *Panama Gunrunning*. 96th Congress, 1st session, 1979.

Index

ABOUT THE AUTHOR

EDWARD A. LYNCH is an assistant professor in the Department of Political Science at Villanova University. He did his graduate work at the University of Virginia. His articles have appeared in *Terrorism: An International Journal*, *Publius: The Journal of Federalism*, *This World*, and *The Journal of Defense and Diplomacy*.